KING OF NOWHERE™

DESIGNERS
SCOTT NEWMAN
& MICHELLE ANKLEY

ASSISTANT EDITOR
RAMIRO PORTNOY

ASSOCIATE EDITOR
AMANDA LAFRANCO

EDITOR
ERIC HARBURN

KING OF NOWHERE, December 2020. Published by BOOM! Studios, a division of Boom Entertainment, Inc. King of Nowhere is ™ & © 2020 W. Maxwell Prince & Tyler Jenkins. Originally published in single magazine form as KING OF NOWHERE No. 1-5. ™ & © 2020 W. Maxwell Prince & Tyler Jenkins. All rights reserved. BOOM! Studios™ and the BOOM! Studios logo are trademarks of Boom Entertainment, Inc., registered in various countries and categories. All characters, events, and institutions depicted herein are fictional. Any similarity between any of the names, characters, persons, events, and/or institutions in this publication to actual names, characters, and persons, whether living or dead, events, and/ or institutions is unintended and purely coincidental. BOOM! Studios does not read or accept unsolicited submissions of ideas, stories, or artwork.

BOOM! Studios, 5670 Wilshire Boulevard, Suite 400, Los Angeles, CA 90036-5679. Printed in USA. First Printing.

ISBN: 978-1-68415-613-9, eISBN: 978-1-64668-025-2

KING NOW

CREATED BY **W. MAXWELL PRINCE** AND TYLER JENKINS

OF HERE

WRITTEN BY
W. MAXWELL PRINCE

ILLUSTRATED BY
TYLER JENKINS

COLORED BY
HILARY JENKINS

LETTERED BY
ANDWORLD DESIGN

COVER BY
TYLER JENKINS
AND HILARY JENKINS

CHAPTER ONE

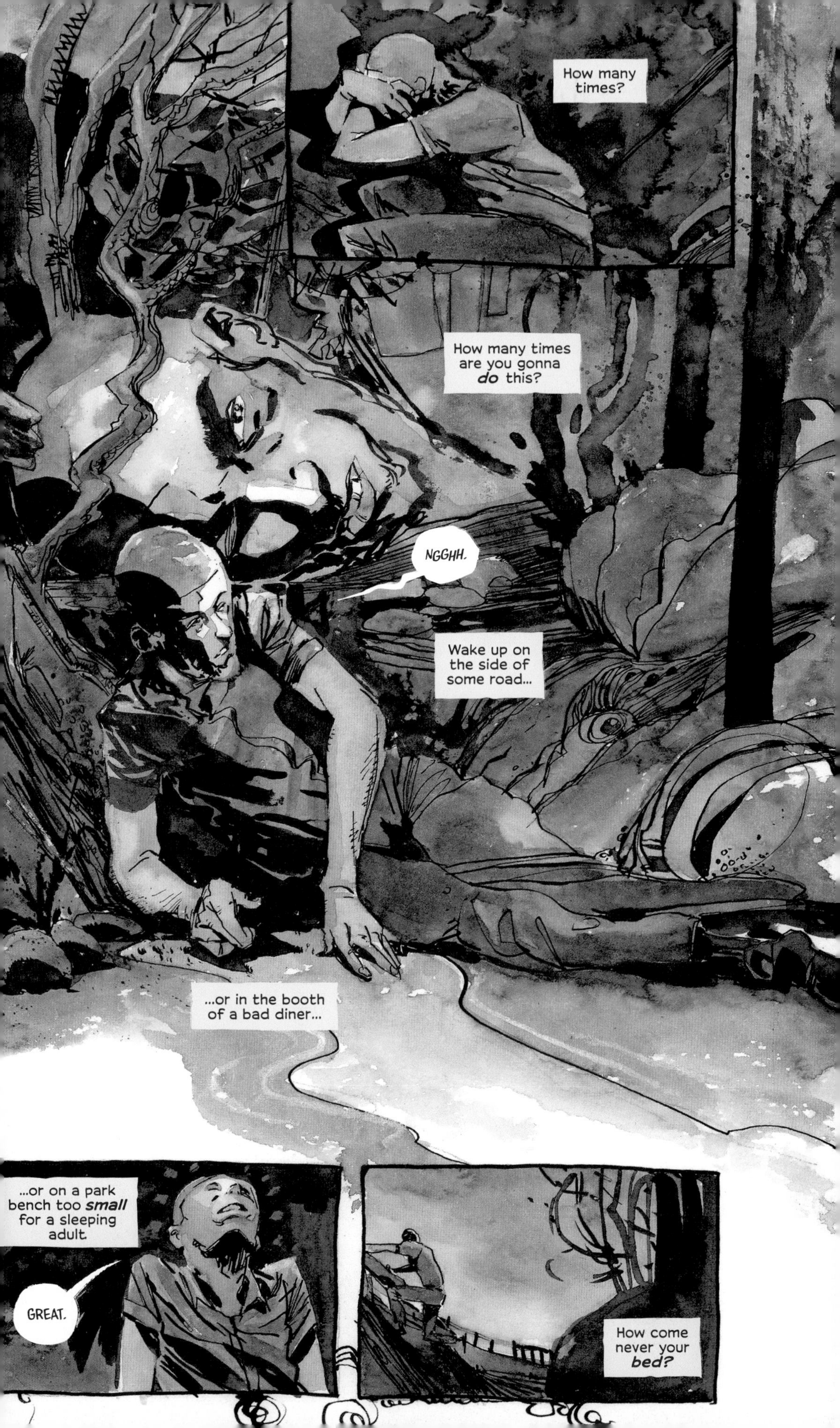
How many times?
How many times are you gonna *do* this?
NGGHH.
Wake up on the side of some road...
...or in the booth of a bad diner...
...or on a park bench too ***small*** for a sleeping adult.
GREAT.
How come never your ***bed?***

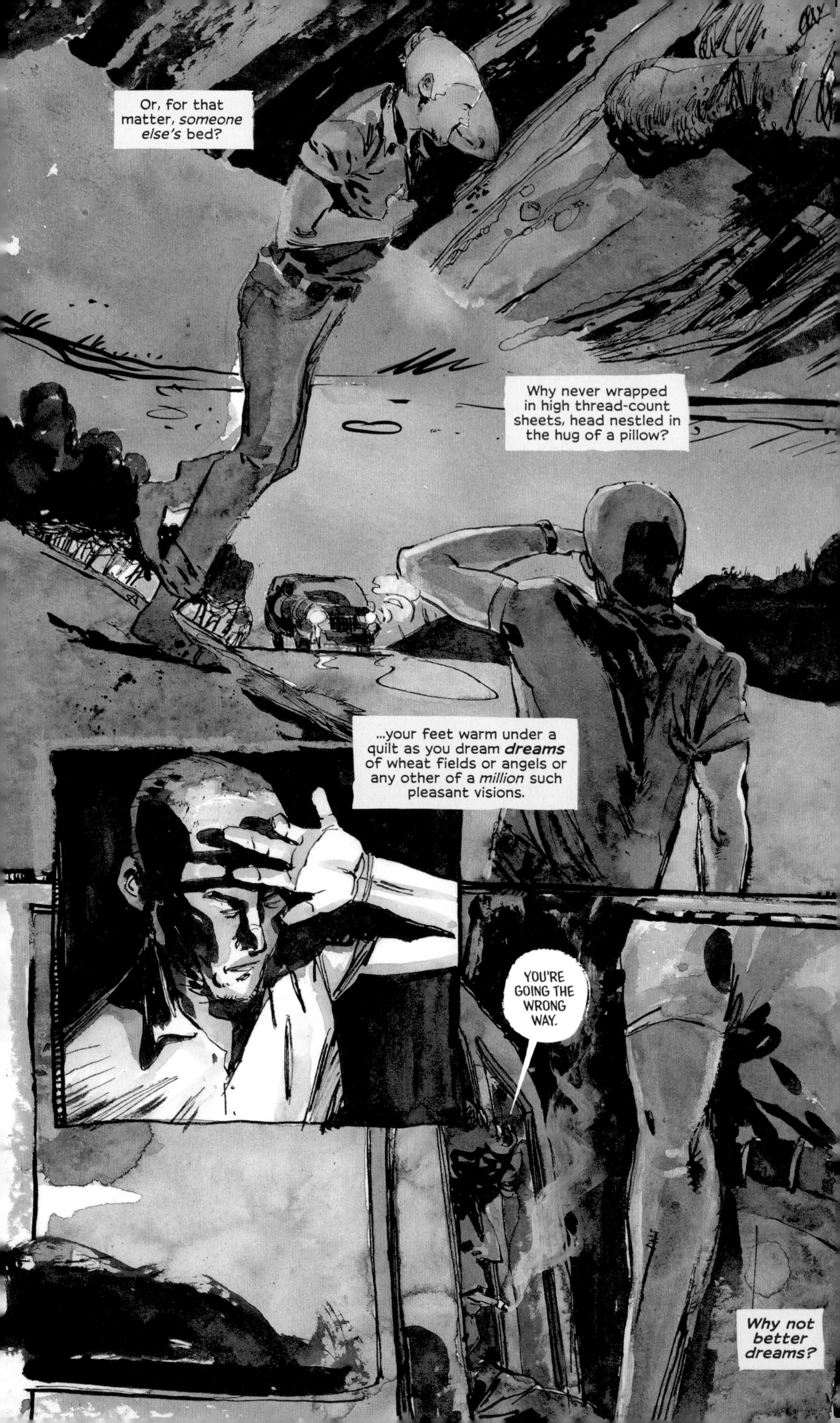
Or, for that matter, *someone else's* bed?
Why never wrapped in high thread-count sheets, head nestled in the hug of a pillow?
...your feet warm under a quilt as you dream ***dreams*** of wheat fields or angels or any other of a *million* such pleasant visions.
YOU'RE GOING THE WRONG WAY.
Why not better dreams?

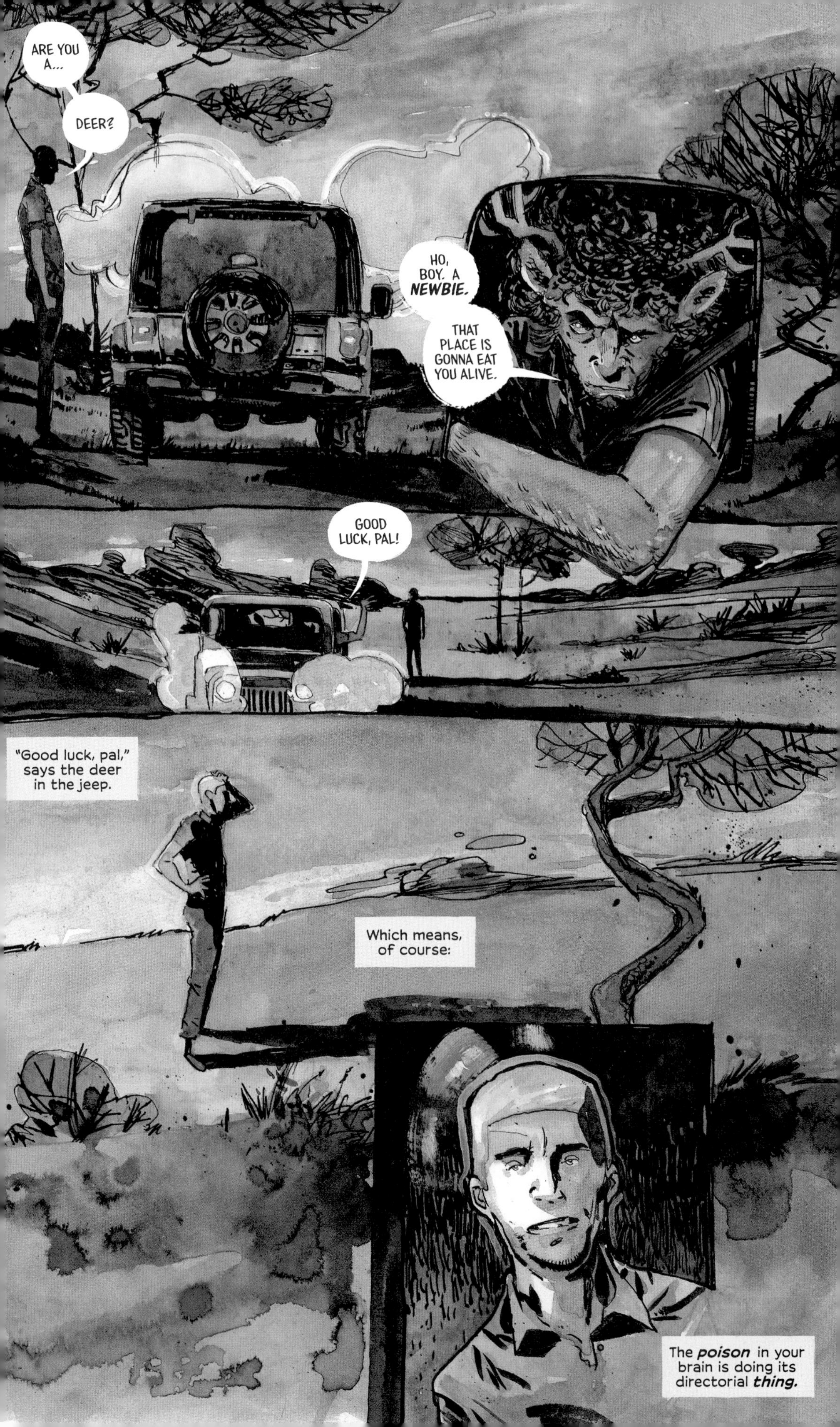
ARE YOU A...
DEER?
HO, BOY. A NEWBIE.
THAT PLACE IS GONNA EAT YOU ALIVE.
GOOD LUCK, PAL!
"Good luck, pal," says the deer in the jeep.
Which means, of course:
The poison in your brain is doing its directorial thing.

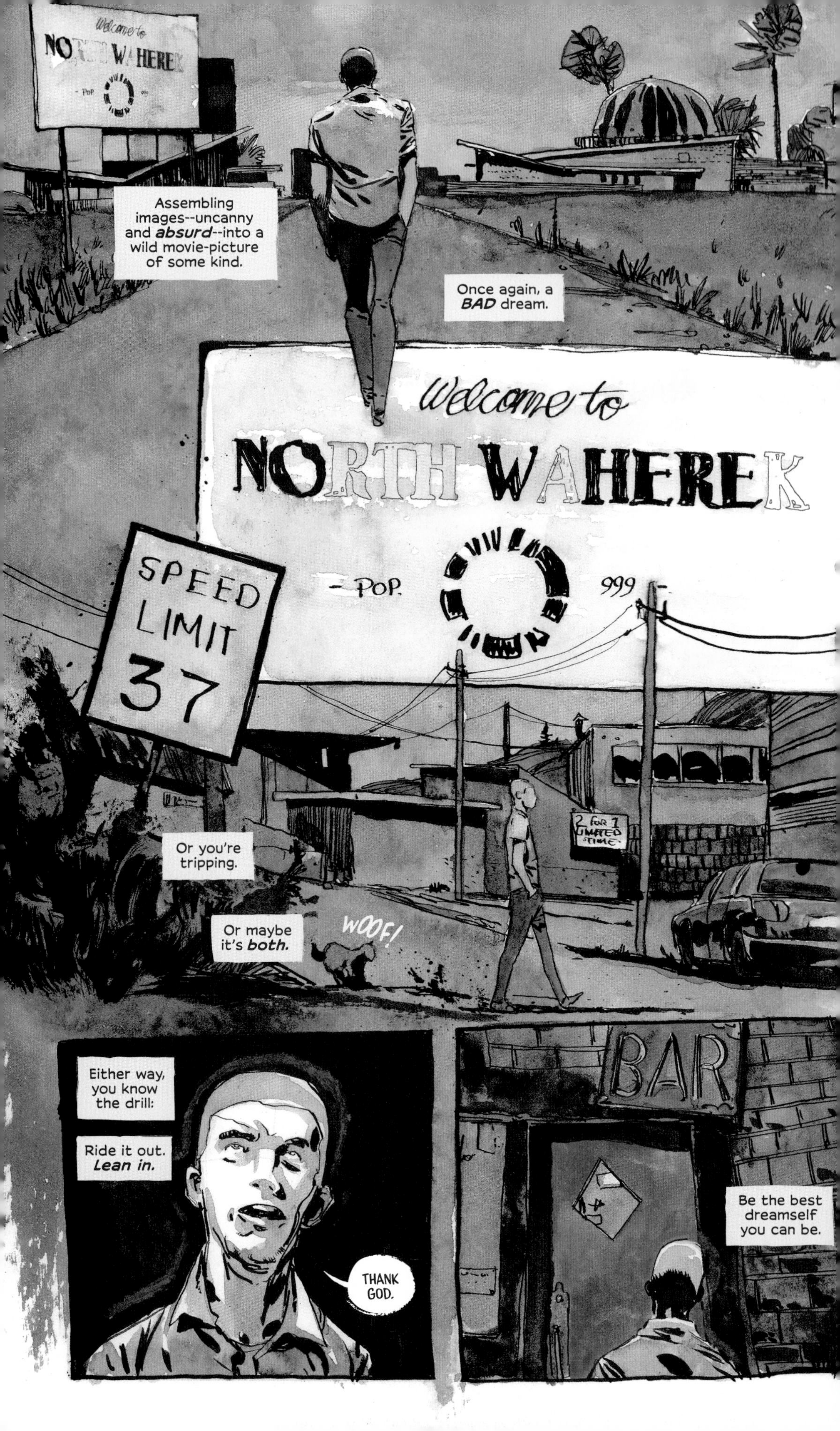

Assembling images--uncanny and *absurd*--into a wild movie-picture of some kind.
Once again, a *BAD* dream.
Welcome to
NORTH WAHEREK
POP. 999
SPEED LIMIT 37
2 FOR 1 LIMITED TIME
Or you're tripping.
Or maybe it's *both.*
WOOF!
Either way, you know the drill:
Ride it out. *Lean in.*
THANK GOD.
BAR
Be the best dreamself you can be.

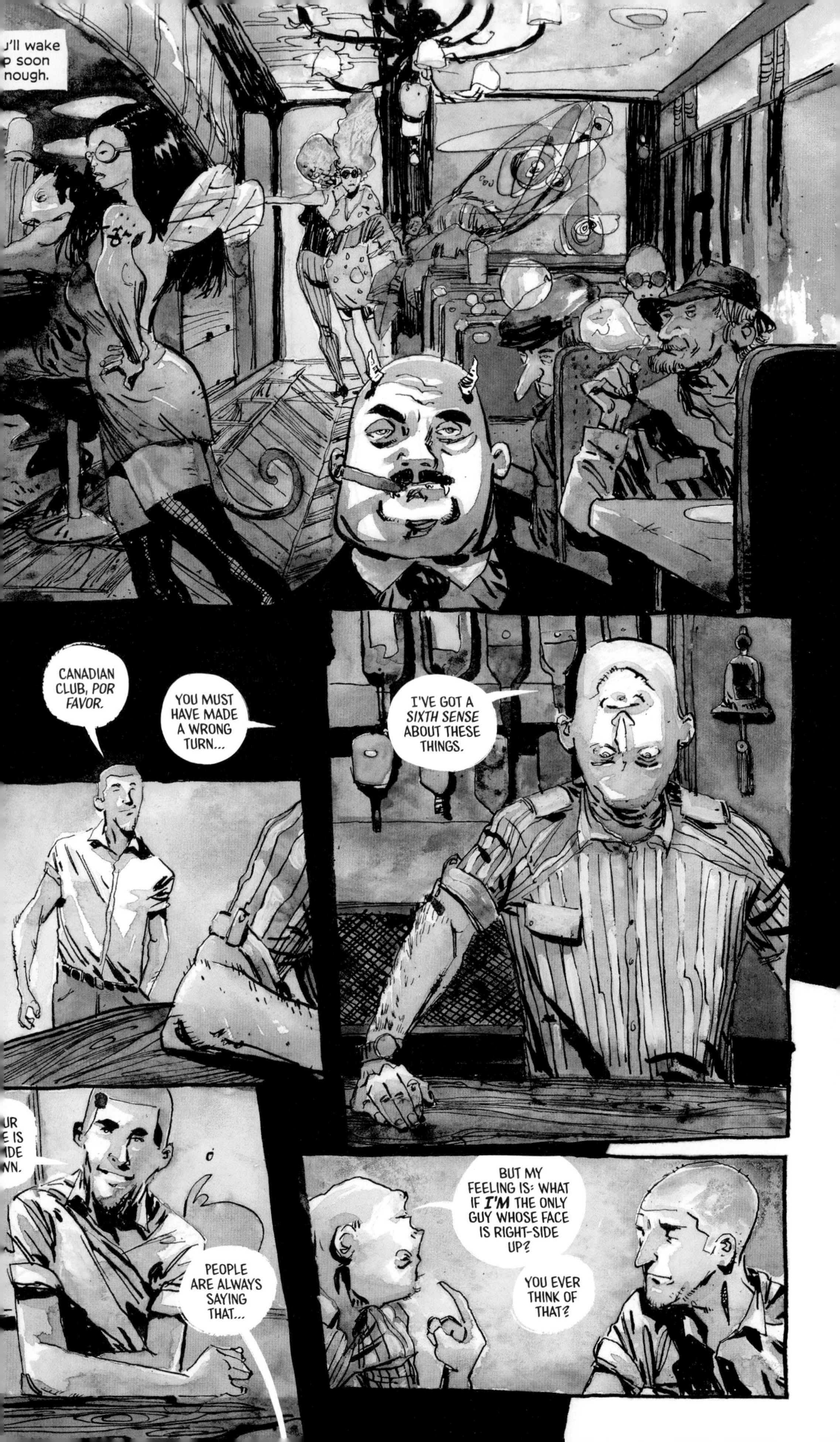

'll wake p soon nough.
CANADIAN CLUB, *POR FAVOR.*
YOU MUST HAVE MADE A WRONG TURN...
I'VE GOT A *SIXTH SENSE* ABOUT THESE THINGS.
UR E IS IDE WN.
PEOPLE ARE ALWAYS SAYING THAT...
BUT MY FEELING IS: WHAT IF ***I'M*** THE ONLY GUY WHOSE FACE IS RIGHT-SIDE UP?
YOU EVER THINK OF THAT?

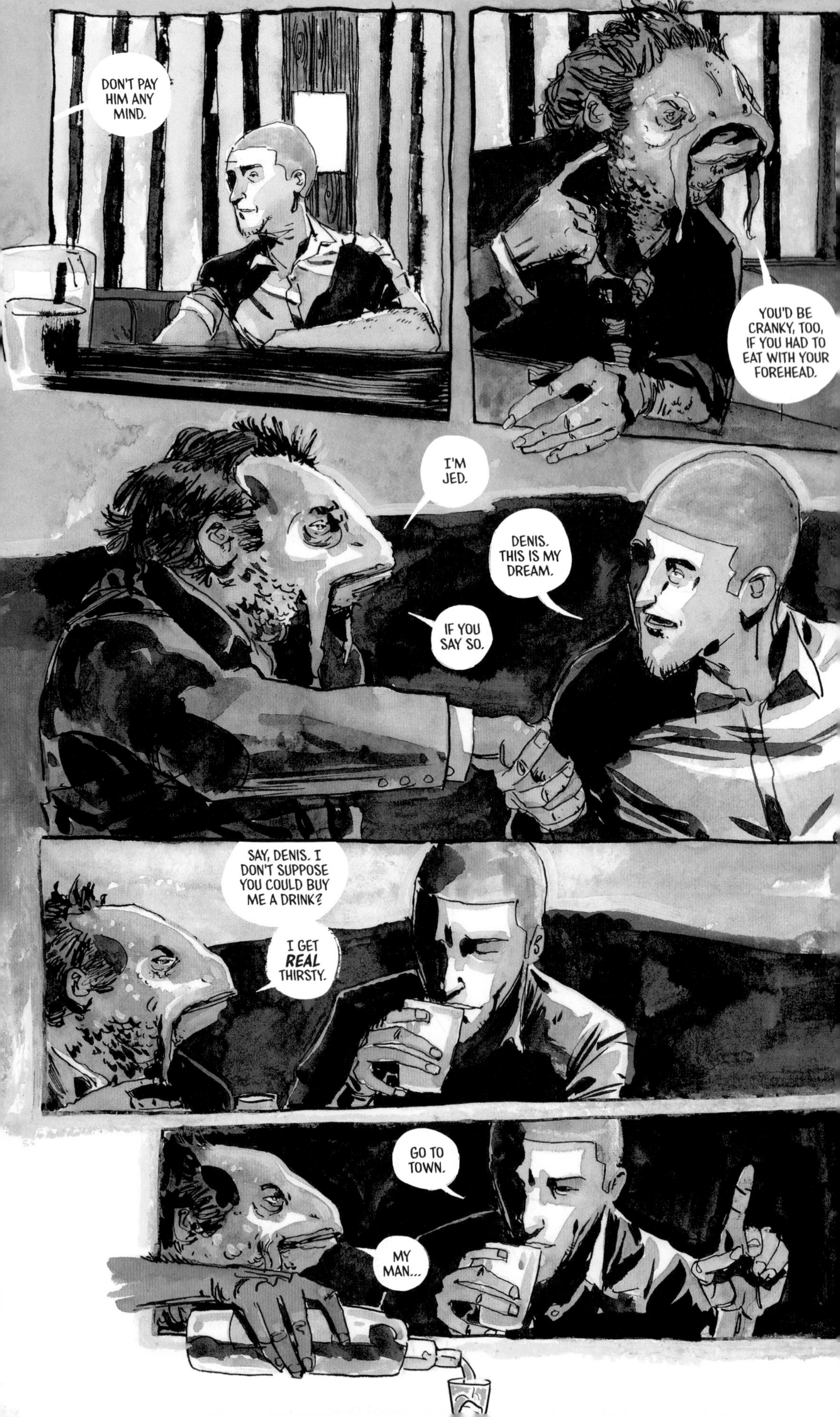
DON'T PAY HIM ANY MIND.
YOU'D BE CRANKY, TOO, IF YOU HAD TO EAT WITH YOUR FOREHEAD.
I'M JED.
DENIS. THIS IS MY DREAM.
IF YOU SAY SO.
SAY, DENIS. I DON'T SUPPOSE YOU COULD BUY ME A DRINK?
I GET REAL THIRSTY.
GO TO TOWN.
MY MAN...

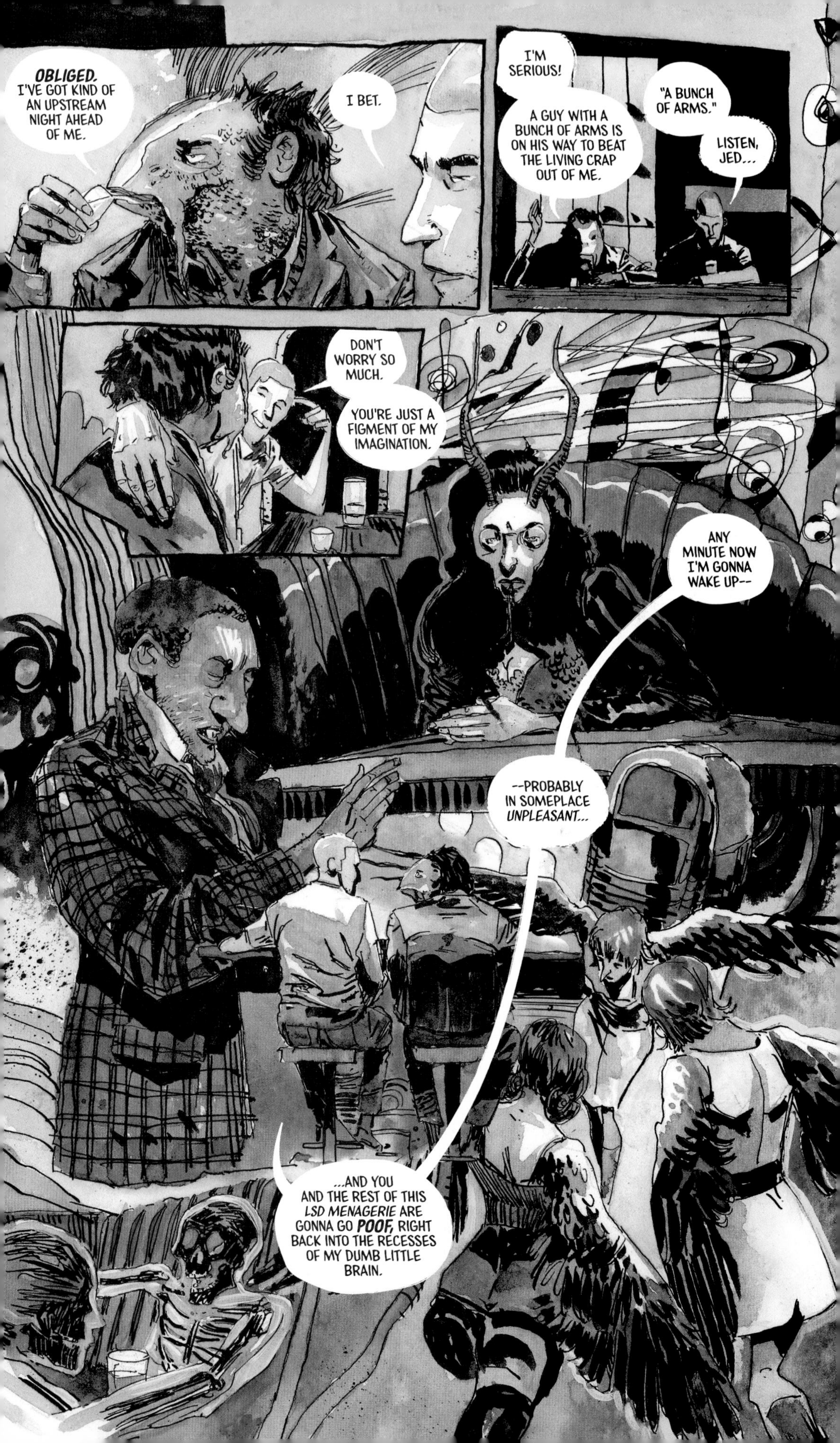
OBLIGED. I'VE GOT KIND OF AN UPSTREAM NIGHT AHEAD OF ME.
I BET.
I'M SERIOUS!
A GUY WITH A BUNCH OF ARMS IS ON HIS WAY TO BEAT THE LIVING CRAP OUT OF ME.
"A BUNCH OF ARMS."
LISTEN, JED...
DON'T WORRY SO MUCH.
YOU'RE JUST A FIGMENT OF MY IMAGINATION.
ANY MINUTE NOW I'M GONNA WAKE UP--
--PROBABLY IN SOMEPLACE *UNPLEASANT*...
...AND YOU AND THE REST OF THIS *LSD MENAGERIE* ARE GONNA GO ***POOF,*** RIGHT BACK INTO THE RECESSES OF MY DUMB LITTLE BRAIN.

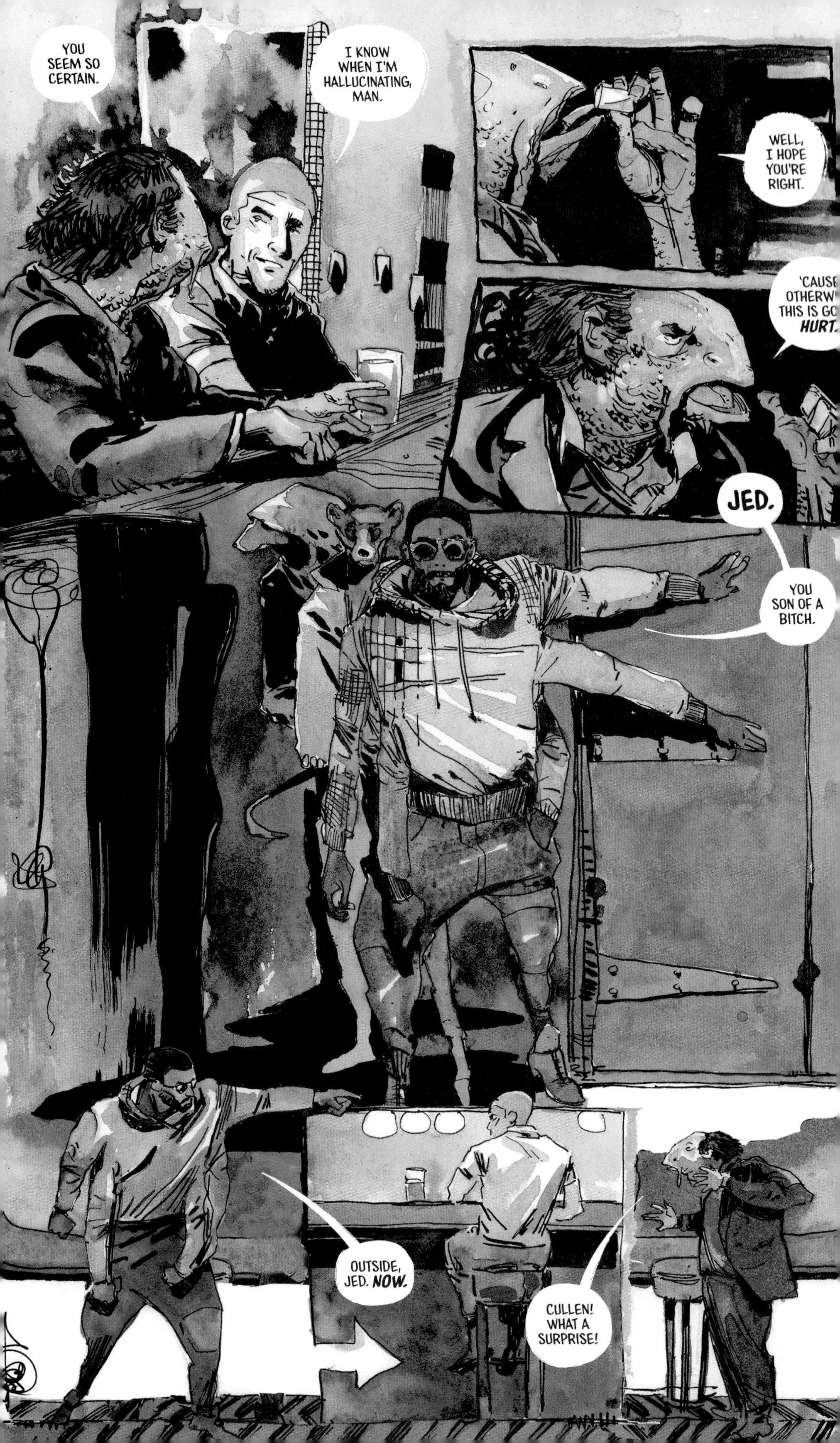
YOU SEEM SO CERTAIN.
I KNOW WHEN I'M HALLUCINATING, MAN.
WELL, I HOPE YOU'RE RIGHT.
'CAUSE OTHERW THIS IS GO HURT.
JED.
YOU SON OF A BITCH.
OUTSIDE, JED. NOW.
CULLEN! WHAT A SURPRISE!

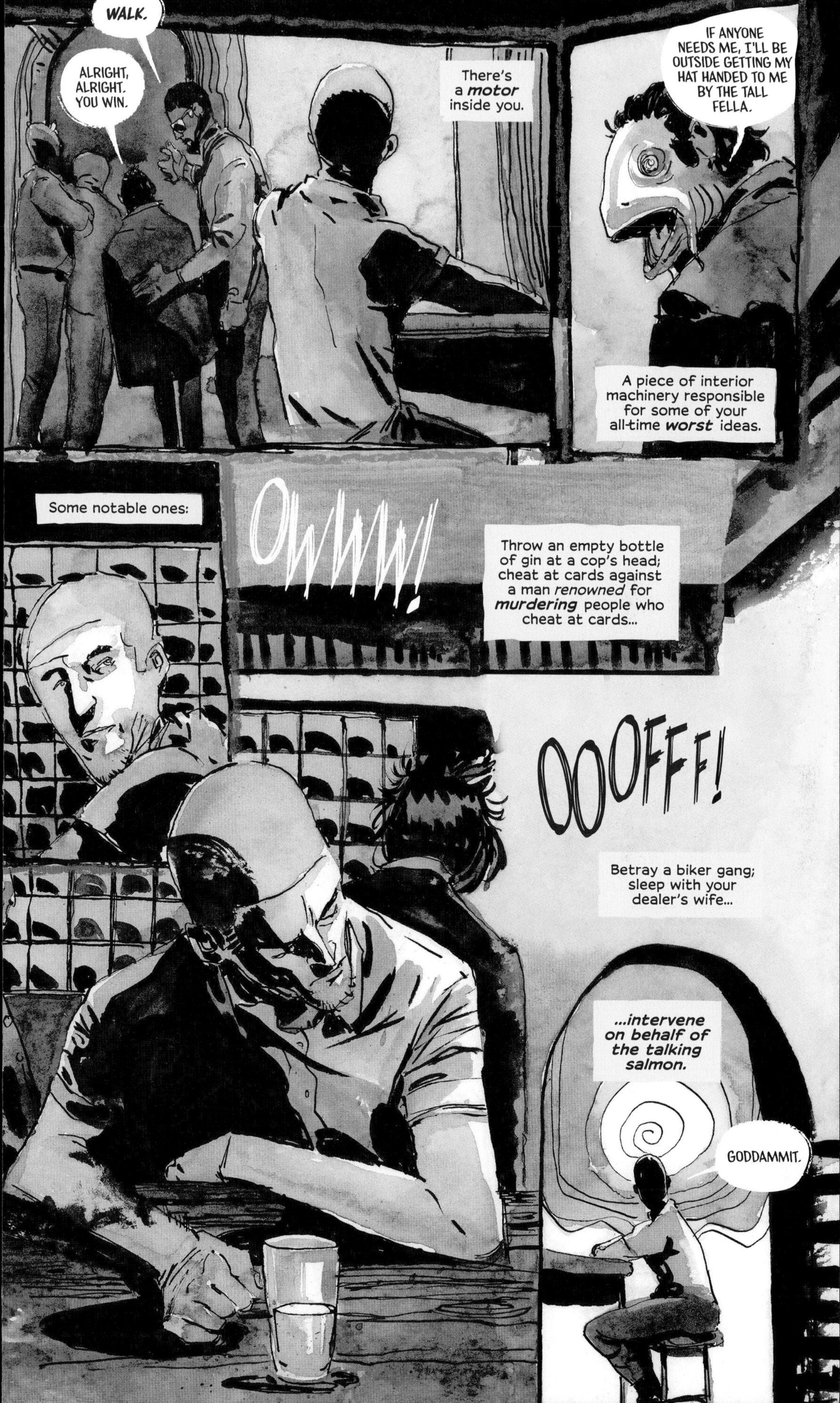
WALK.
ALRIGHT, ALRIGHT. YOU WIN.
There's a *motor* inside you.
IF ANYONE NEEDS ME, I'LL BE OUTSIDE GETTING MY HAT HANDED TO ME BY THE TALL FELLA.
A piece of interior machinery responsible for some of your all-time *worst* ideas.
Some notable ones:
OWWW!
Throw an empty bottle of gin at a cop's head; cheat at cards against a man *renowned* for *murdering* people who cheat at cards...
OOOFFF!
Betray a biker gang; sleep with your dealer's wife...
...intervene on behalf of the talking salmon.
GODDAMMIT.

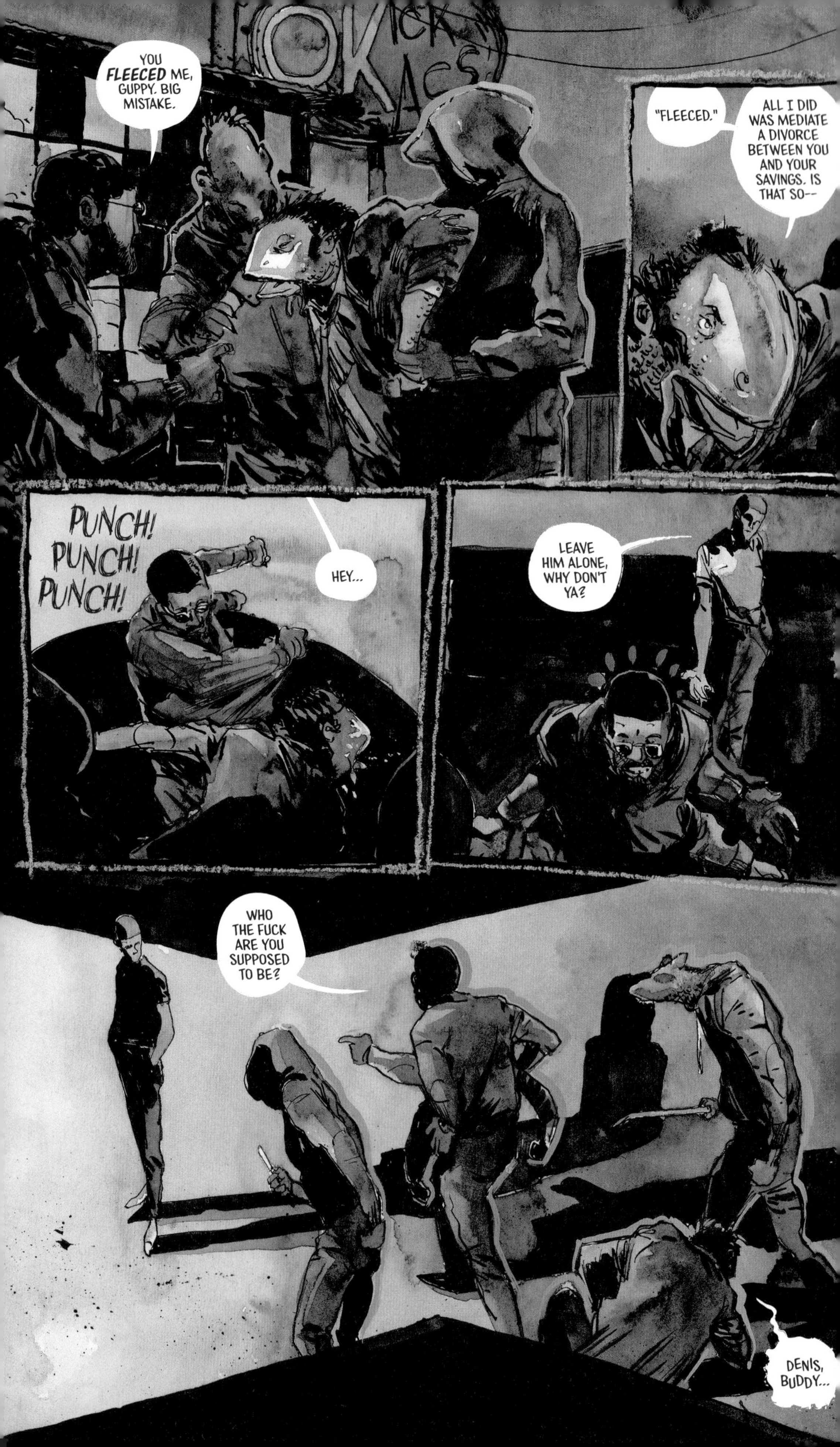
YOU FLEECED ME, GUPPY. BIG MISTAKE.
"FLEECED."
ALL I DID WAS MEDIATE A DIVORCE BETWEEN YOU AND YOUR SAVINGS. IS THAT SO--
PUNCH! PUNCH! PUNCH!
HEY...
LEAVE HIM ALONE, WHY DON'T YA?
WHO THE FUCK ARE YOU SUPPOSED TO BE?
DENIS, BUDDY...

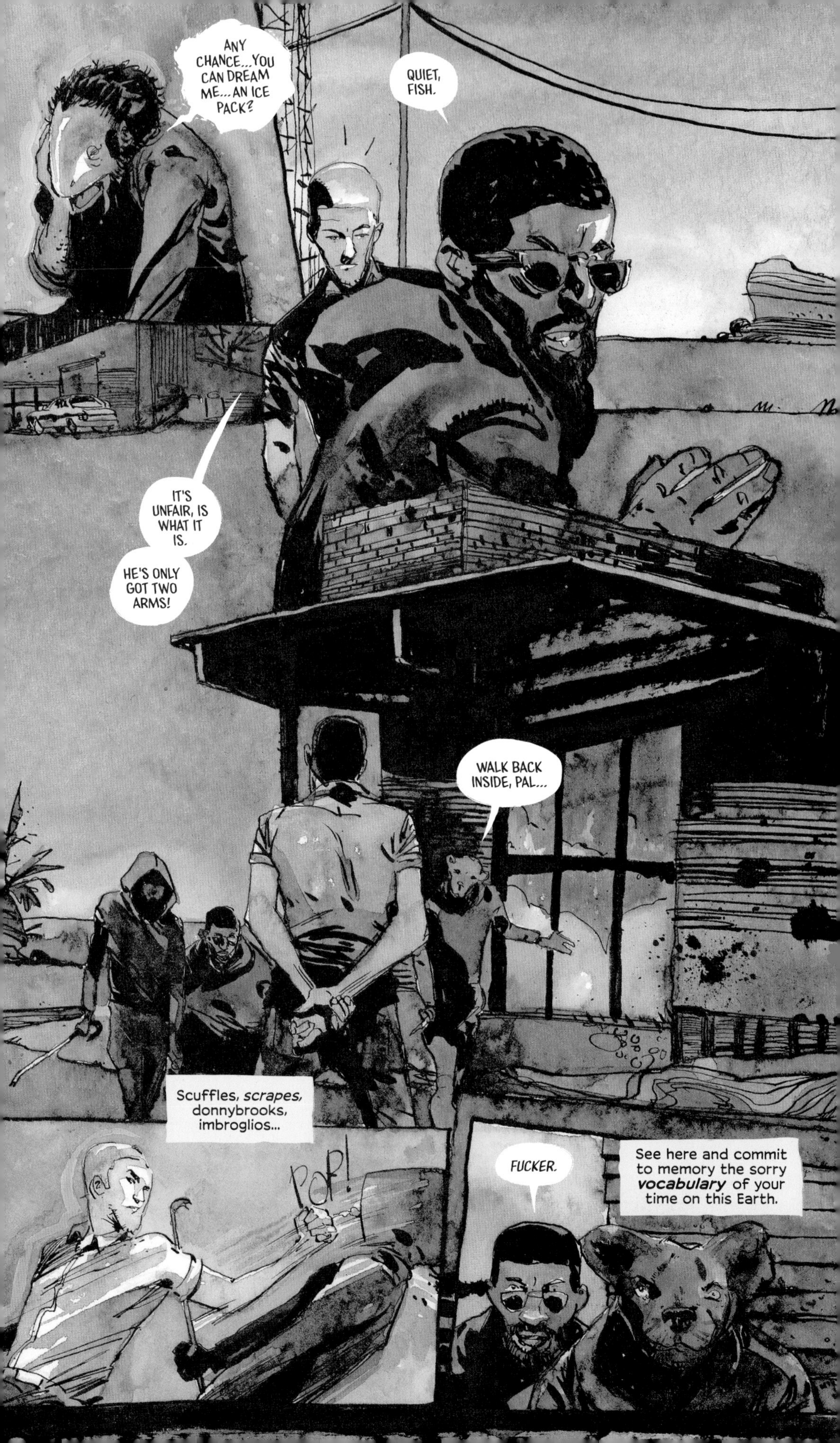
ANY CHANCE... YOU CAN DREAM ME... AN ICE PACK?
QUIET, FISH.
IT'S UNFAIR, IS WHAT IT IS.
HE'S ONLY GOT TWO ARMS!
WALK BACK INSIDE, PAL...
Scuffles, *scrapes,* donnybrooks, imbroglios...
POP!
FUCKER.
See here and commit to memory the sorry ***vocabulary*** of your time on this Earth.

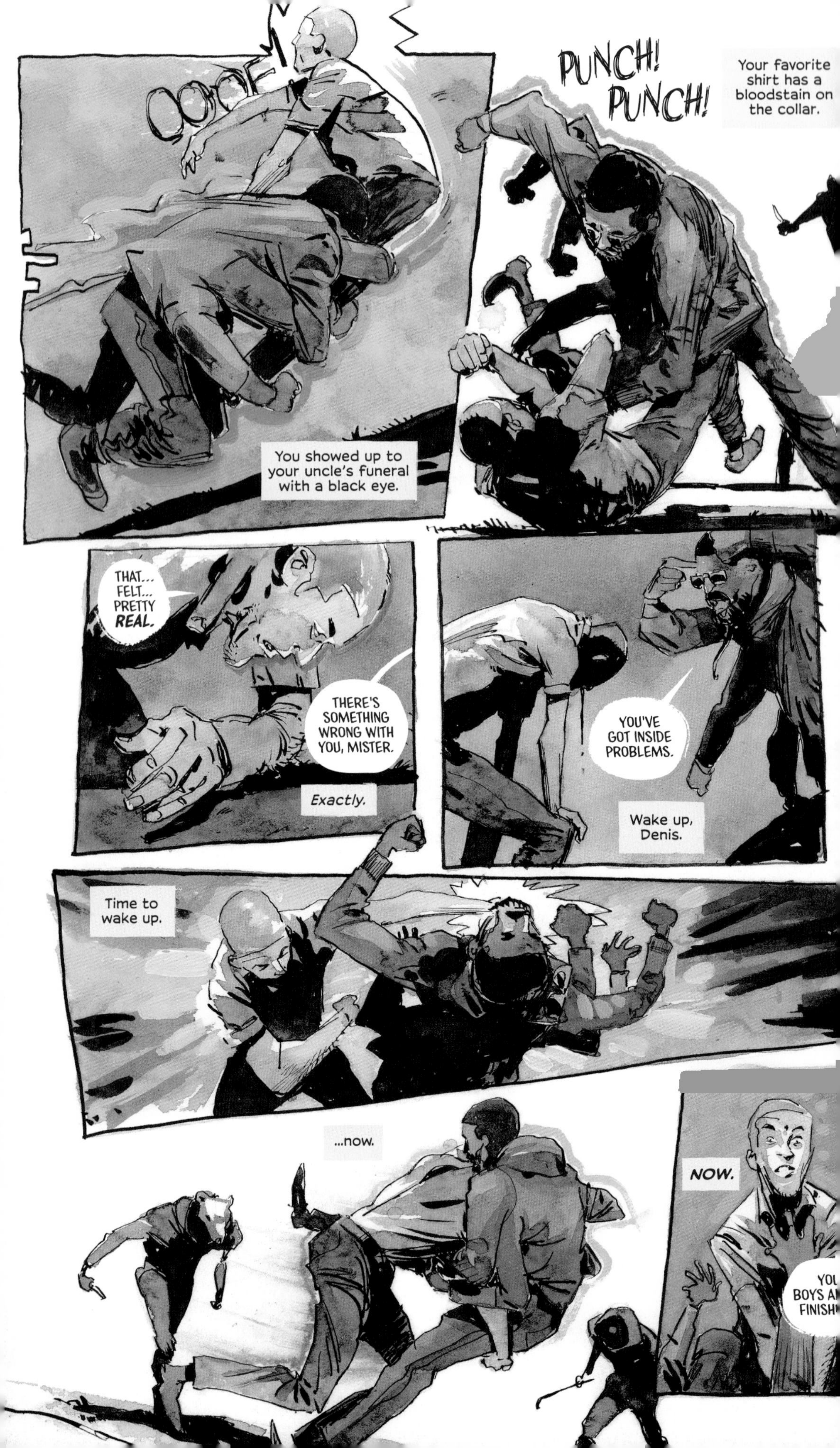
OOOOF!
You showed up to your uncle's funeral with a black eye.
PUNCH! PUNCH!
Your favorite shirt has a bloodstain on the collar.
THAT... FELT... PRETTY REAL.
THERE'S SOMETHING WRONG WITH YOU, MISTER.
Exactly.
YOU'VE GOT INSIDE PROBLEMS.
Wake up, Denis.
Time to wake up.
...now.
NOW.

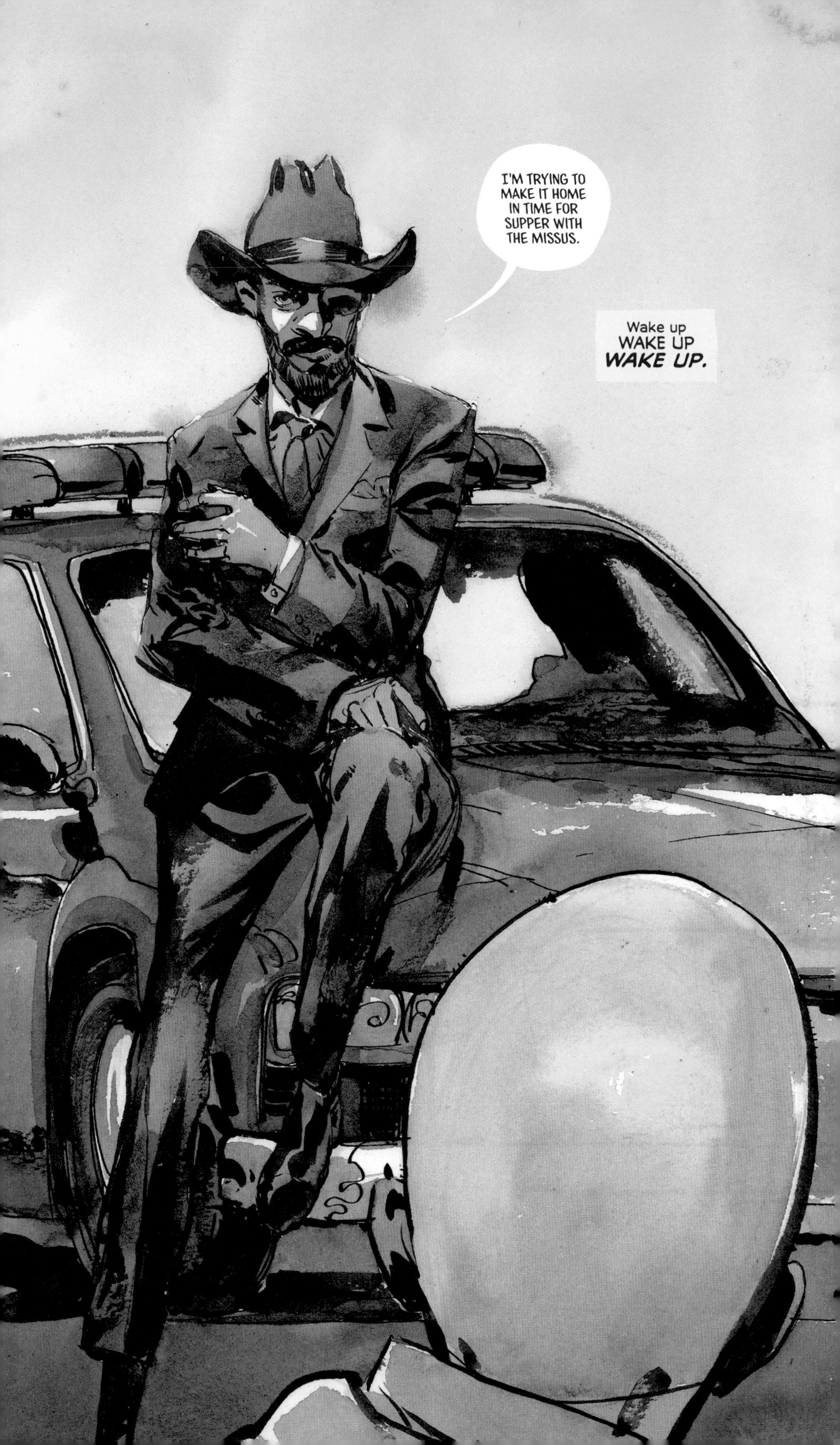
I'M TRYING TO MAKE IT HOME IN TIME FOR SUPPER WITH THE MISSUS.
Wake up WAKE UP WAKE UP.

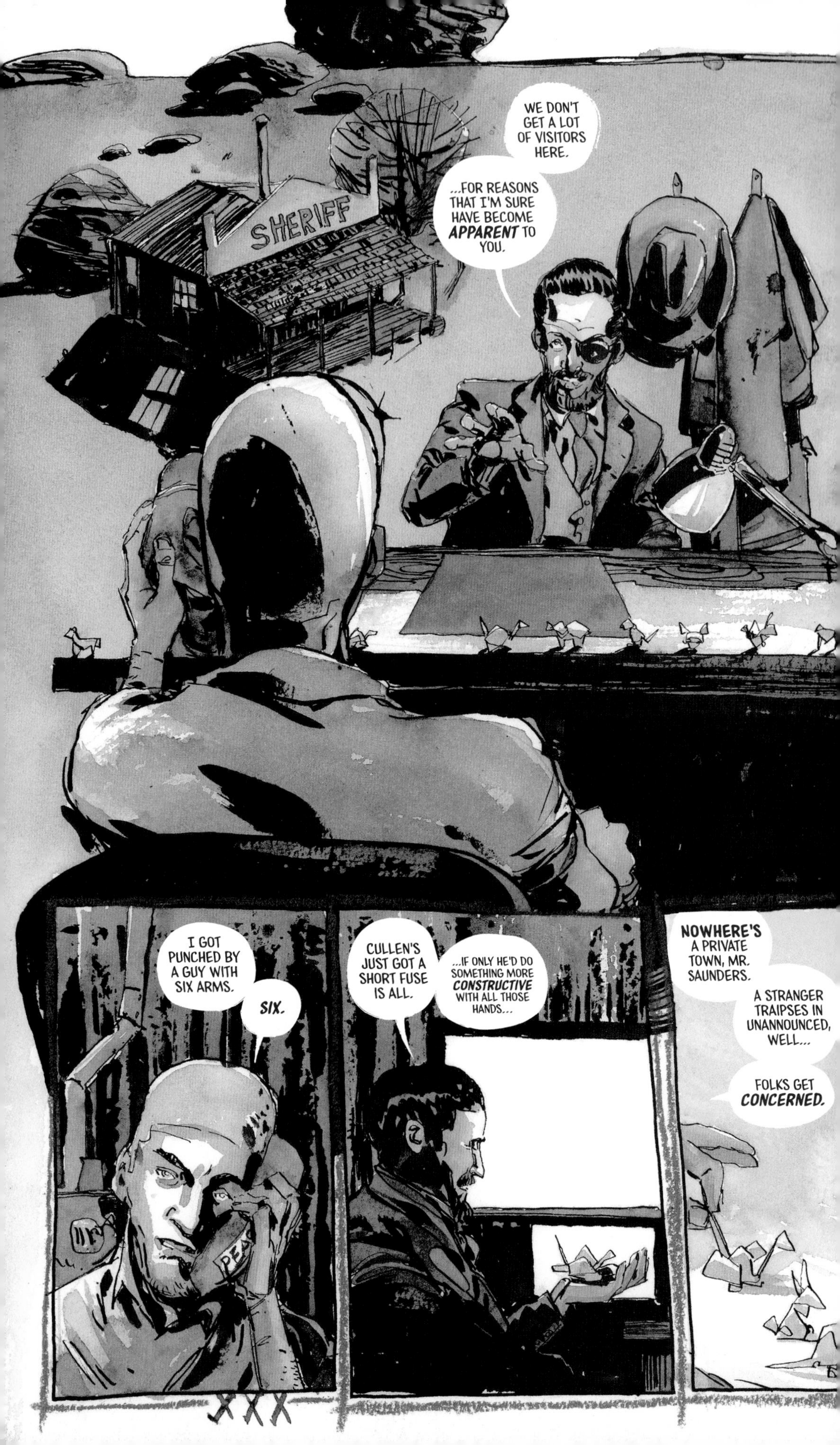
SHERIFF
WE DON'T GET A LOT OF VISITORS HERE.
...FOR REASONS THAT I'M SURE HAVE BECOME **APPARENT** TO YOU.
I GOT PUNCHED BY A GUY WITH SIX ARMS.
SIX.
CULLEN'S JUST GOT A SHORT FUSE IS ALL.
...IF ONLY HE'D DO SOMETHING MORE ***CONSTRUCTIVE*** WITH ALL THOSE HANDS...
NOWHERE'S A PRIVATE TOWN, MR. SAUNDERS.
A STRANGER TRAIPSES IN UNANNOUNCED, WELL...
FOLKS GET ***CONCERNED.***

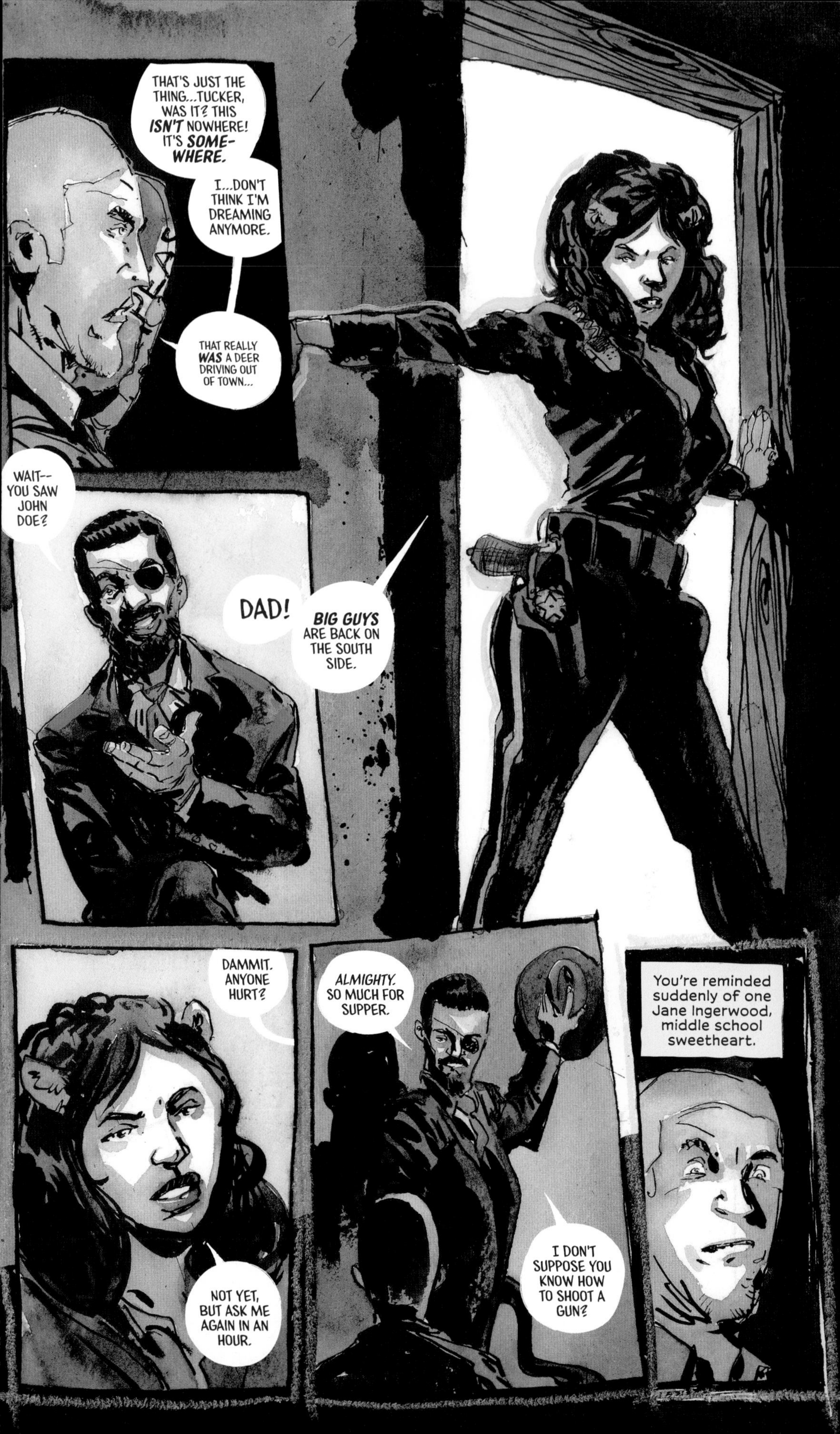
THAT'S JUST THE THING...TUCKER, WAS IT? THIS ISN'T NOWHERE! IT'S SOME-WHERE.
I...DON'T THINK I'M DREAMING ANYMORE.
THAT REALLY WAS A DEER DRIVING OUT OF TOWN...
WAIT--YOU SAW JOHN DOE?
DAD!
BIG GUYS ARE BACK ON THE SOUTH SIDE.
DAMMIT. ANYONE HURT?
NOT YET, BUT ASK ME AGAIN IN AN HOUR.
ALMIGHTY. SO MUCH FOR SUPPER.
I DON'T SUPPOSE YOU KNOW HOW TO SHOOT A GUN?
You're reminded suddenly of one Jane Ingerwood, middle school sweetheart.

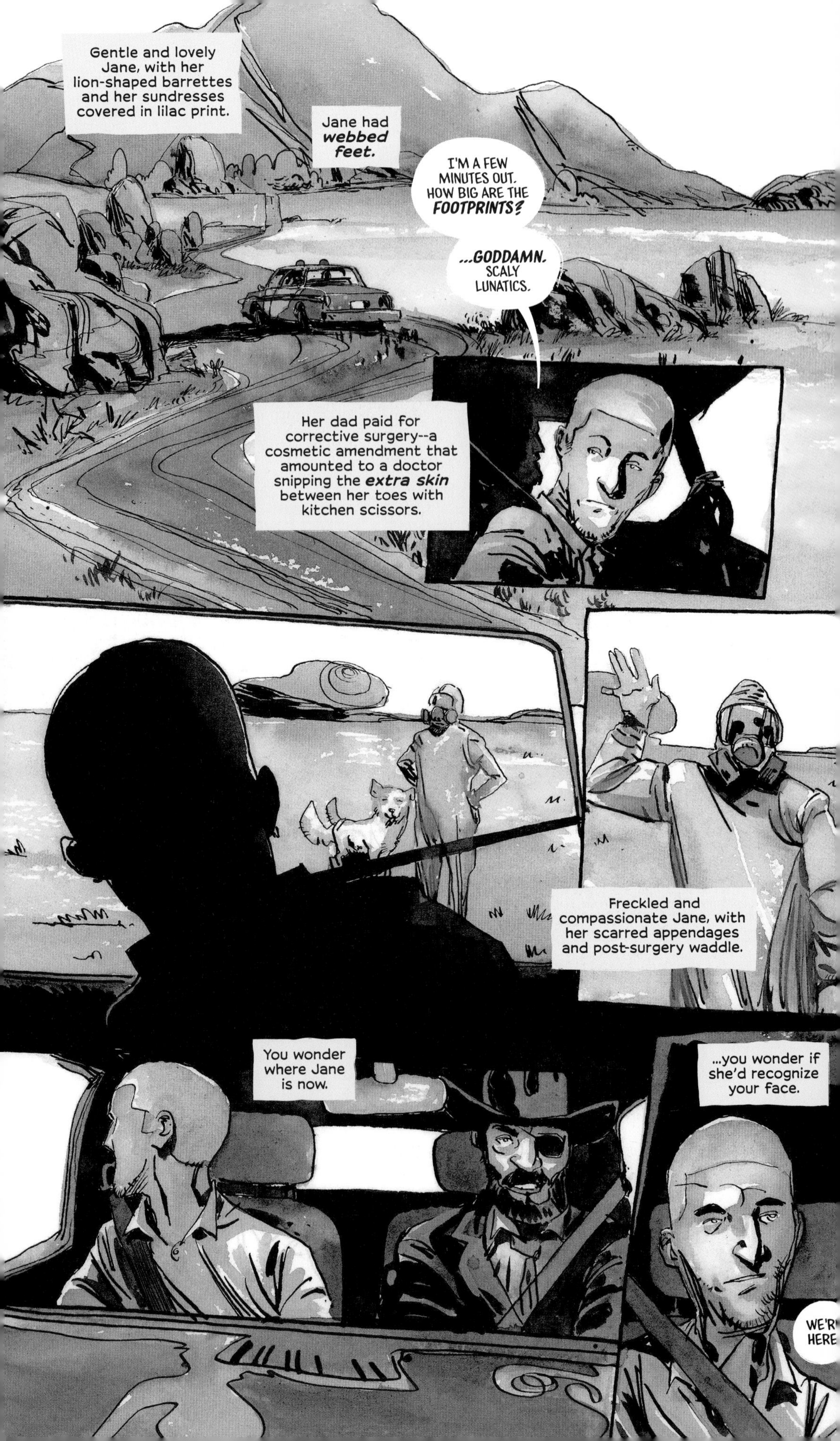

Gentle and lovely Jane, with her lion-shaped barrettes and her sundresses covered in lilac print.
Jane had *webbed feet.*
I'M A FEW MINUTES OUT. HOW BIG ARE THE *FOOTPRINTS?*
...GODDAMN. SCALY LUNATICS.
Her dad paid for corrective surgery--a cosmetic amendment that amounted to a doctor snipping the *extra skin* between her toes with kitchen scissors.
Freckled and compassionate Jane, with her scarred appendages and post-surgery waddle.
You wonder where Jane is now.
...you wonder if she'd recognize your face.
WE'R
HERE

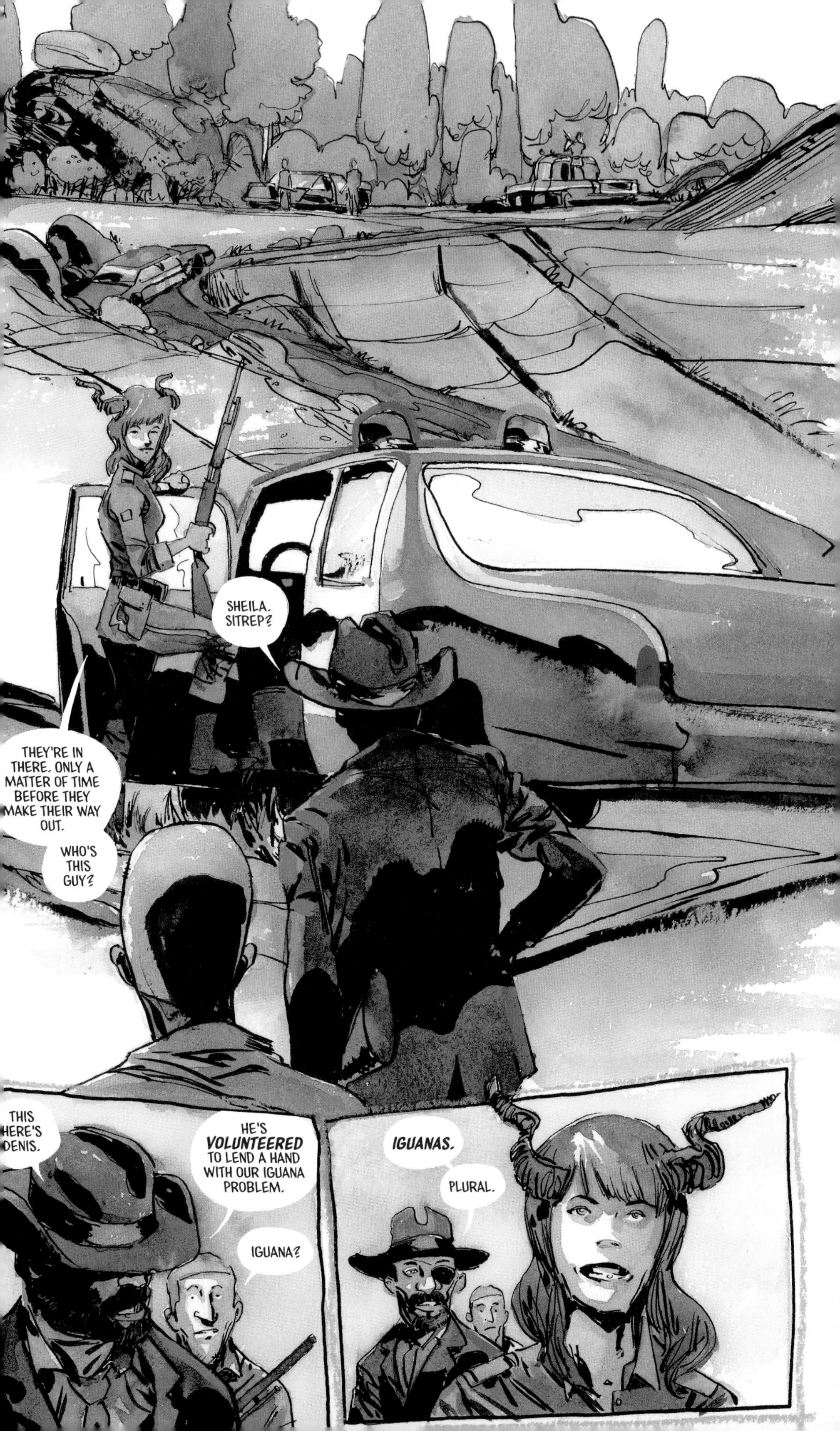
SHEILA. SITREP?
THEY'RE IN THERE. ONLY A MATTER OF TIME BEFORE THEY MAKE THEIR WAY OUT.
WHO'S THIS GUY?
THIS HERE'S DENIS.
HE'S *VOLUNTEERED* TO LEND A HAND WITH OUR IGUANA PROBLEM.
IGUANA?
IGUANAS.
PLURAL.

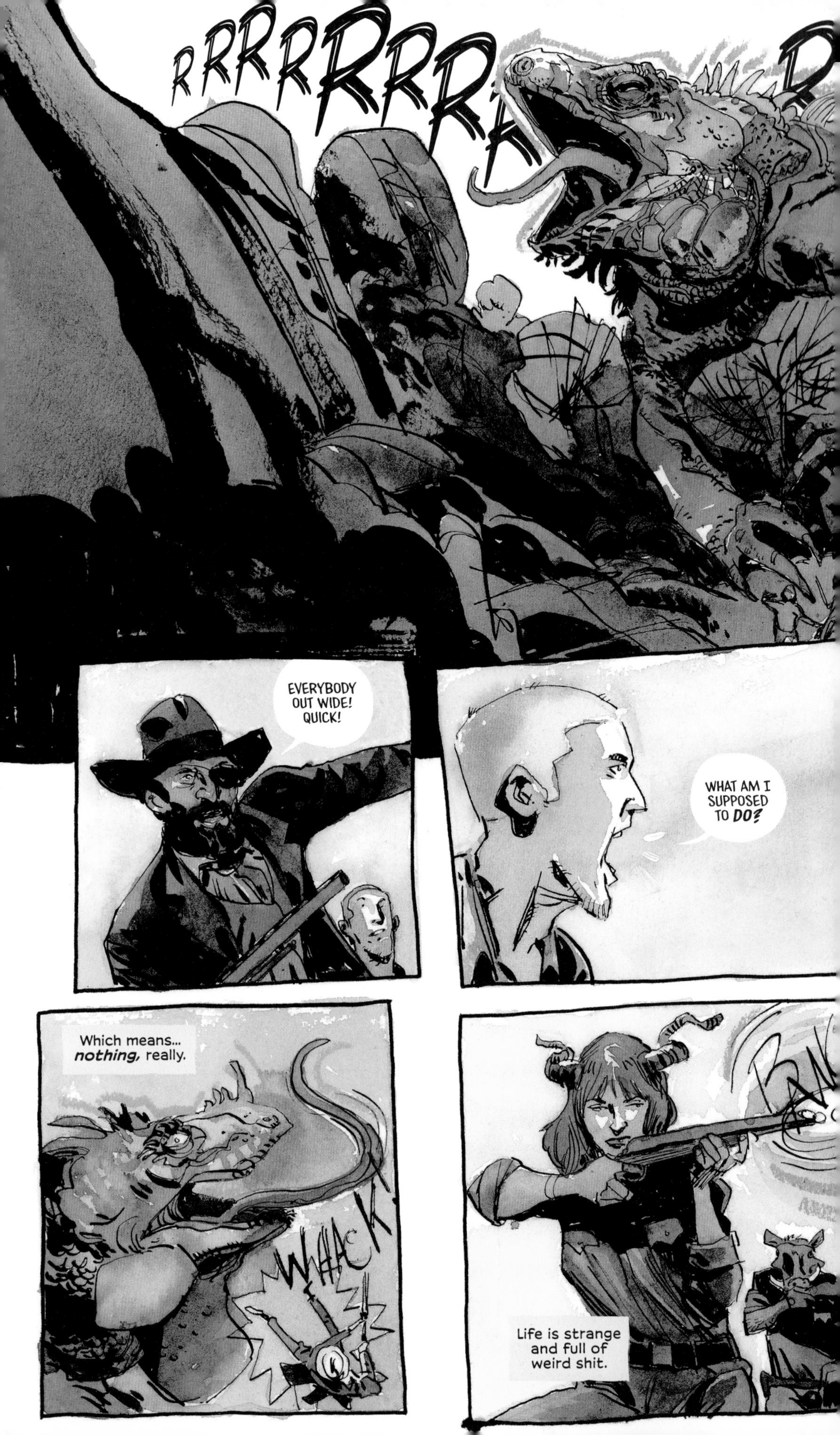
EVERYBODY OUT WIDE! QUICK!
WHAT AM I SUPPOSED TO *DO?*
Which means... ***nothing,*** really.
WHACK
Life is strange and full of weird shit.

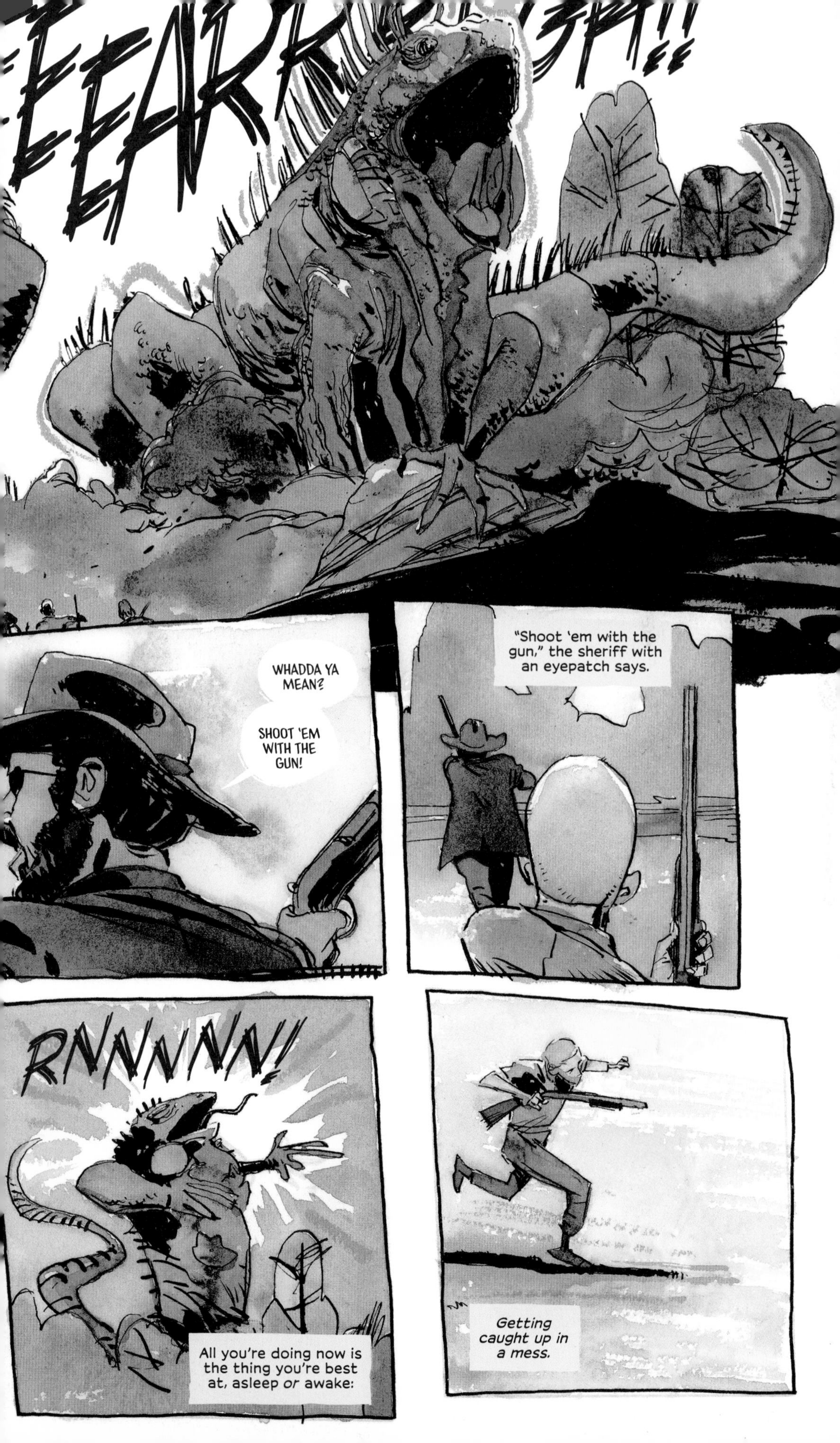

WHADDA YA MEAN?
SHOOT 'EM WITH THE GUN!
"Shoot 'em with the gun," the sheriff with an eyepatch says.
RNNNNN!
All you're doing now is the thing you're best at, asleep *or* awake:
Getting caught up in a mess.

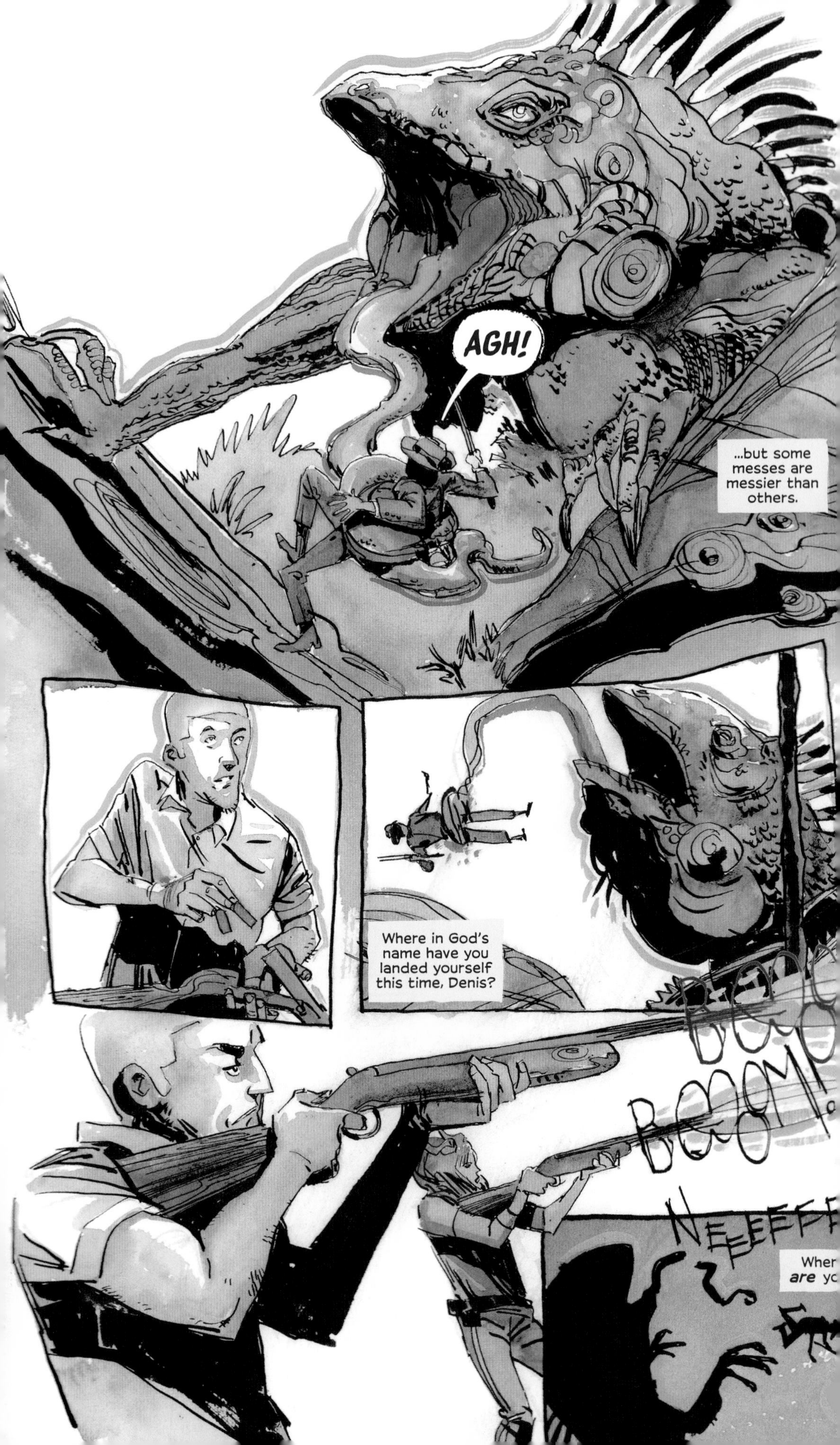
AGH!
...but some messes are messier than others.
Where in God's name have you landed yourself this time, Denis?

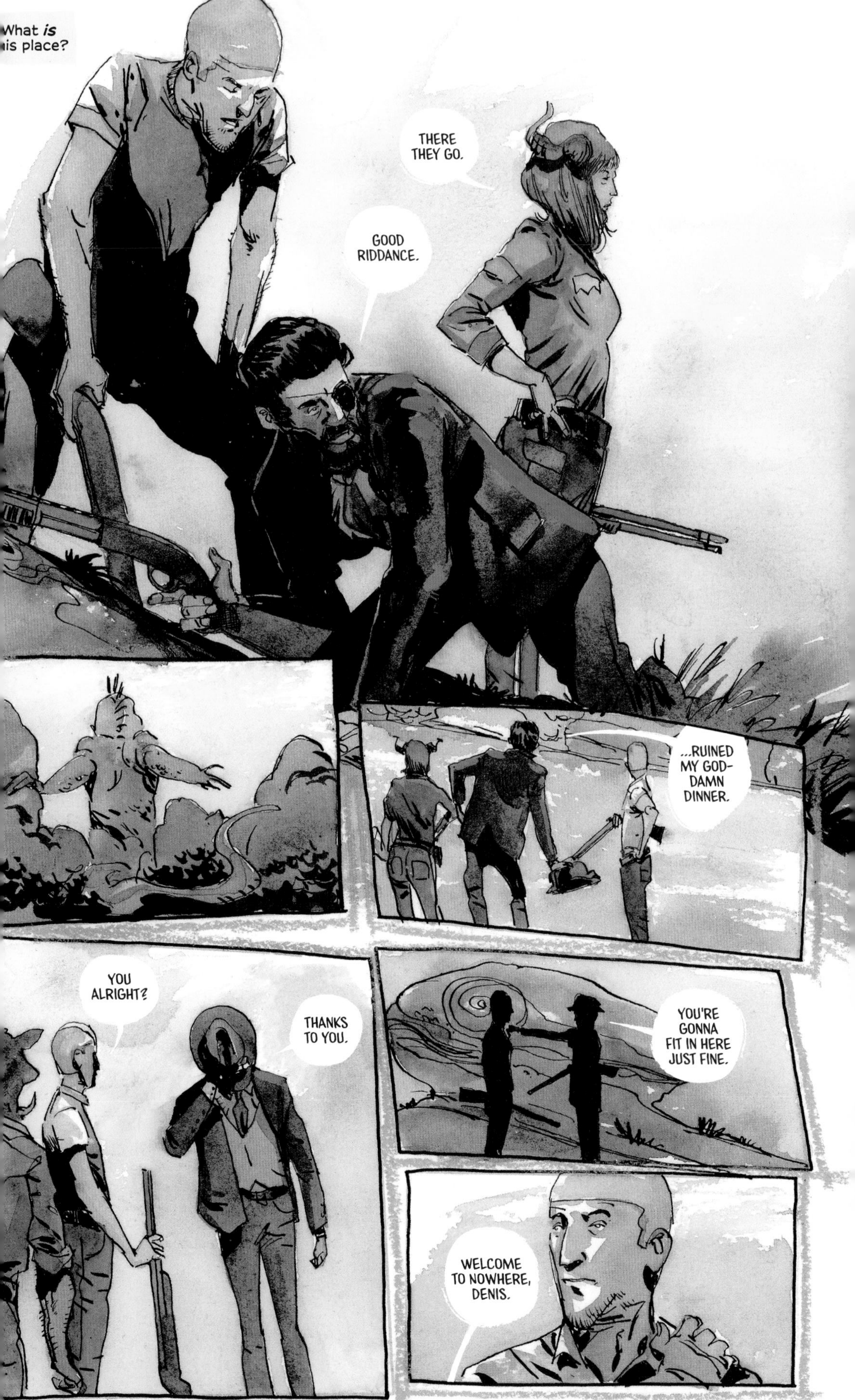
What *is*
is place?
THERE THEY GO.
GOOD RIDDANCE.
...RUINED MY GOD-DAMN DINNER.
YOU ALRIGHT?
THANKS TO YOU.
YOU'RE GONNA FIT IN HERE JUST FINE.
WELCOME TO NOWHERE, DENIS.

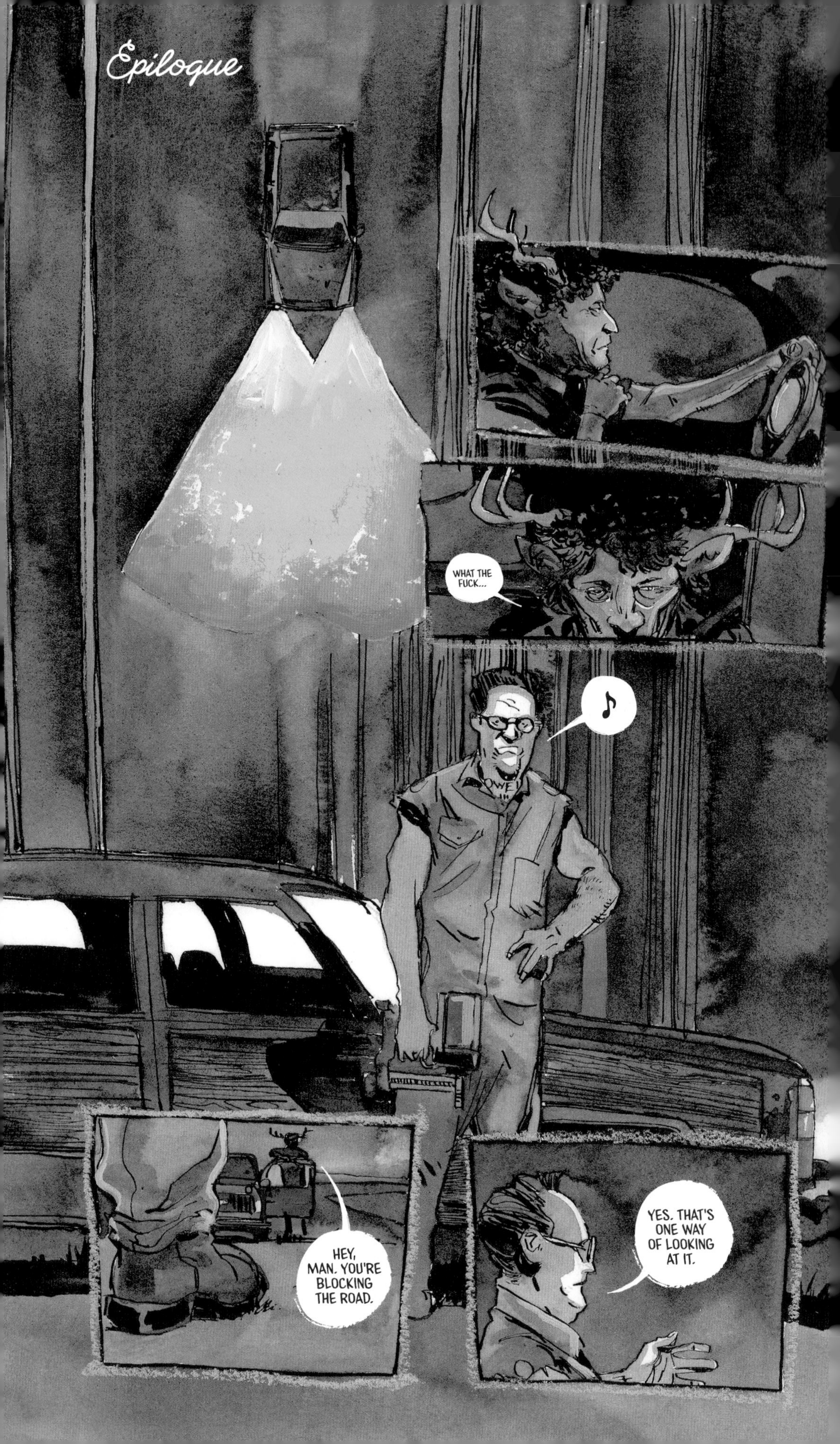
Epilogue
WHAT THE FUCK...
♪
HEY, MAN. YOU'RE BLOCKING THE ROAD.
YES. THAT'S ONE WAY OF LOOKING AT IT.

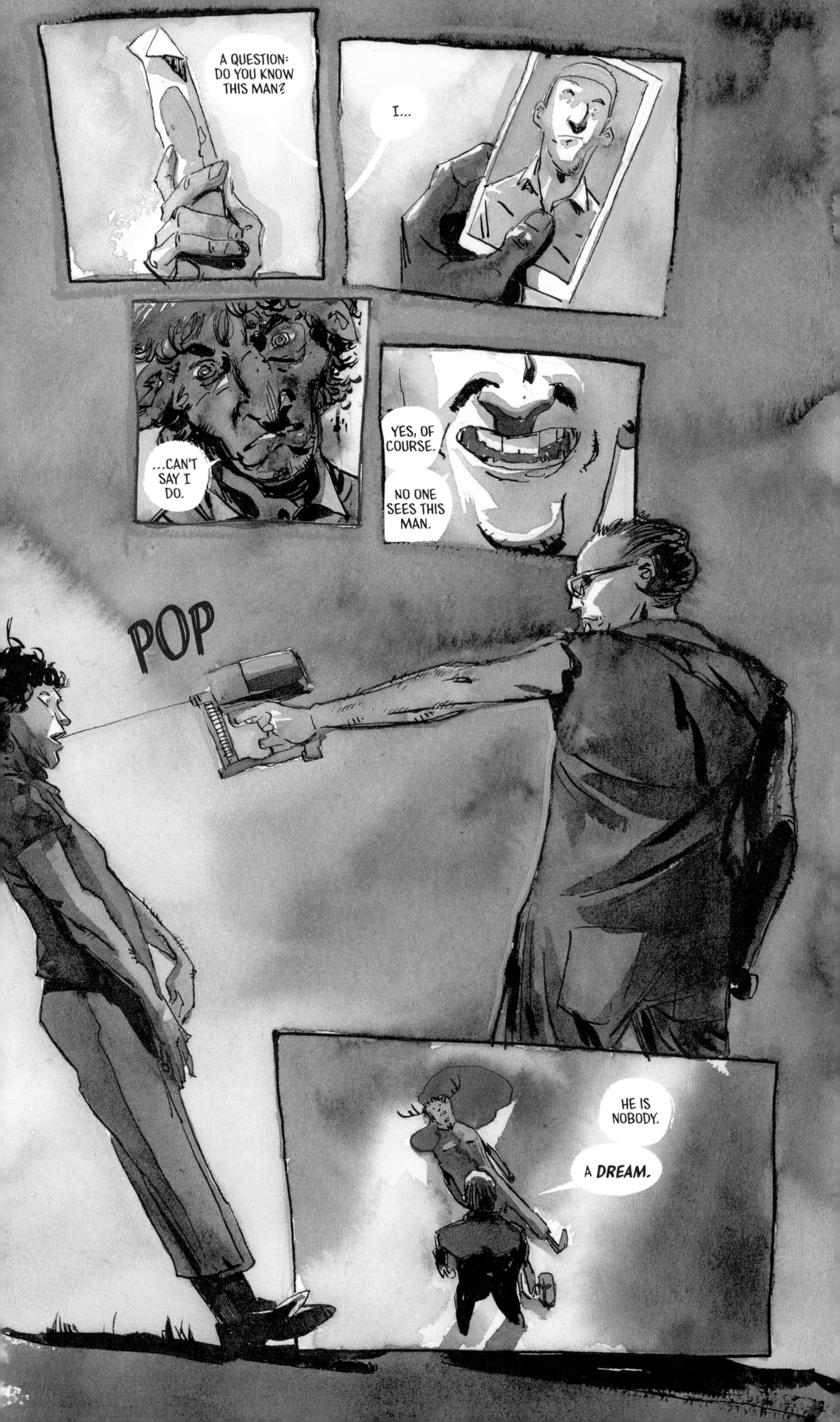
A QUESTION:
DO YOU KNOW THIS MAN?
I...
...CAN'T SAY I DO.
YES, OF COURSE.
NO ONE SEES THIS MAN.
POP
HE IS NOBODY.
A **DREAM.**

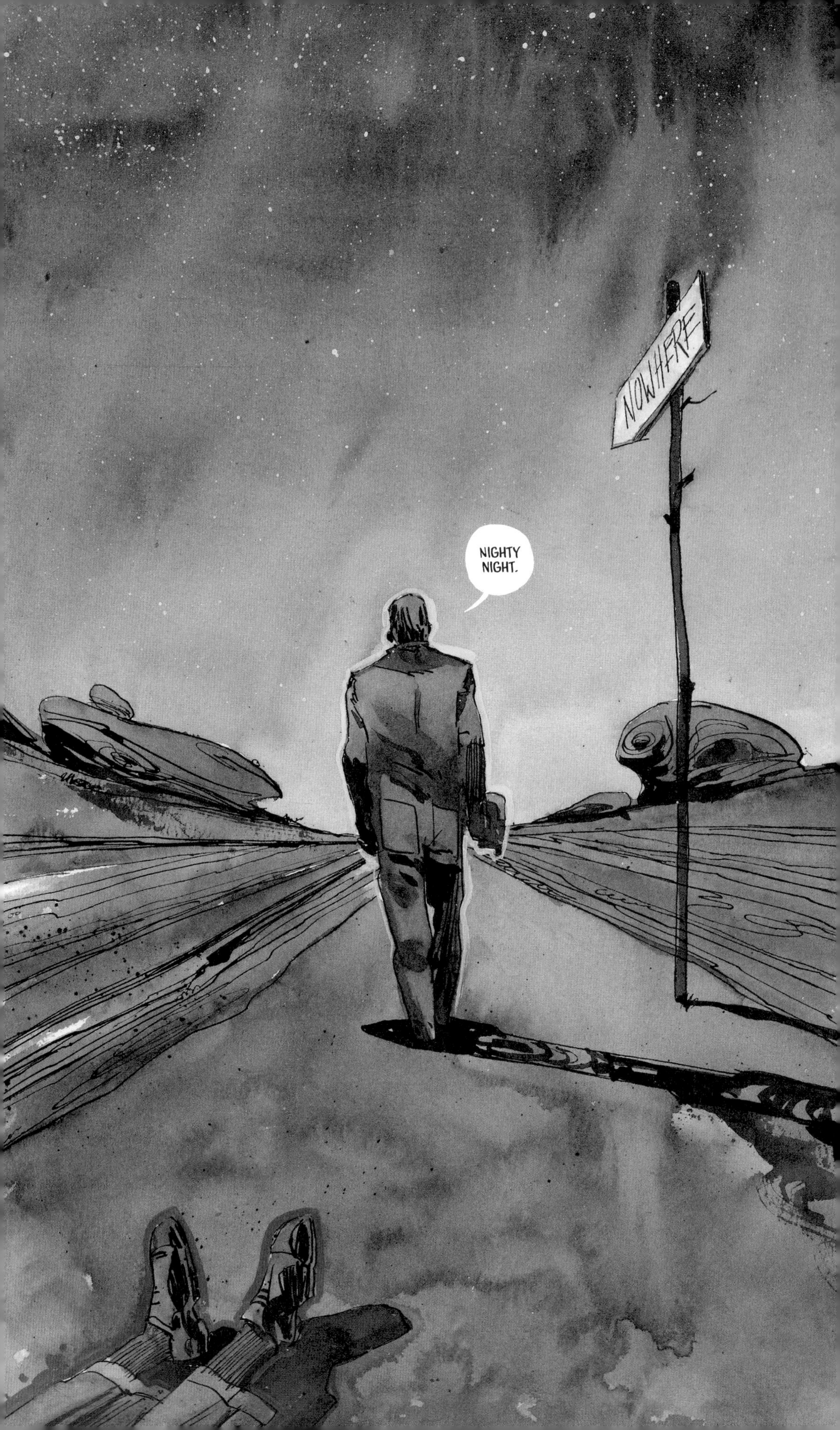
NOWHERE
NIGHTY NIGHT.

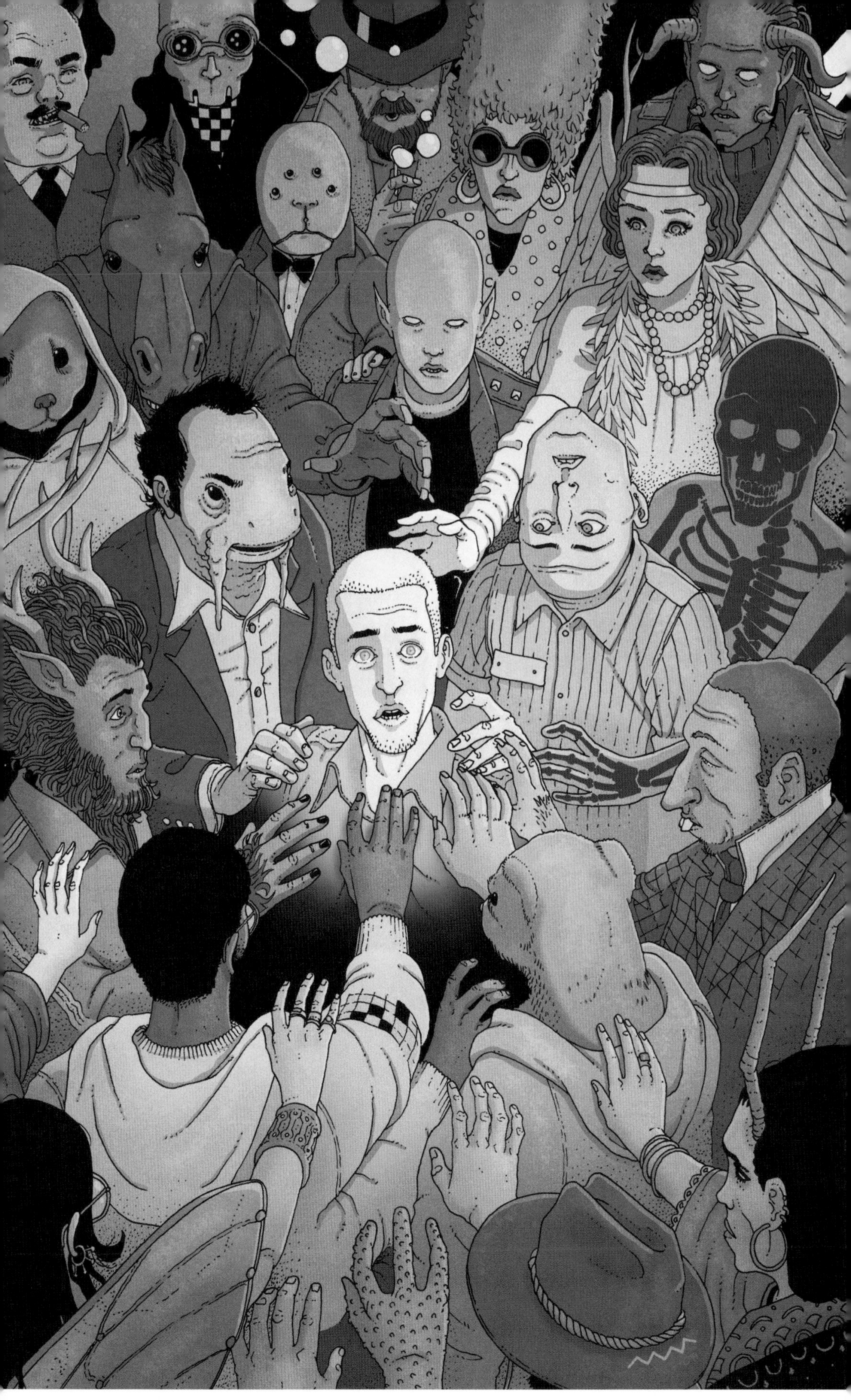

ISSUE ONE COVER BY **MARTÍN MORAZZO** WITH COLORS BY **CHRIS O'HALLORAN**

CHAPTER TWO

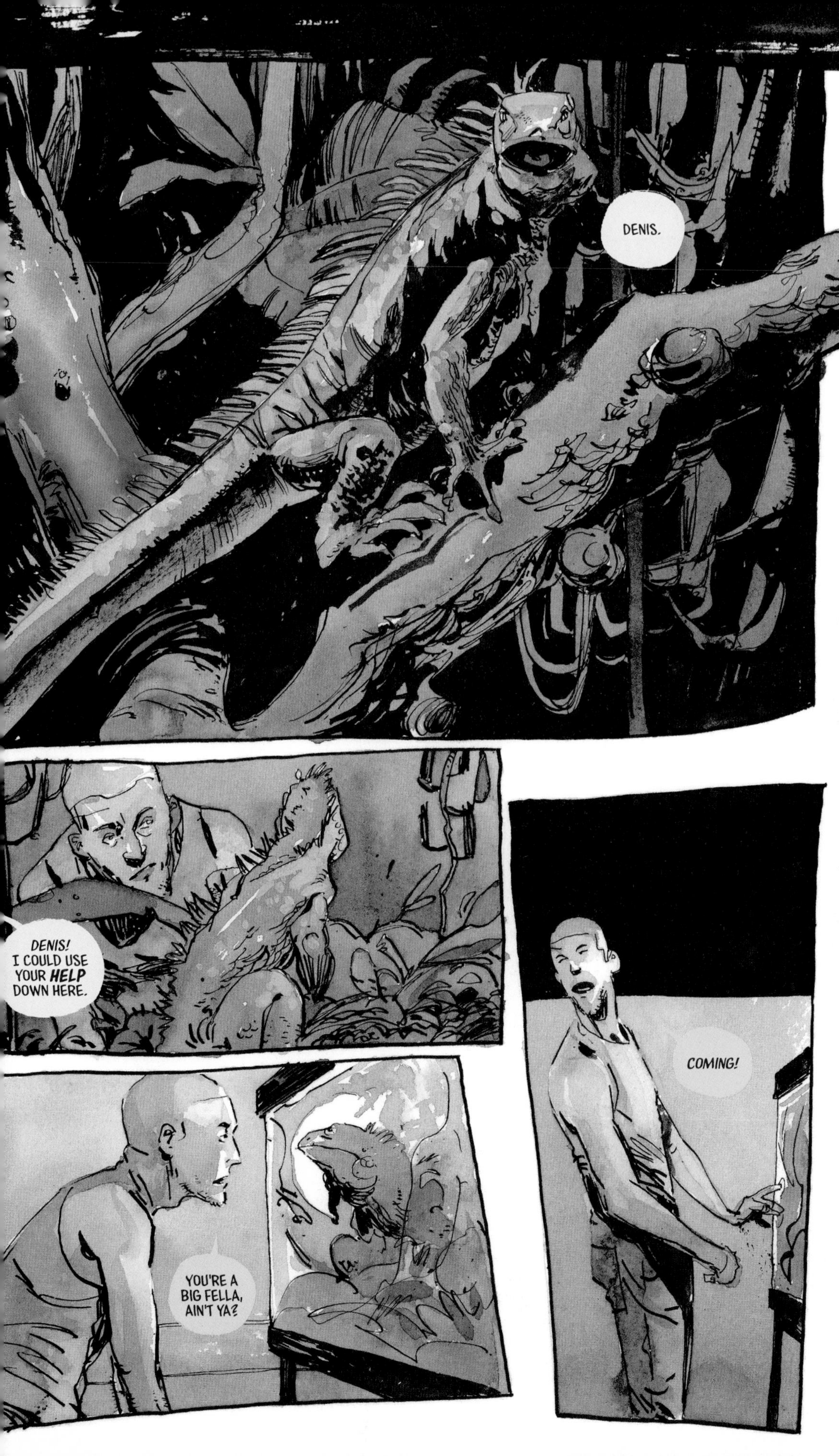
DENIS.
DENIS! I COULD USE YOUR **HELP** DOWN HERE.
YOU'RE A BIG FELLA, AIN'T YA?
COMING!

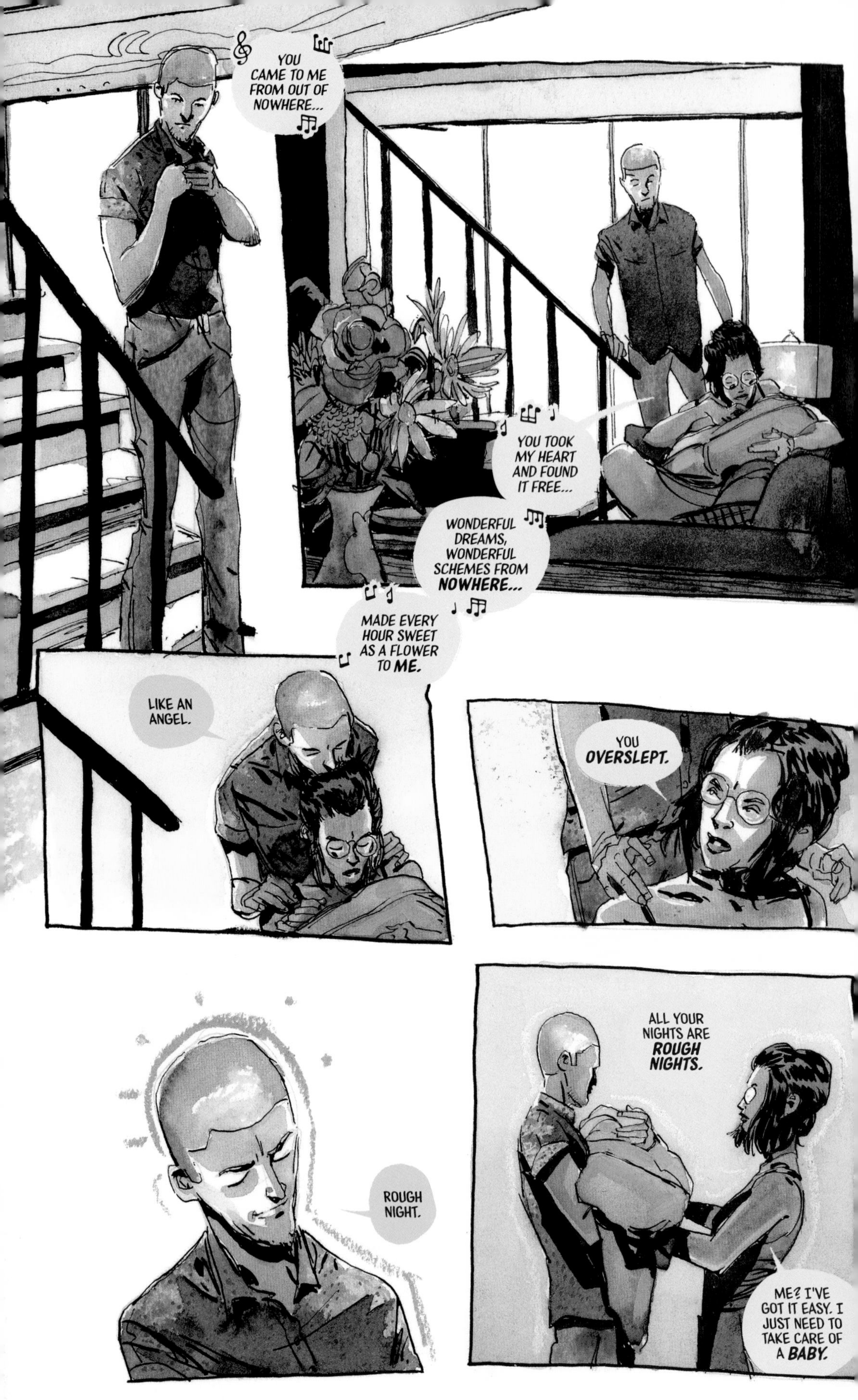
YOU CAME TO ME FROM OUT OF NOWHERE...
YOU TOOK MY HEART AND FOUND IT FREE...
WONDERFUL DREAMS, WONDERFUL SCHEMES FROM NOWHERE...
MADE EVERY HOUR SWEET AS A FLOWER TO ME.
LIKE AN ANGEL.
YOU OVERSLEPT.
ROUGH NIGHT.
ALL YOUR NIGHTS ARE ROUGH NIGHTS.
ME? I'VE GOT IT EASY. I JUST NEED TO TAKE CARE OF A BABY.

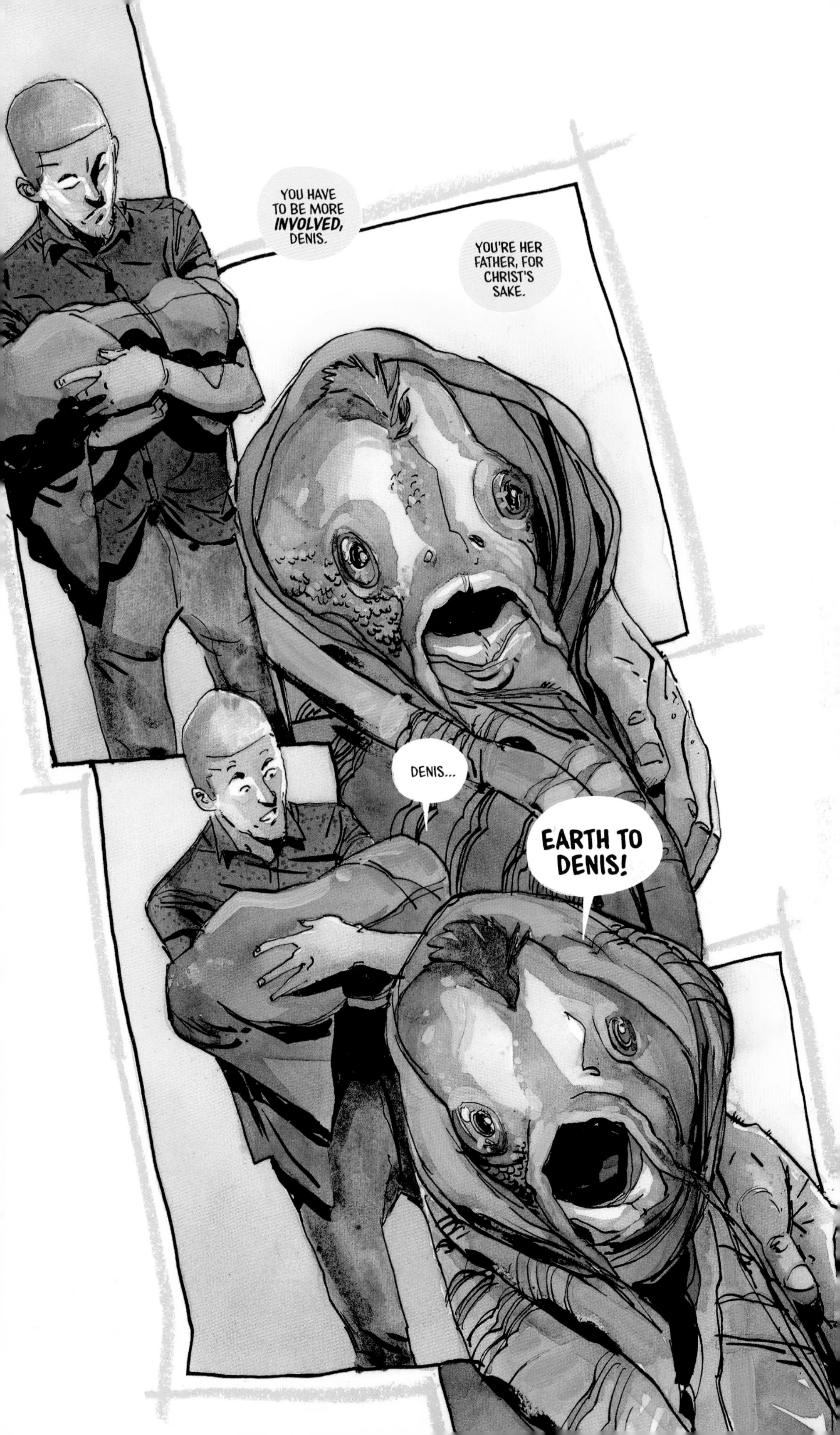
YOU HAVE TO BE MORE *INVOLVED,* DENIS.
YOU'RE HER FATHER, FOR CHRIST'S SAKE.
DENIS...
EARTH TO DENIS!

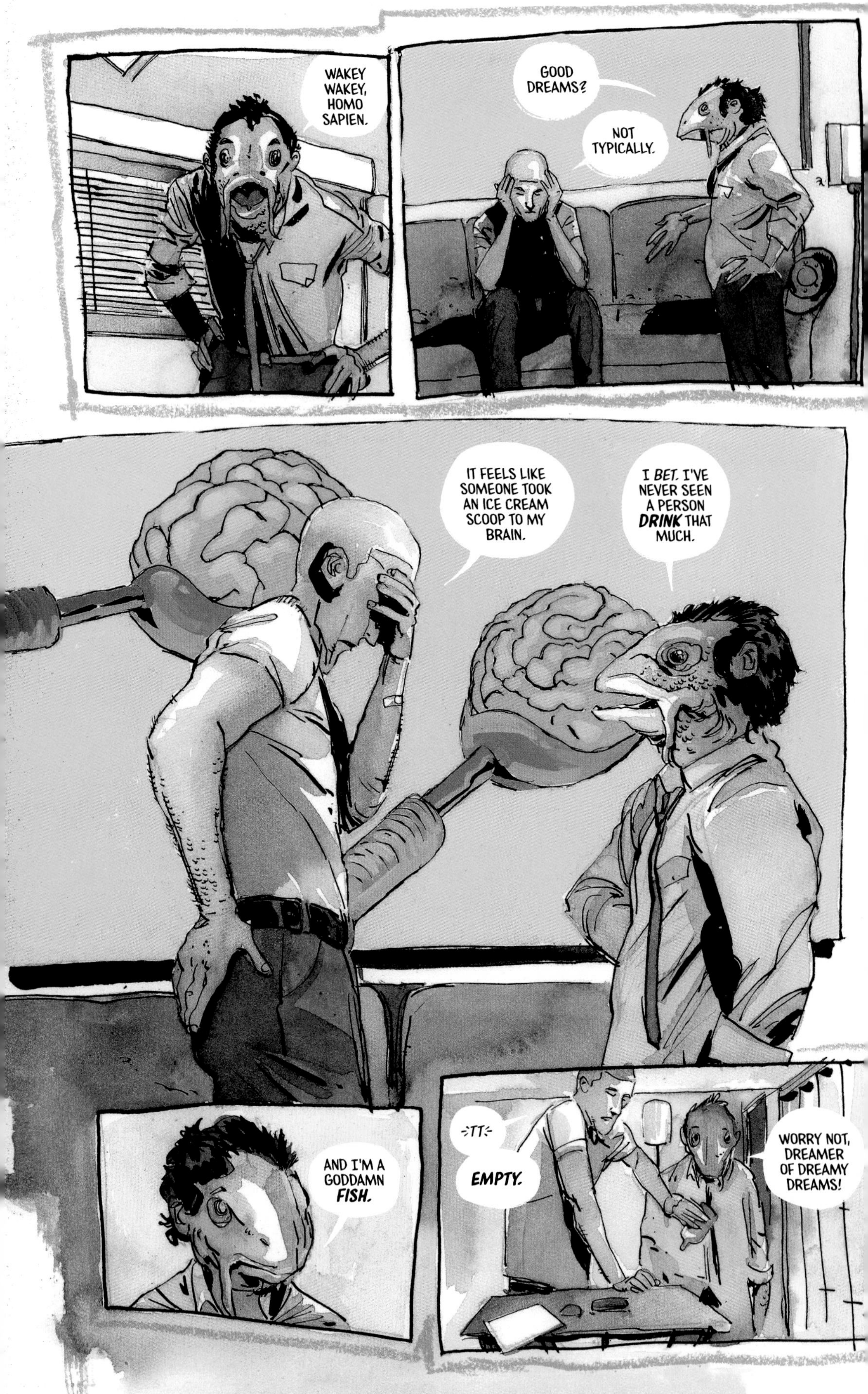
WAKEY WAKEY, HOMO SAPIEN.
GOOD DREAMS?
NOT TYPICALLY.
IT FEELS LIKE SOMEONE TOOK AN ICE CREAM SCOOP TO MY BRAIN.
I *BET.* I'VE NEVER SEEN A PERSON ***DRINK*** THAT MUCH.
AND I'M A GODDAMN ***FISH.***
TT
EMPTY.
WORRY NOT, DREAMER OF DREAMY DREAMS!

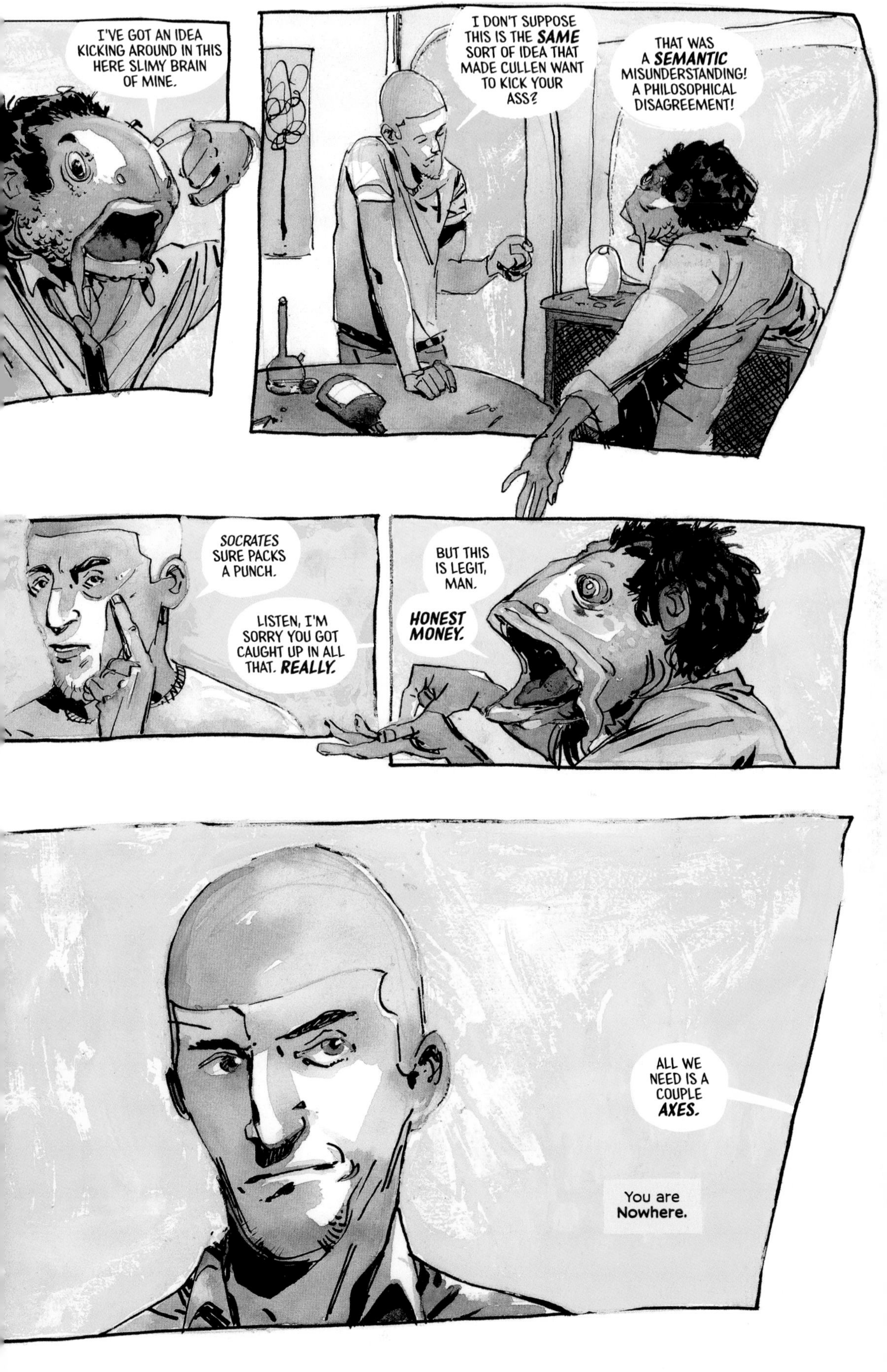
I'VE GOT AN IDEA KICKING AROUND IN THIS HERE SLIMY BRAIN OF MINE.
I DON'T SUPPOSE THIS IS THE SAME SORT OF IDEA THAT MADE CULLEN WANT TO KICK YOUR ASS?
THAT WAS A SEMANTIC MISUNDERSTANDING! A PHILOSOPHICAL DISAGREEMENT!
SOCRATES SURE PACKS A PUNCH.
LISTEN, I'M SORRY YOU GOT CAUGHT UP IN ALL THAT. REALLY.
BUT THIS IS LEGIT, MAN.
HONEST MONEY.
ALL WE NEED IS A COUPLE AXES.
You are Nowhere.

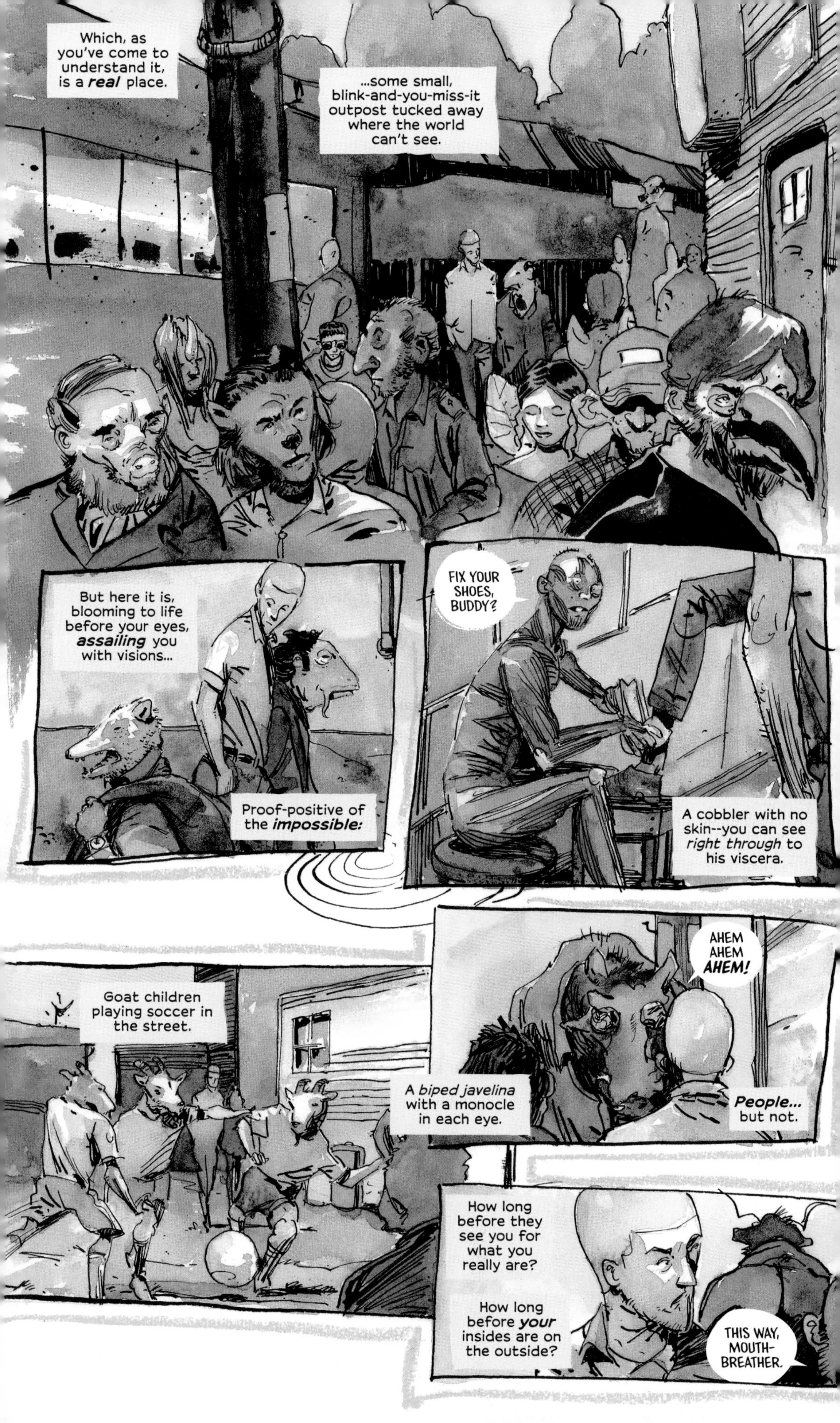

Which, as you've come to understand it, is a ***real*** place.
...some small, blink-and-you-miss-it outpost tucked away where the world can't see.
But here it is, blooming to life before your eyes, ***assailing*** you with visions...
Proof-positive of the ***impossible:***
FIX YOUR SHOES, BUDDY?
A cobbler with no skin--you can see *right through* to his viscera.
Goat children playing soccer in the street.
AHEM AHEM ***AHEM!***
A *biped javelina* with a monocle in each eye.
People... but not.
How long before they see you for what you really are?
How long before ***your*** insides are on the outside?
THIS WAY, MOUTH-BREATHER.

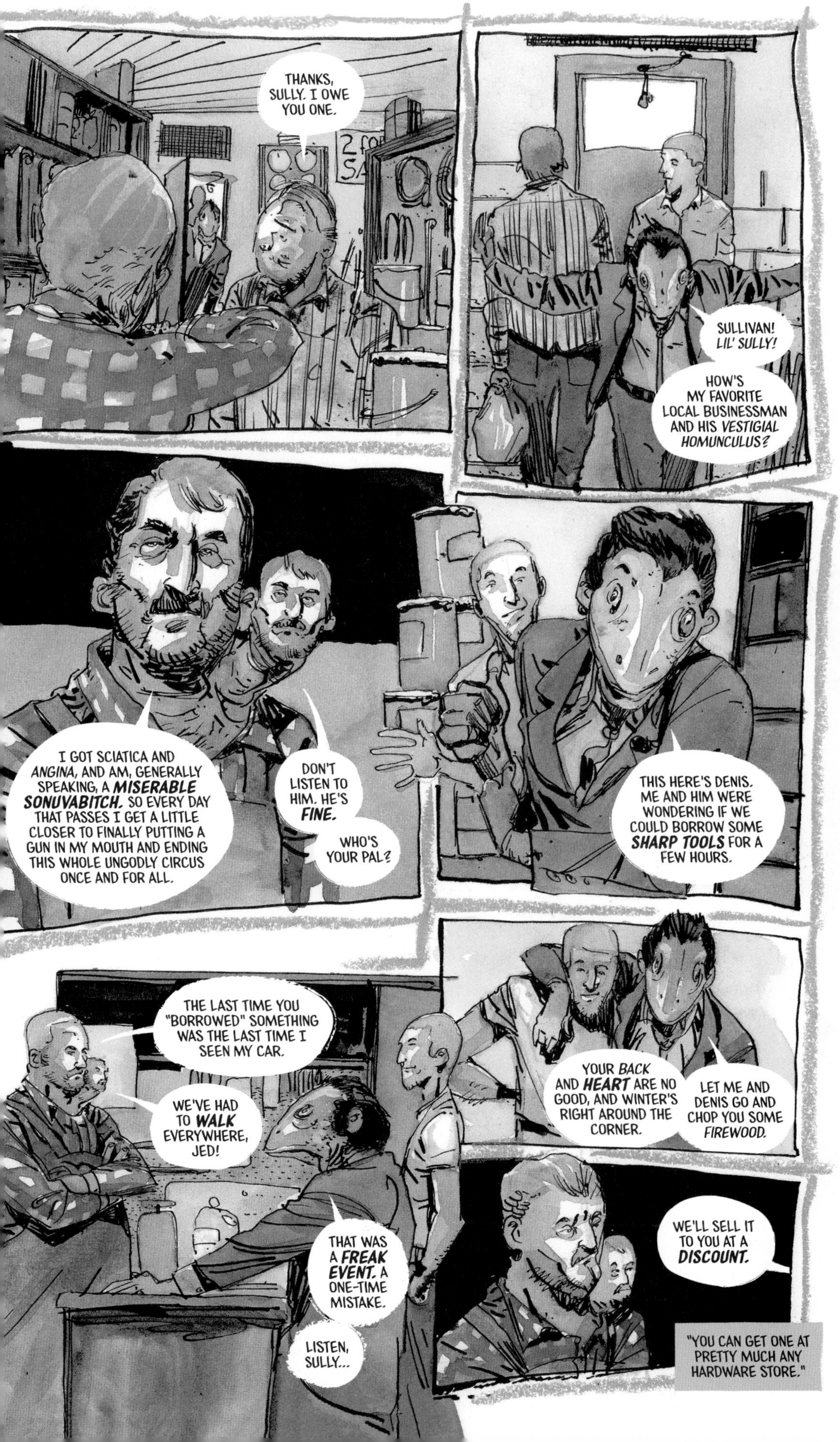
THANKS, SULLY. I OWE YOU ONE.
SULLIVAN! LIL' SULLY!
HOW'S MY FAVORITE LOCAL BUSINESSMAN AND HIS VESTIGIAL HOMUNCULUS?
I GOT SCIATICA AND ANGINA, AND AM, GENERALLY SPEAKING, A MISERABLE SONUVABITCH. SO EVERY DAY THAT PASSES I GET A LITTLE CLOSER TO FINALLY PUTTING A GUN IN MY MOUTH AND ENDING THIS WHOLE UNGODLY CIRCUS ONCE AND FOR ALL.
DON'T LISTEN TO HIM. HE'S FINE.
WHO'S YOUR PAL?
THIS HERE'S DENIS. ME AND HIM WERE WONDERING IF WE COULD BORROW SOME SHARP TOOLS FOR A FEW HOURS.
THE LAST TIME YOU "BORROWED" SOMETHING WAS THE LAST TIME I SEEN MY CAR.
WE'VE HAD TO WALK EVERYWHERE, JED!
THAT WAS A FREAK EVENT. A ONE-TIME MISTAKE.
LISTEN, SULLY...
YOUR BACK AND HEART ARE NO GOOD, AND WINTER'S RIGHT AROUND THE CORNER.
LET ME AND DENIS GO AND CHOP YOU SOME FIREWOOD.
WE'LL SELL IT TO YOU AT A DISCOUNT.
"YOU CAN GET ONE AT PRETTY MUCH ANY HARDWARE STORE."

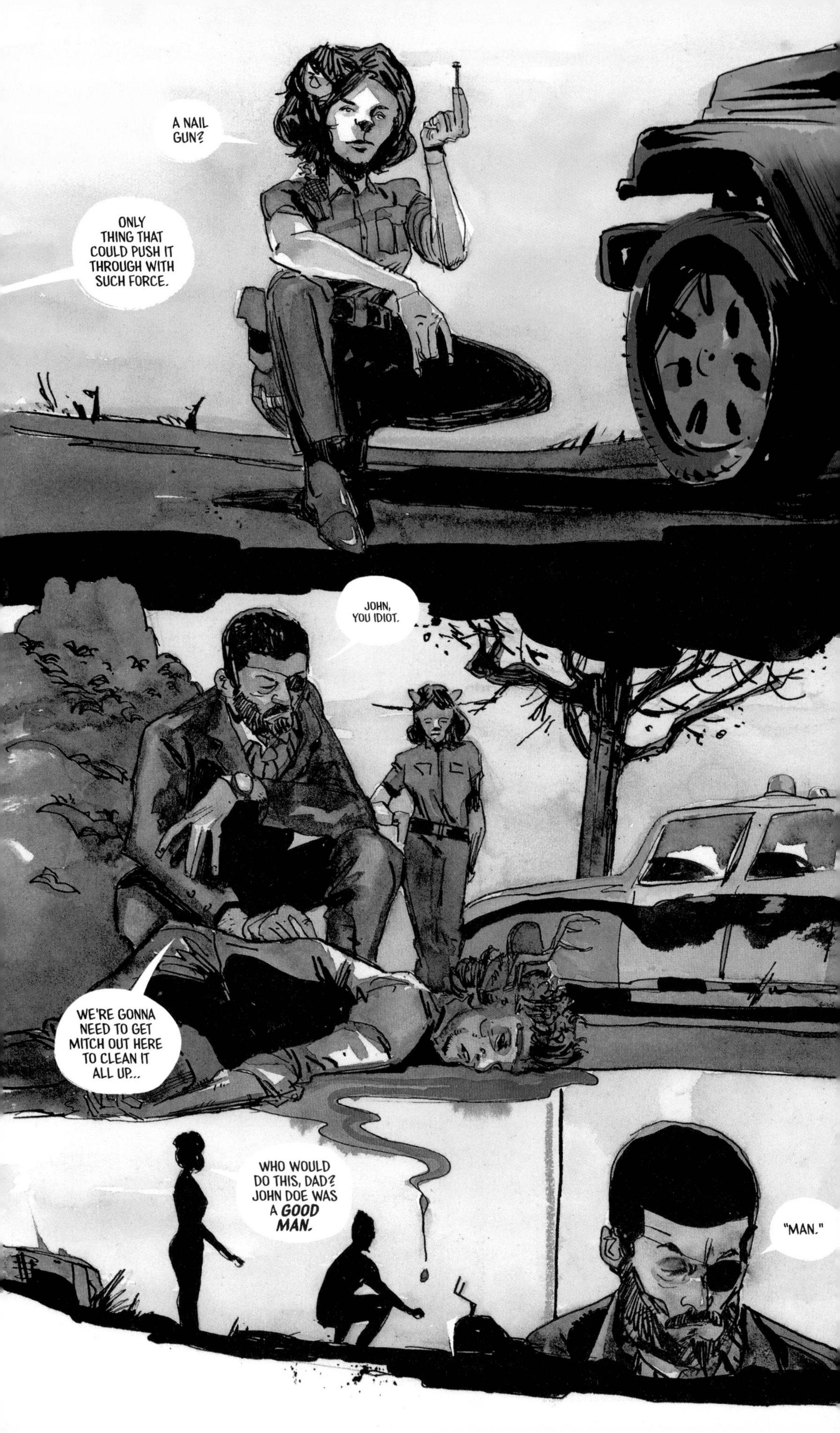
A NAIL GUN?
ONLY THING THAT COULD PUSH IT THROUGH WITH SUCH FORCE.
JOHN, YOU IDIOT.
WE'RE GONNA NEED TO GET MITCH OUT HERE TO CLEAN IT ALL UP...
WHO WOULD DO THIS, DAD? JOHN DOE WAS A GOOD MAN.
"MAN."

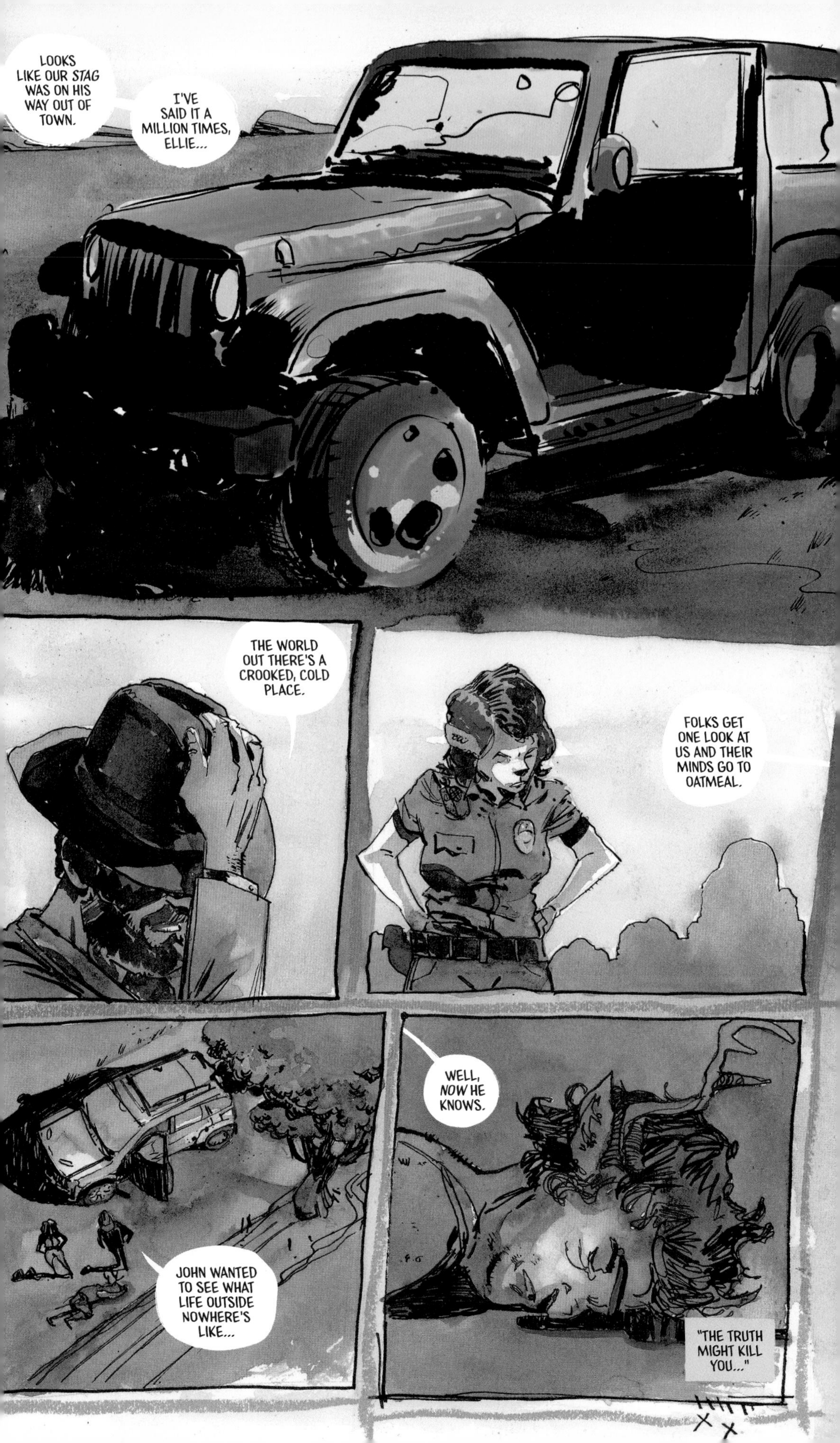
LOOKS LIKE OUR *STAG* WAS ON HIS WAY OUT OF TOWN.
I'VE SAID IT A MILLION TIMES, ELLIE...
THE WORLD OUT THERE'S A CROOKED, COLD PLACE.
FOLKS GET ONE LOOK AT US AND THEIR MINDS GO TO OATMEAL.
JOHN WANTED TO SEE WHAT LIFE OUTSIDE NOWHERE'S LIKE...
WELL, *NOW* HE KNOWS.
"THE TRUTH MIGHT KILL YOU..."

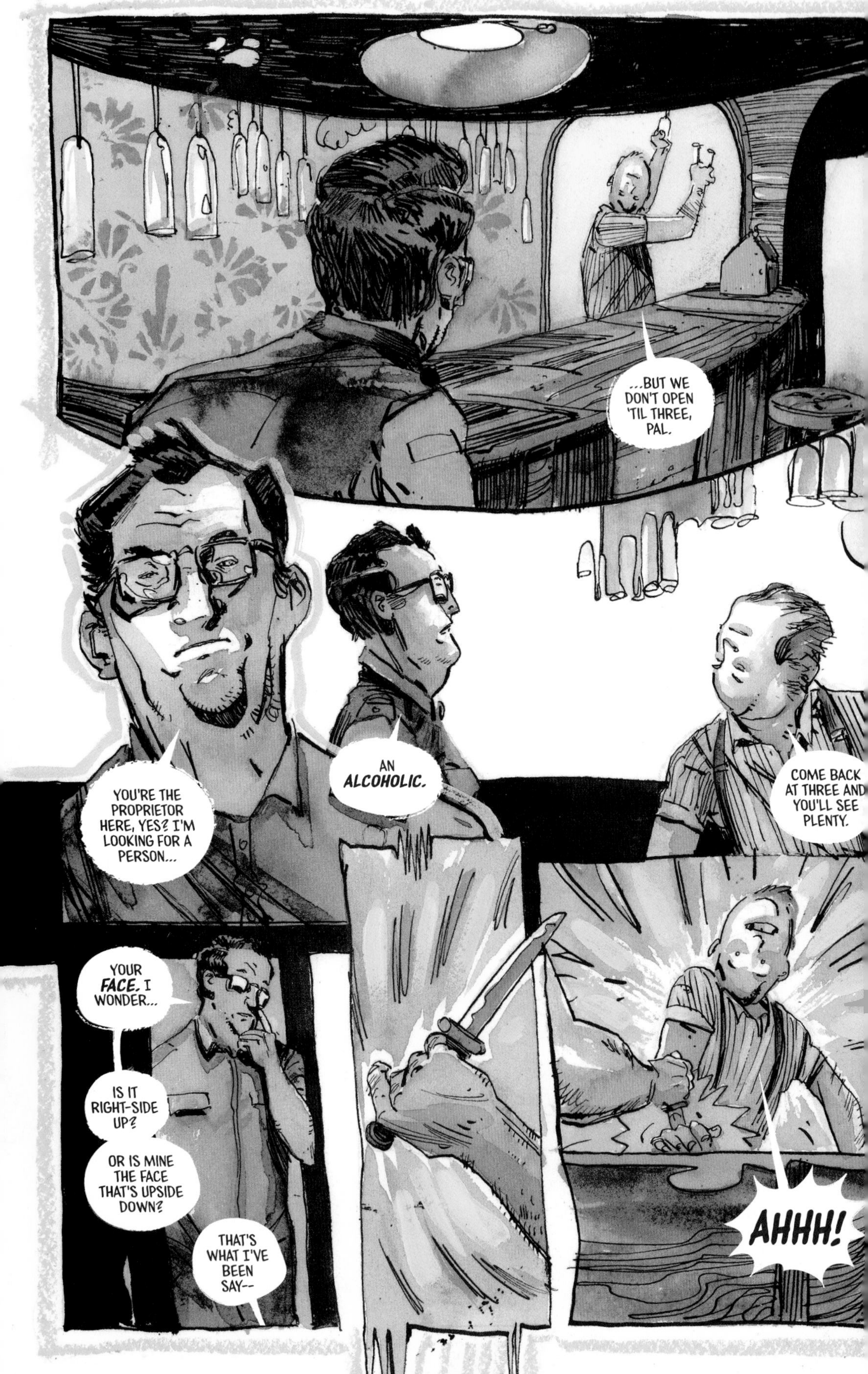
...BUT WE DON'T OPEN 'TIL THREE, PAL.
YOU'RE THE PROPRIETOR HERE, YES? I'M LOOKING FOR A PERSON...
AN ALCOHOLIC.
COME BACK AT THREE AND YOU'LL SEE PLENTY.
YOUR FACE. I WONDER...
IS IT RIGHT-SIDE UP?
OR IS MINE THE FACE THAT'S UPSIDE DOWN?
THAT'S WHAT I'VE BEEN SAY--
AHHH!

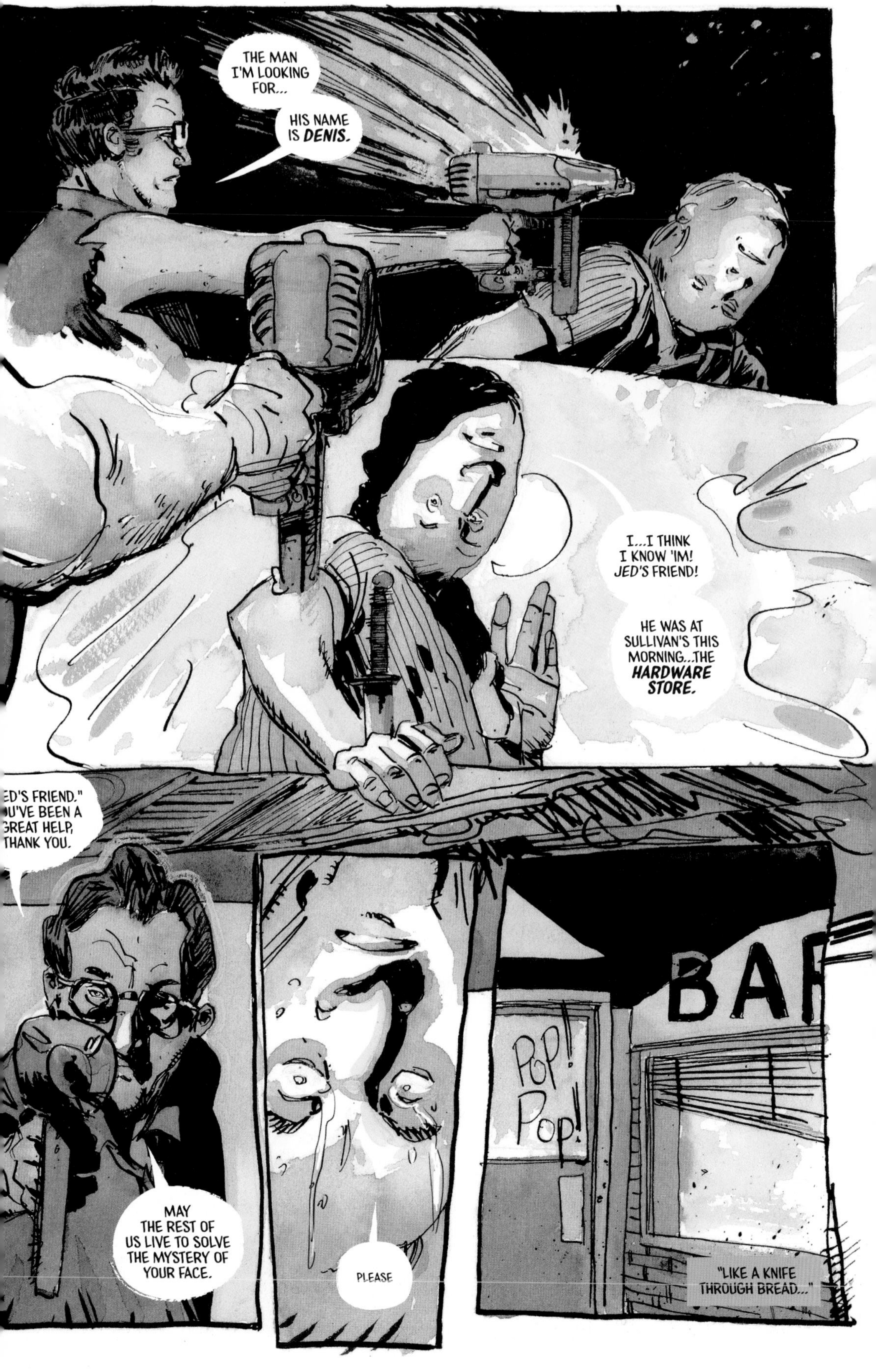
THE MAN I'M LOOKING FOR...
HIS NAME IS DENIS.
I...I THINK I KNOW 'IM! JED'S FRIEND!
HE WAS AT SULLIVAN'S THIS MORNING...THE HARDWARE STORE.
ED'S FRIEND." OU'VE BEEN A GREAT HELP, THANK YOU.
MAY THE REST OF US LIVE TO SOLVE THE MYSTERY OF YOUR FACE.
PLEASE
BAR
POP! POP!
"LIKE A KNIFE THROUGH BREAD..."

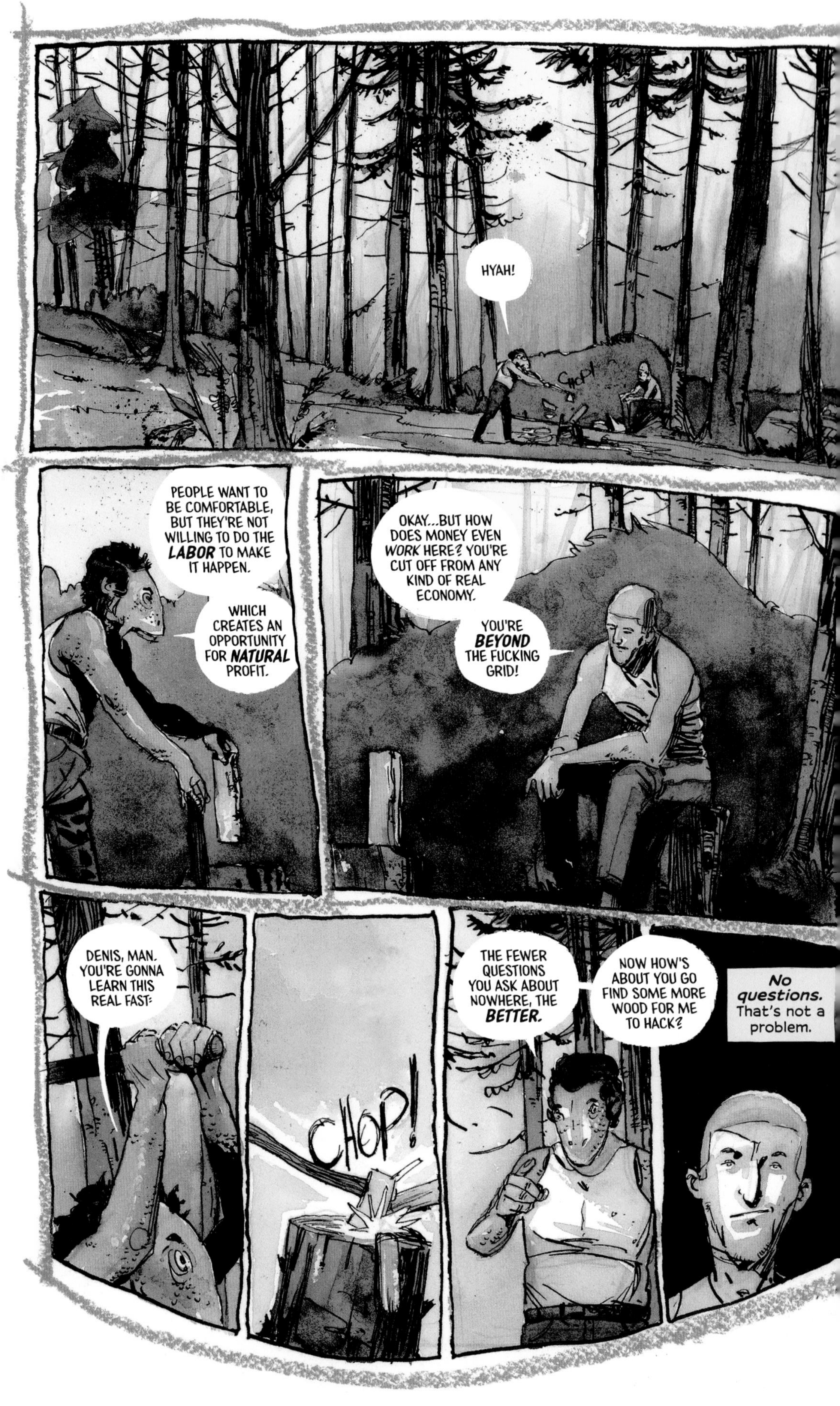
HYAH!
CHOP!
PEOPLE WANT TO BE COMFORTABLE, BUT THEY'RE NOT WILLING TO DO THE **LABOR** TO MAKE IT HAPPEN.
WHICH CREATES AN OPPORTUNITY FOR **NATURAL** PROFIT.
OKAY...BUT HOW DOES MONEY EVEN *WORK* HERE? YOU'RE CUT OFF FROM ANY KIND OF REAL ECONOMY.
YOU'RE **BEYOND** THE FUCKING GRID!
DENIS, MAN. YOU'RE GONNA LEARN THIS REAL FAST:
CHOP!
THE FEWER QUESTIONS YOU ASK ABOUT NOWHERE, THE **BETTER.**
NOW HOW'S ABOUT YOU GO FIND SOME MORE WOOD FOR ME TO HACK?
No questions. That's not a problem.

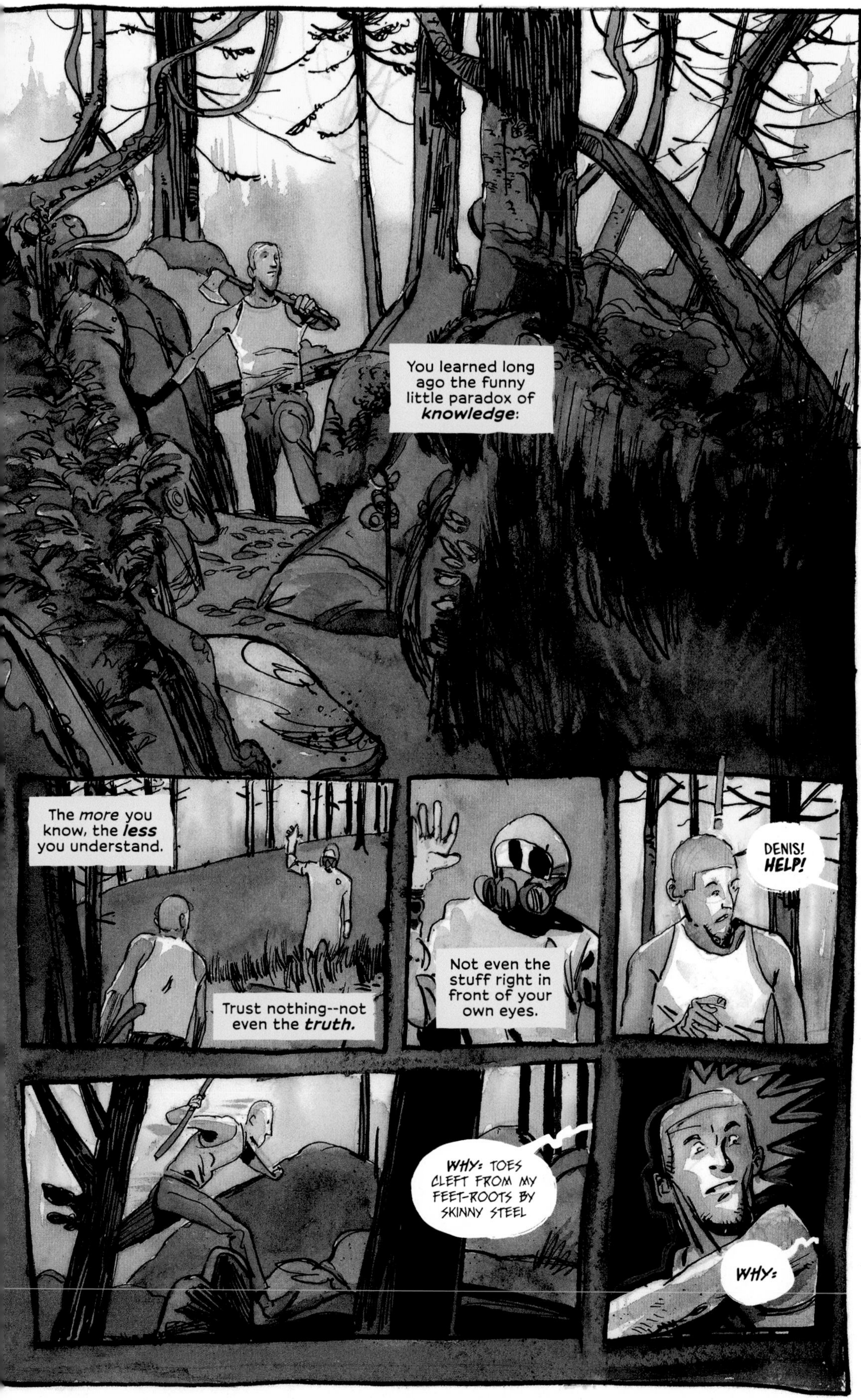
You learned long ago the funny little paradox of ***knowledge***:
The *more* you know, the ***less*** you understand.
Trust nothing--not even the ***truth.***
Not even the stuff right in front of your own eyes.
DENIS! **HELP!**
WHY: TOES CLEFT FROM MY FEET-ROOTS BY SKINNY STEEL
WHY:

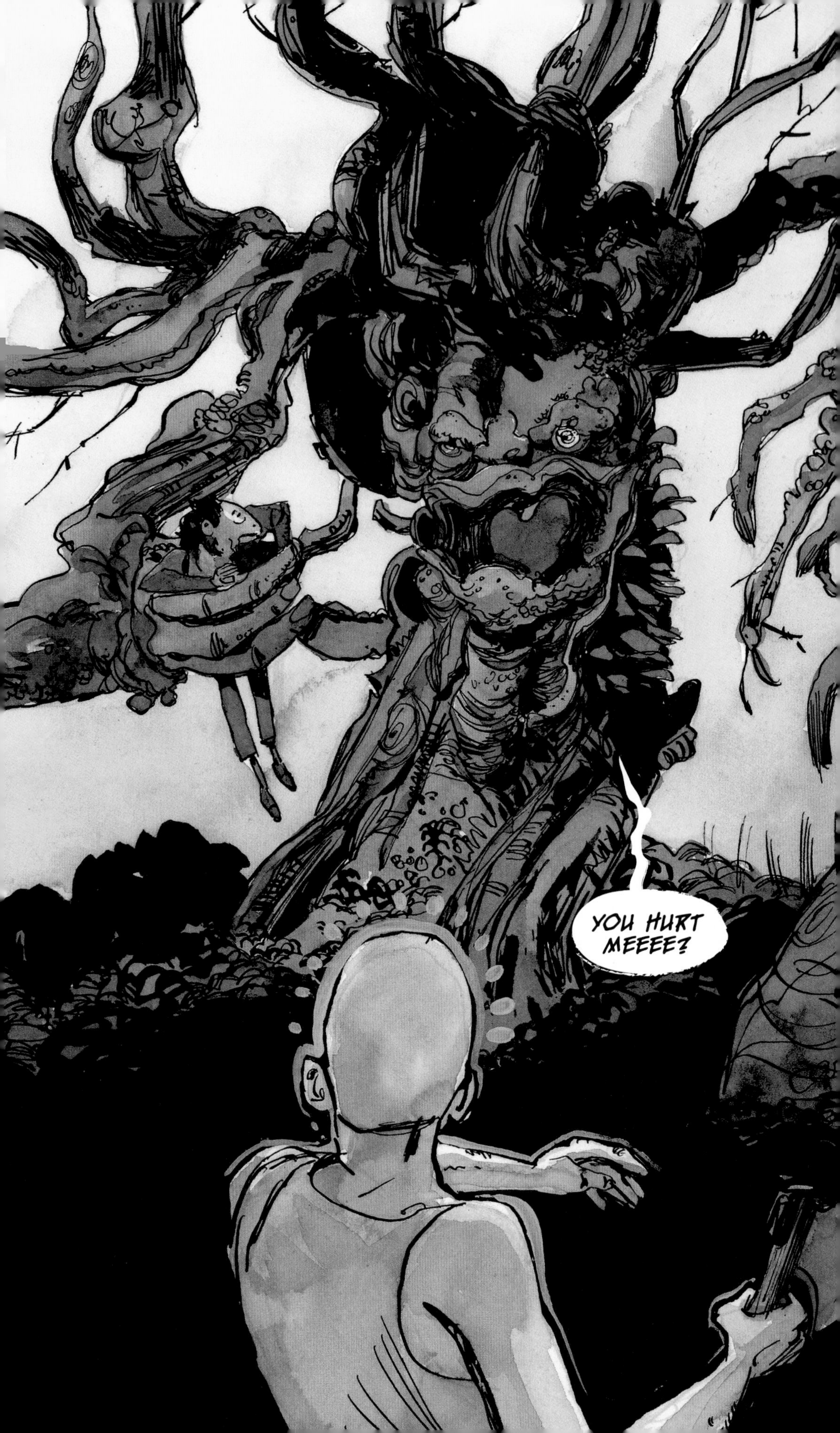
YOU HURT MEEEE?

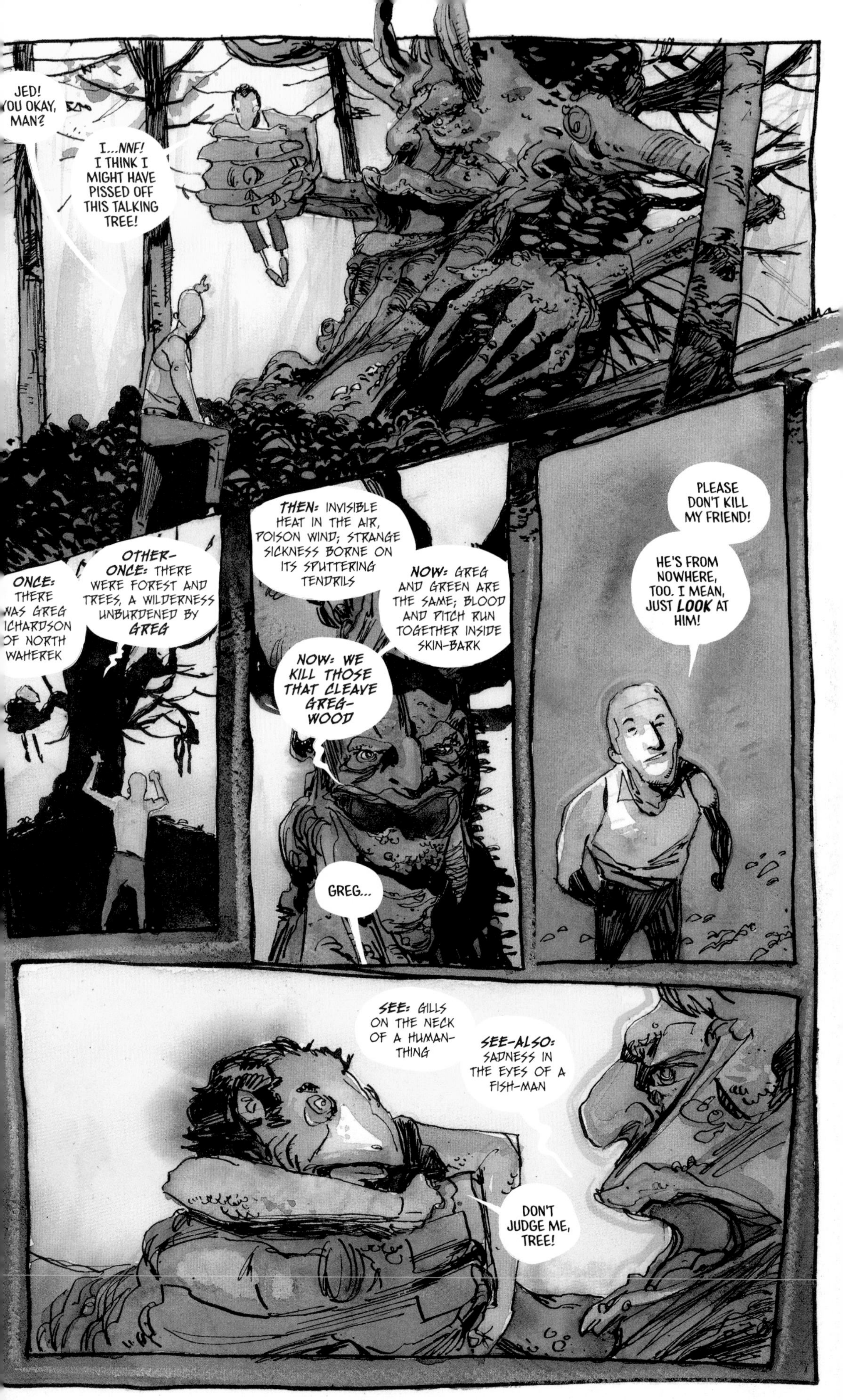
JED! YOU OKAY, MAN?
I...NNF! I THINK I MIGHT HAVE PISSED OFF THIS TALKING TREE!
ONCE: THERE WAS GREG RICHARDSON OF NORTH WAHEREK
OTHER-ONCE: THERE WERE FOREST AND TREES, A WILDERNESS UNBURDENED BY GREG
THEN: INVISIBLE HEAT IN THE AIR, POISON WIND; STRANGE SICKNESS BORNE ON ITS SPUTTERING TENDRILS
NOW: GREG AND GREEN ARE THE SAME; BLOOD AND PITCH RUN TOGETHER INSIDE SKIN-BARK
NOW: WE KILL THOSE THAT CLEAVE GREG-WOOD
GREG...
PLEASE DON'T KILL MY FRIEND!
HE'S FROM NOWHERE, TOO. I MEAN, JUST LOOK AT HIM!
SEE: GILLS ON THE NECK OF A HUMAN-THING
SEE-ALSO: SADNESS IN THE EYES OF A FISH-MAN
DON'T JUDGE ME, TREE!

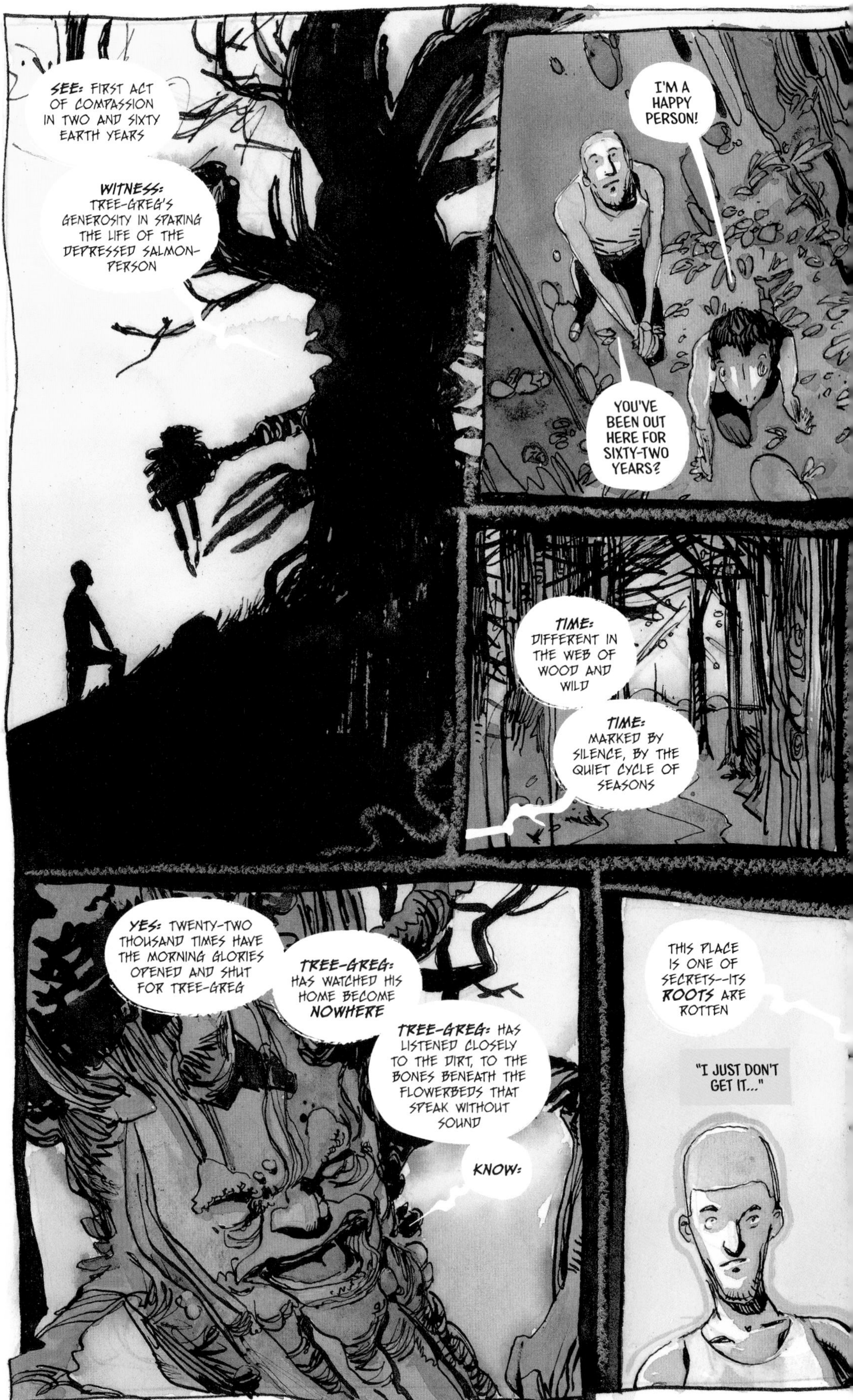

SEE: FIRST ACT OF COMPASSION IN TWO AND SIXTY EARTH YEARS
WITNESS: TREE-GREG'S GENEROSITY IN SPARING THE LIFE OF THE DEPRESSED SALMON-PERSON
I'M A HAPPY PERSON!
YOU'VE BEEN OUT HERE FOR SIXTY-TWO YEARS?
TIME: DIFFERENT IN THE WEB OF WOOD AND WILD
TIME: MARKED BY SILENCE, BY THE QUIET CYCLE OF SEASONS
YES: TWENTY-TWO THOUSAND TIMES HAVE THE MORNING GLORIES OPENED AND SHUT FOR TREE-GREG
TREE-GREG: HAS WATCHED HIS HOME BECOME NOWHERE
TREE-GREG: HAS LISTENED CLOSELY TO THE DIRT, TO THE BONES BENEATH THE FLOWERBEDS THAT SPEAK WITHOUT SOUND
KNOW:
THIS PLACE IS ONE OF SECRETS--ITS ROOTS ARE ROTTEN
"I JUST DON'T GET IT..."

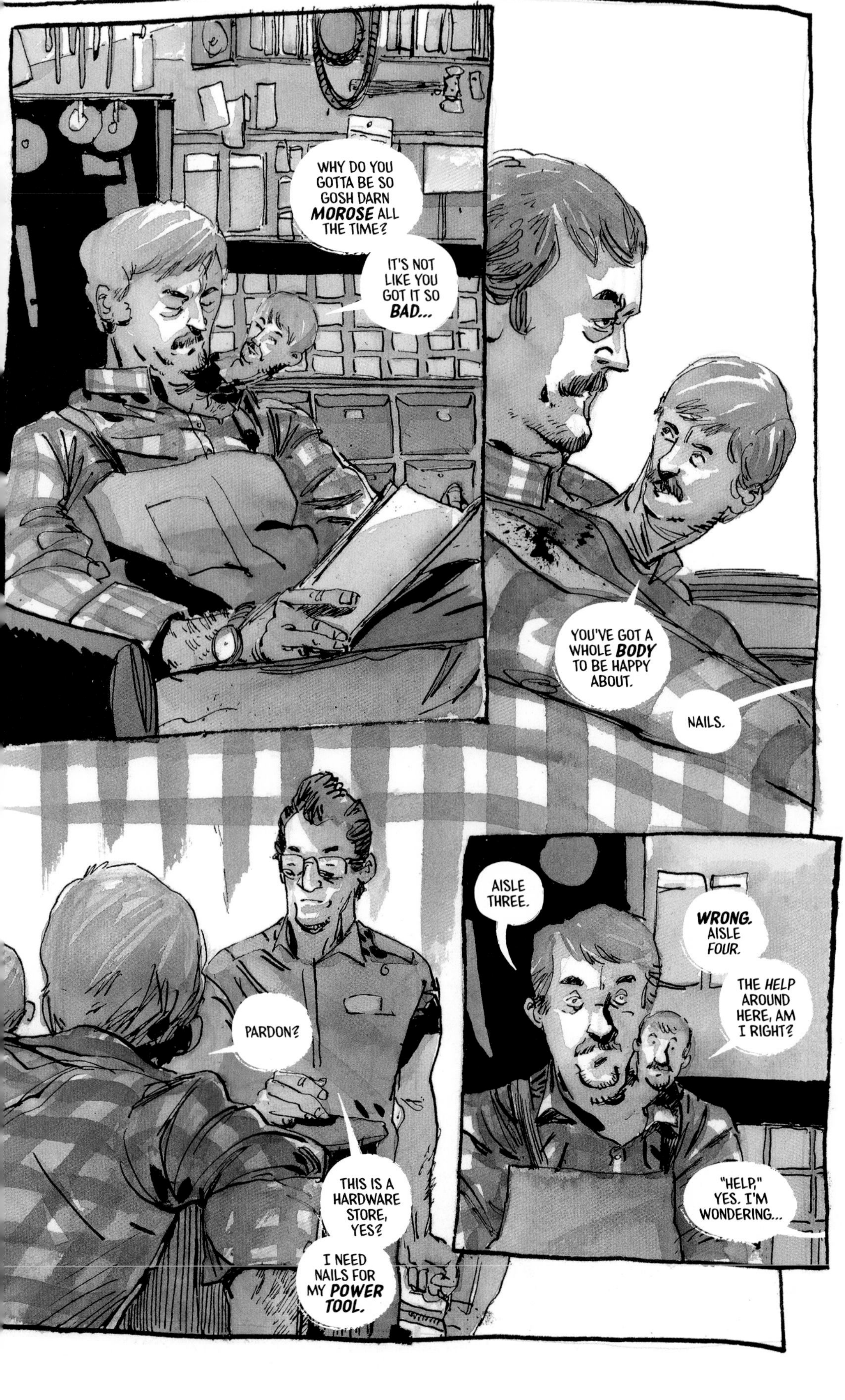
WHY DO YOU GOTTA BE SO GOSH DARN MOROSE ALL THE TIME?
IT'S NOT LIKE YOU GOT IT SO BAD...
YOU'VE GOT A WHOLE BODY TO BE HAPPY ABOUT.
NAILS.
PARDON?
THIS IS A HARDWARE STORE, YES?
I NEED NAILS FOR MY POWER TOOL.
AISLE THREE.
WRONG. AISLE FOUR.
THE HELP AROUND HERE, AM I RIGHT?
"HELP," YES. I'M WONDERING...

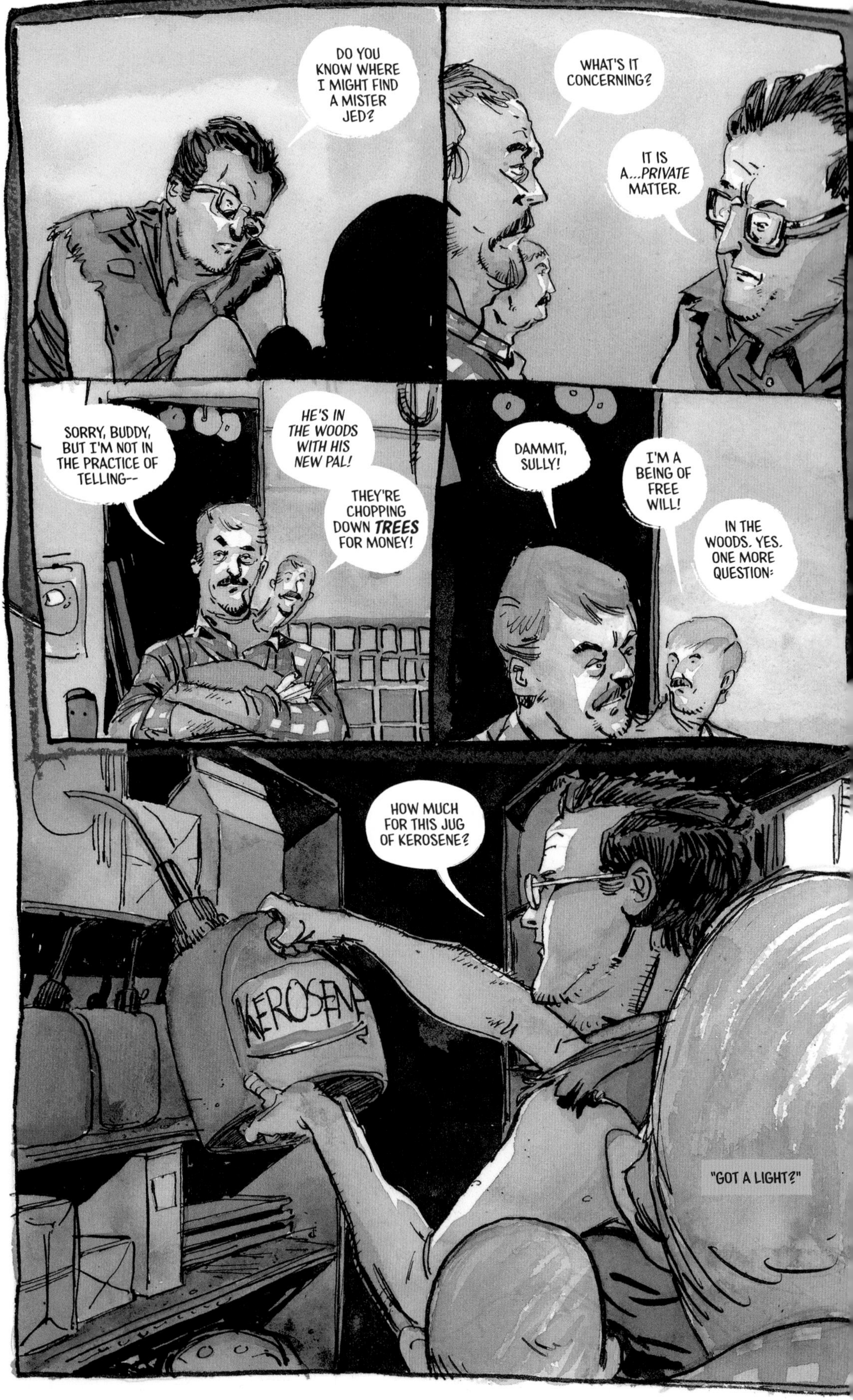
DO YOU KNOW WHERE I MIGHT FIND A MISTER JED?
WHAT'S IT CONCERNING?
IT IS A...*PRIVATE* MATTER.
SORRY, BUDDY, BUT I'M NOT IN THE PRACTICE OF TELLING--
HE'S IN THE WOODS WITH HIS NEW PAL!
THEY'RE CHOPPING DOWN ***TREES*** FOR MONEY!
DAMMIT, SULLY!
I'M A BEING OF FREE WILL!
IN THE WOODS. YES. ONE MORE QUESTION:
HOW MUCH FOR THIS JUG OF KEROSENE?
KEROSENE
"GOT A LIGHT?"

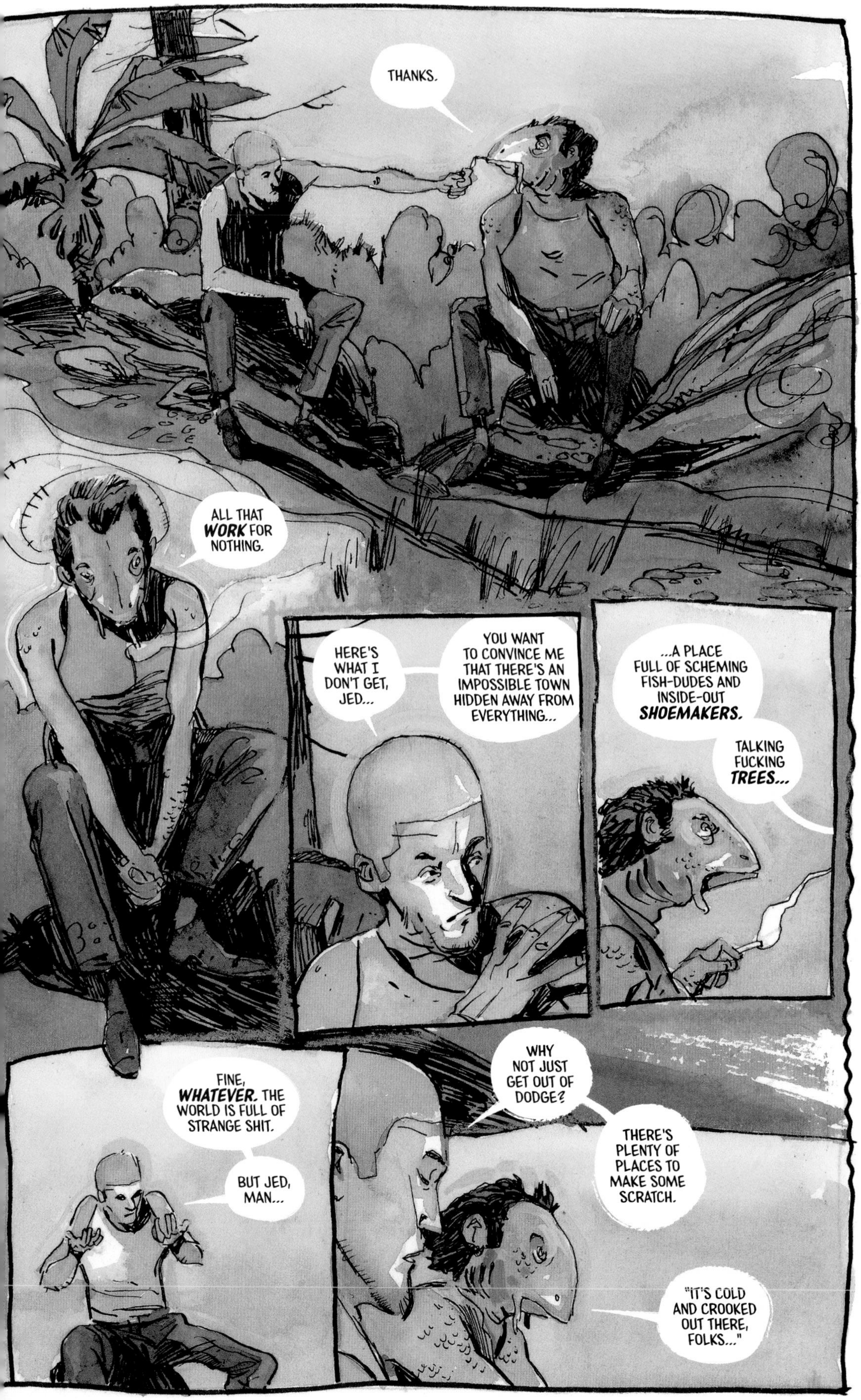
THANKS.
ALL THAT WORK FOR NOTHING.
HERE'S WHAT I DON'T GET, JED...
YOU WANT TO CONVINCE ME THAT THERE'S AN IMPOSSIBLE TOWN HIDDEN AWAY FROM EVERYTHING...
...A PLACE FULL OF SCHEMING FISH-DUDES AND INSIDE-OUT SHOEMAKERS.
TALKING FUCKING TREES...
FINE, WHATEVER. THE WORLD IS FULL OF STRANGE SHIT.
BUT JED, MAN...
WHY NOT JUST GET OUT OF DODGE?
THERE'S PLENTY OF PLACES TO MAKE SOME SCRATCH.
"IT'S COLD AND CROOKED OUT THERE, FOLKS..."

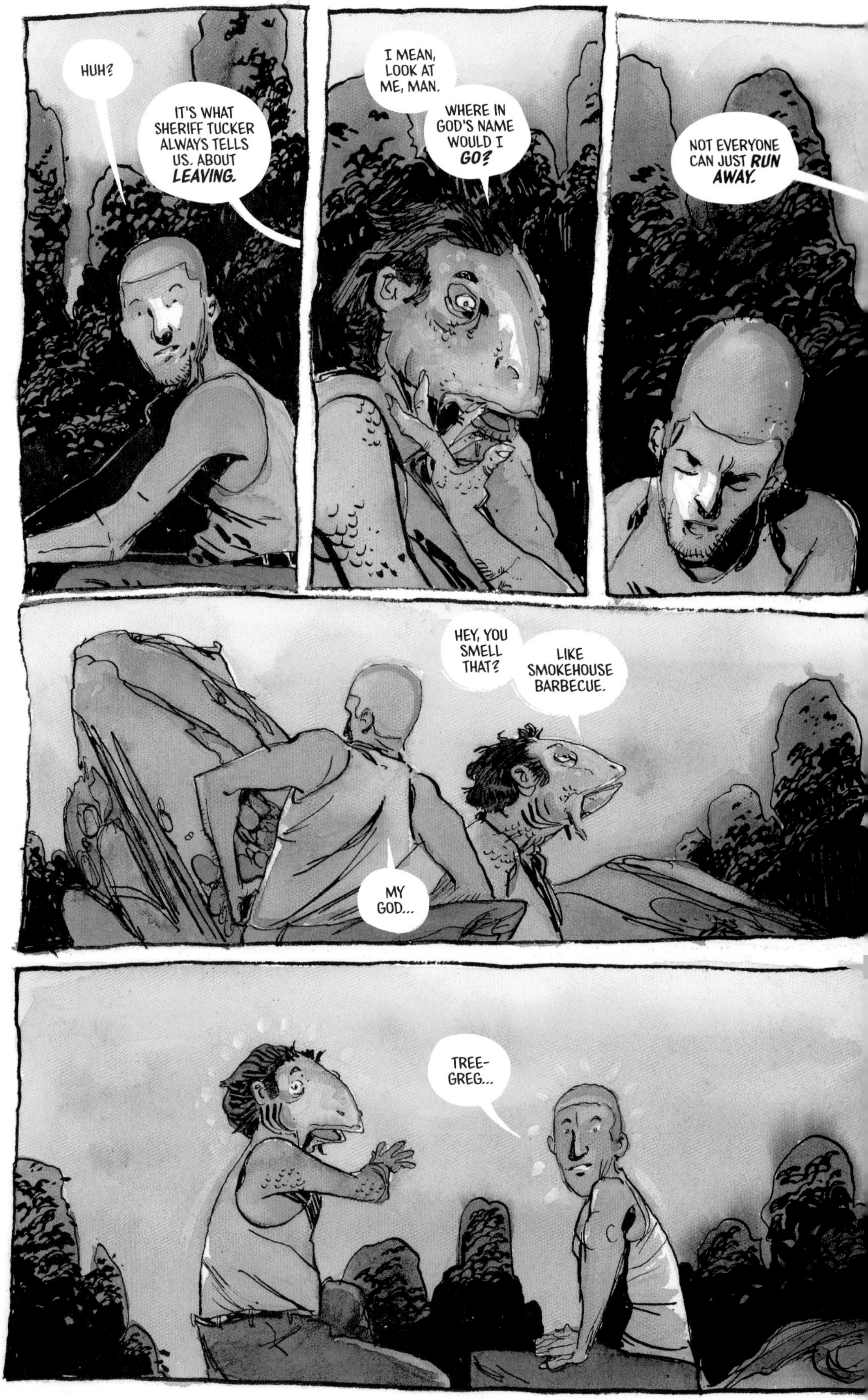
HUH?
IT'S WHAT SHERIFF TUCKER ALWAYS TELLS US. ABOUT LEAVING.
I MEAN, LOOK AT ME, MAN.
WHERE IN GOD'S NAME WOULD I GO?
NOT EVERYONE CAN JUST RUN AWAY.
HEY, YOU SMELL THAT?
LIKE SMOKEHOUSE BARBECUE.
MY GOD...
TREE-GREG...

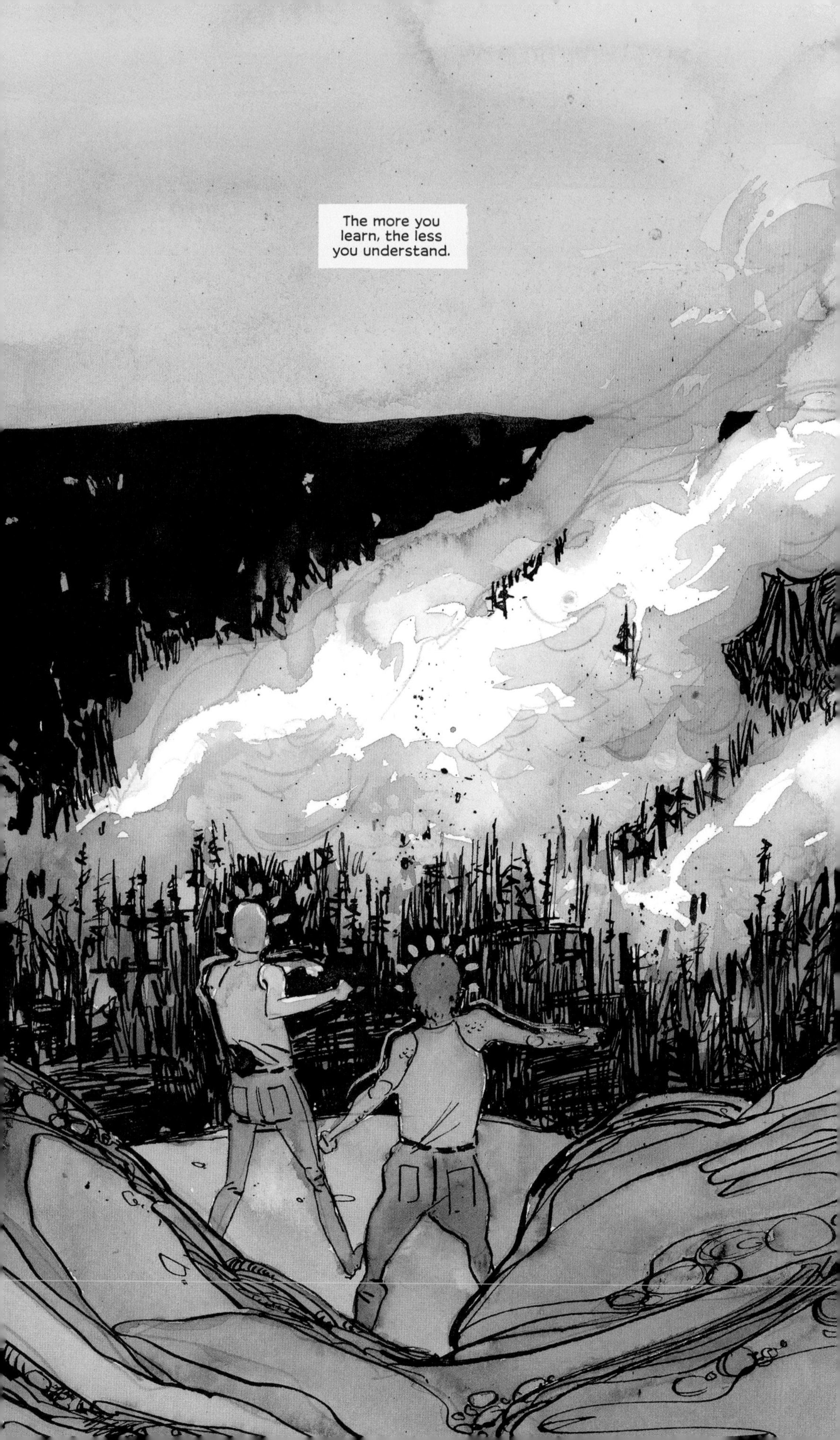
The more you learn, the less you understand.

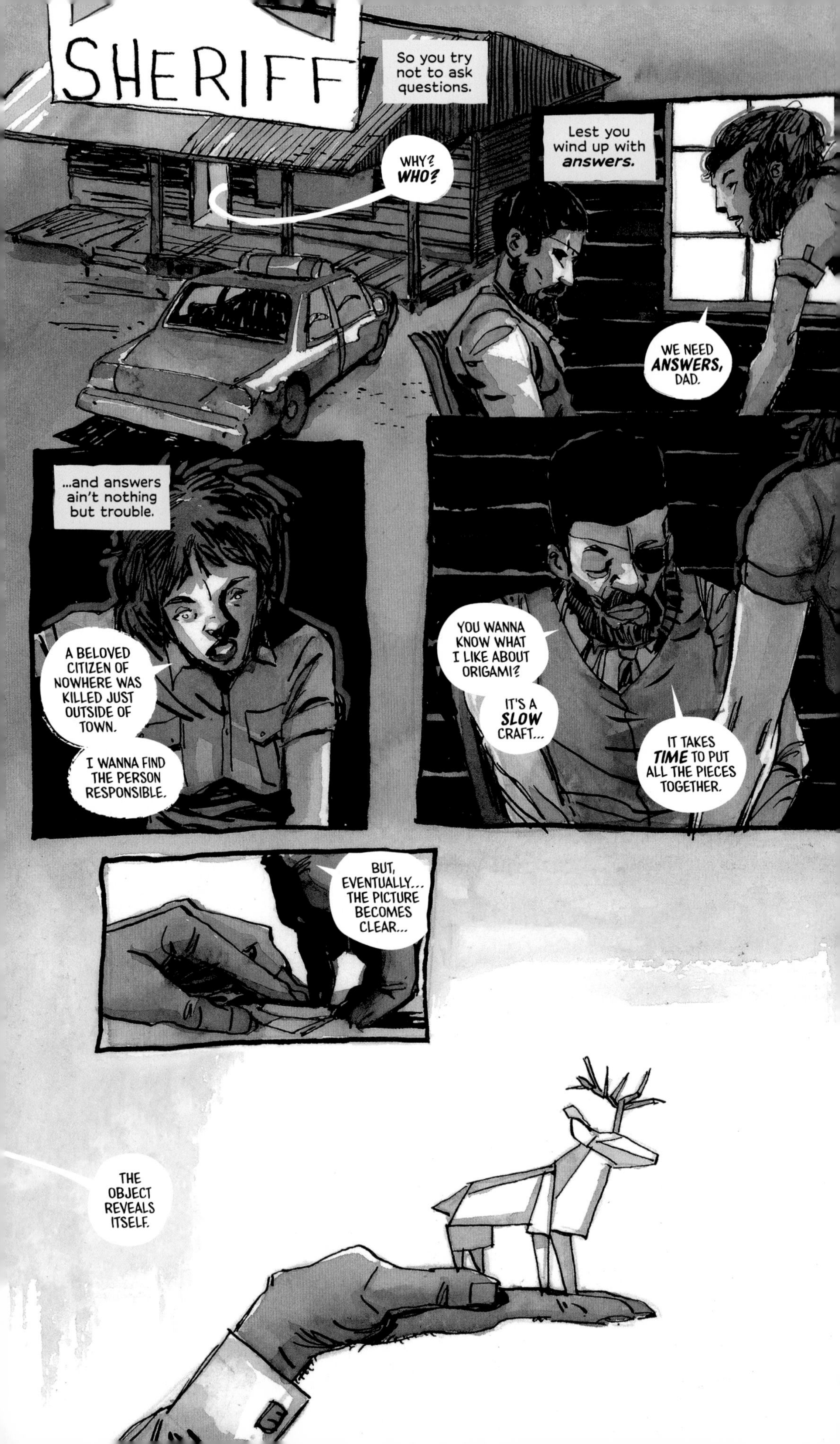
SHERIFF
So you try not to ask questions.
Lest you wind up with *answers.*
WHY? WHO?
WE NEED ANSWERS, DAD.
...and answers ain't nothing but trouble.
A BELOVED CITIZEN OF NOWHERE WAS KILLED JUST OUTSIDE OF TOWN.
I WANNA FIND THE PERSON RESPONSIBLE.
YOU WANNA KNOW WHAT I LIKE ABOUT ORIGAMI?
IT'S A SLOW CRAFT...
IT TAKES TIME TO PUT ALL THE PIECES TOGETHER.
BUT, EVENTUALLY... THE PICTURE BECOMES CLEAR...
THE OBJECT REVEALS ITSELF.

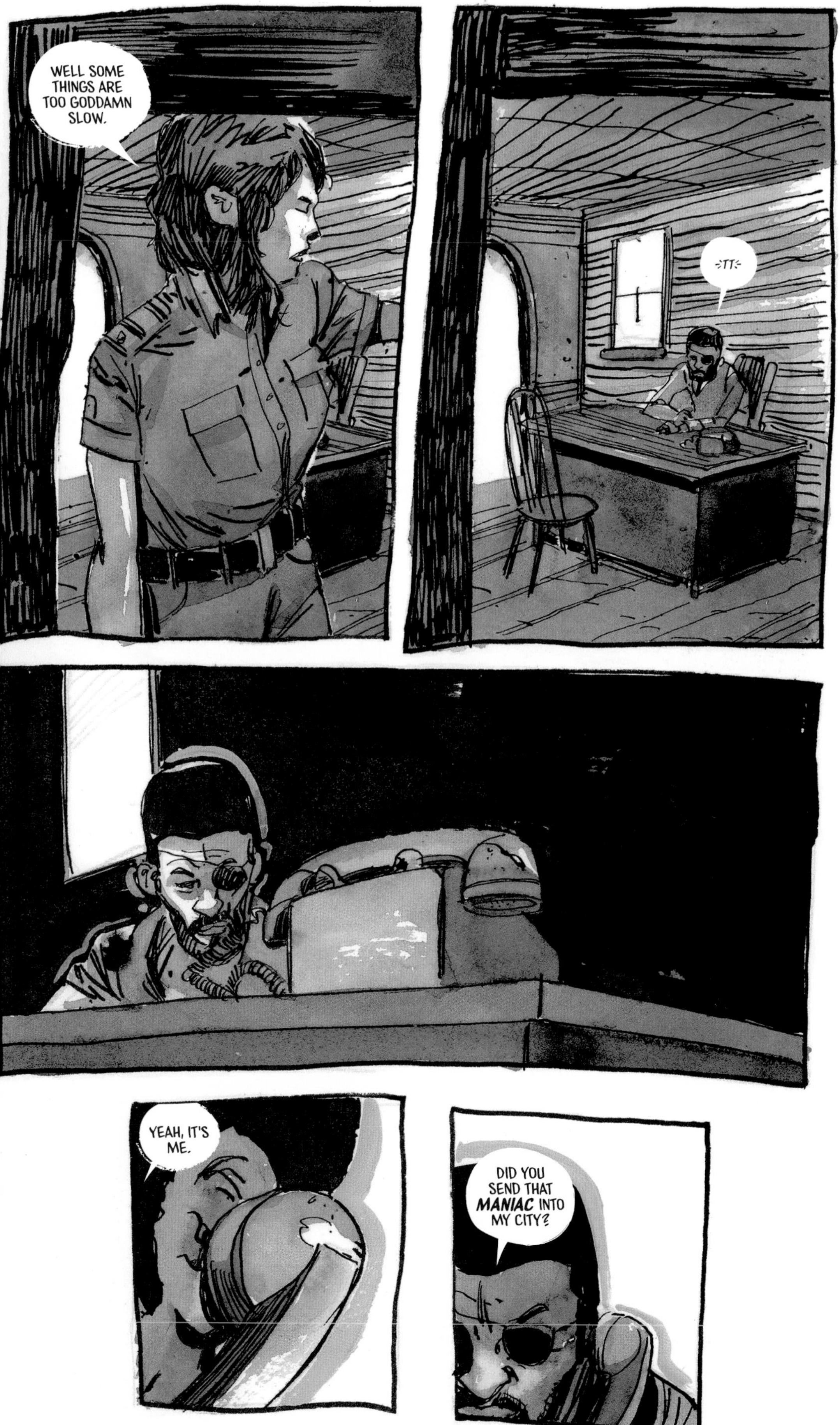
WELL SOME THINGS ARE TOO GODDAMN SLOW.
TT
YEAH, IT'S ME.
DID YOU SEND THAT MANIAC INTO MY CITY?

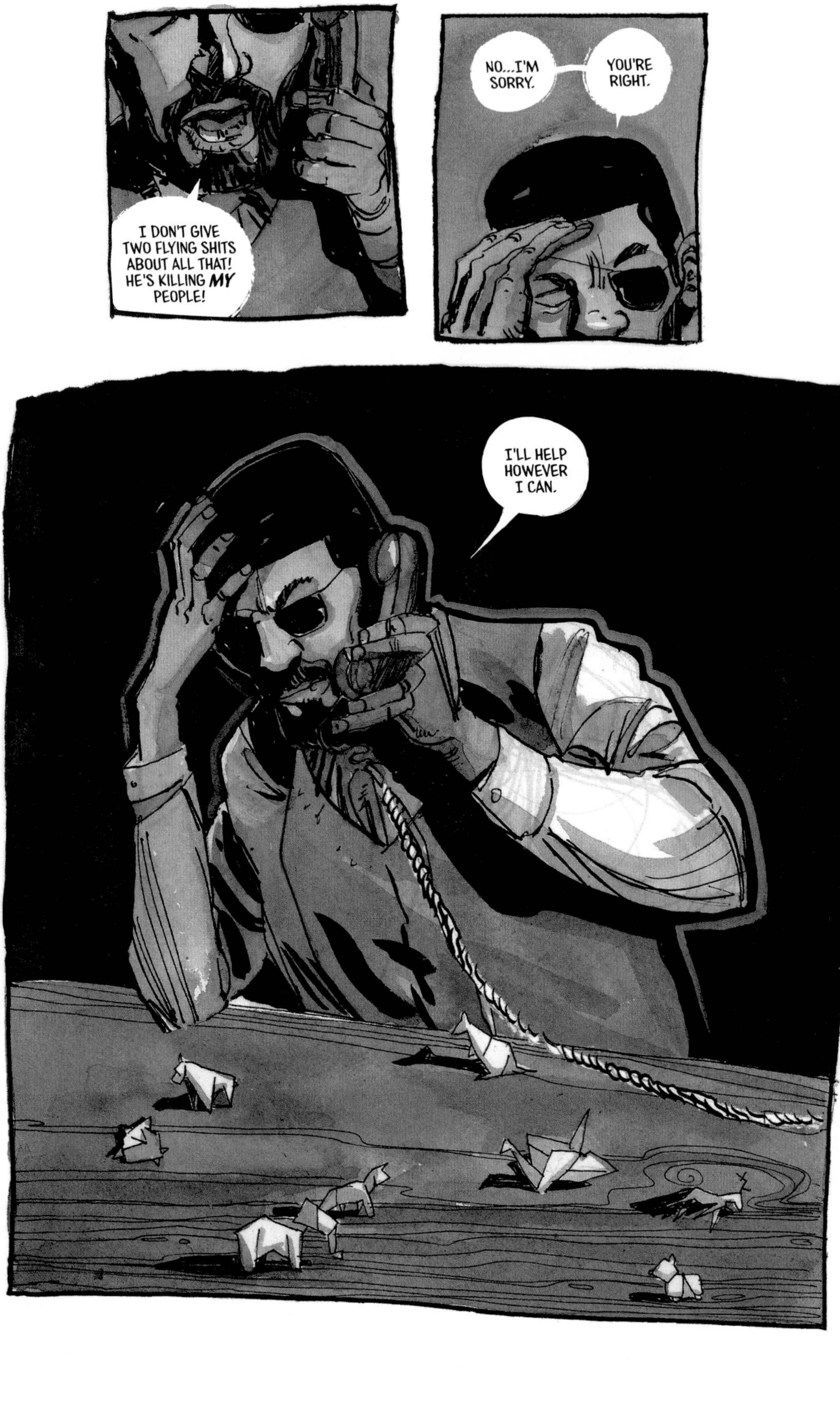
I DON'T GIVE TWO FLYING SHITS ABOUT ALL THAT! HE'S KILLING MY PEOPLE!
NO...I'M SORRY.
YOU'RE RIGHT.
I'LL HELP HOWEVER I CAN.

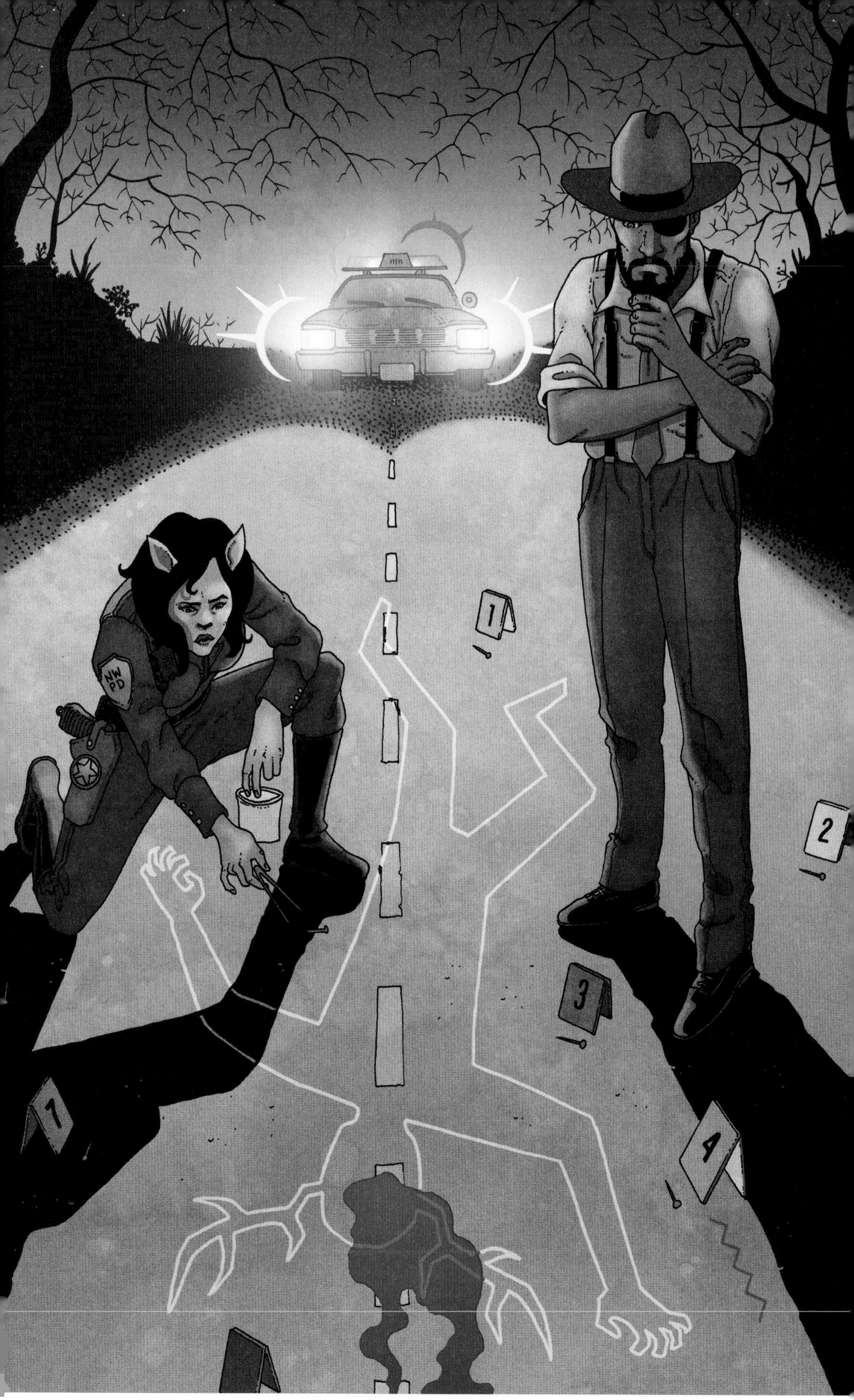

NW
PD
1
2
3
4
7

ISSUE TWO COVER BY **MARTÍN MORAZZO** WITH COLORS BY **CHRIS O'HALLORAN**

CHAPTER THREE

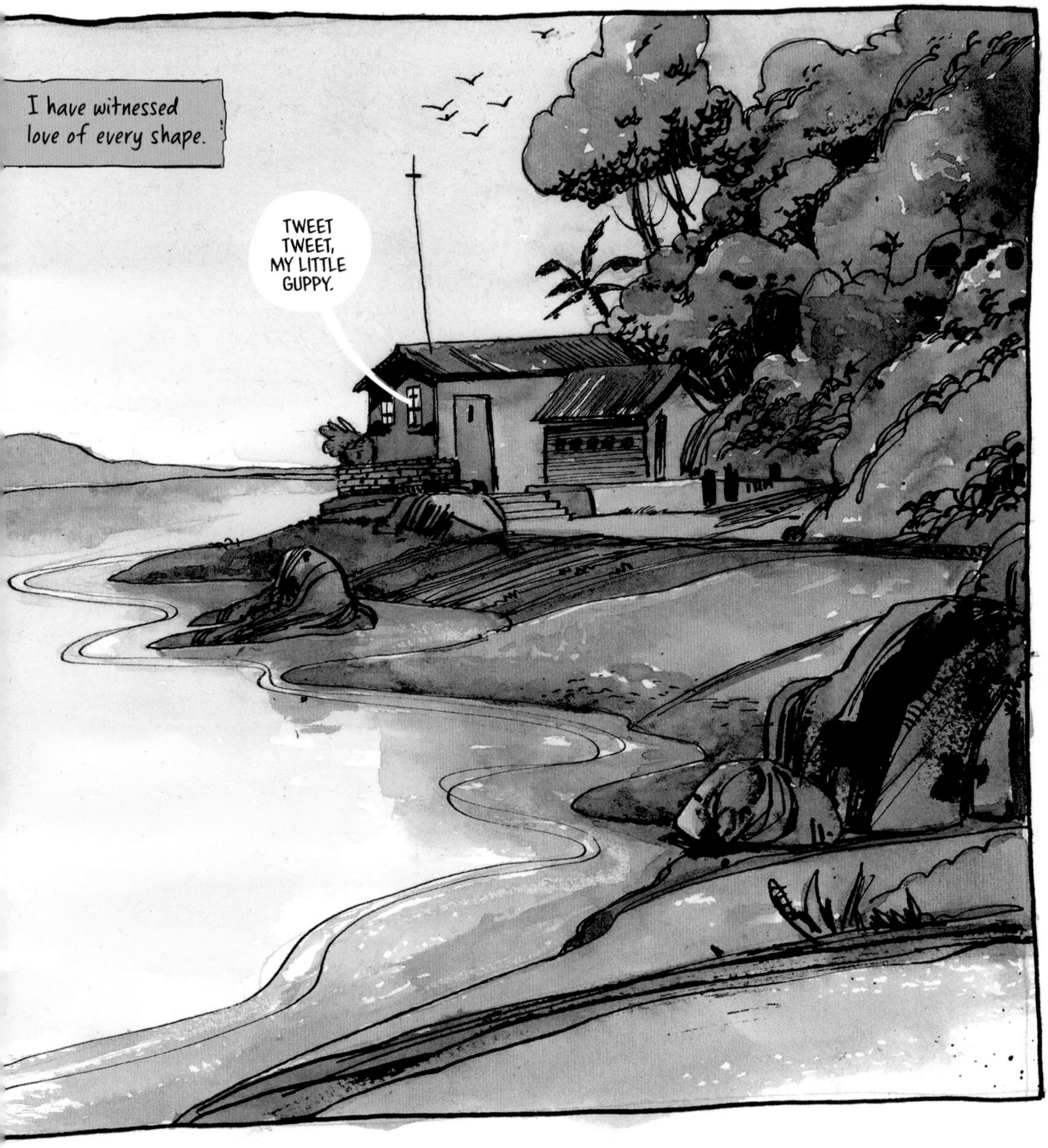
I have witnessed love of every shape.
TWEET TWEET, MY LITTLE GUPPY.

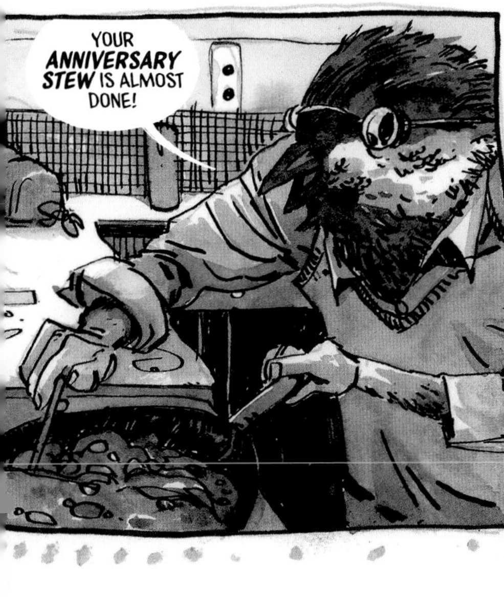
YOUR ANNIVERSARY STEW IS ALMOST DONE!

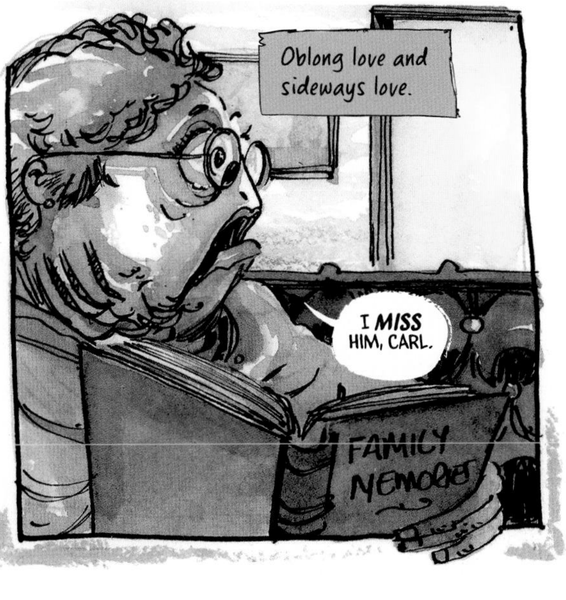
Oblong love and sideways love.
I MISS HIM, CARL.
FAMILY MEMORIES

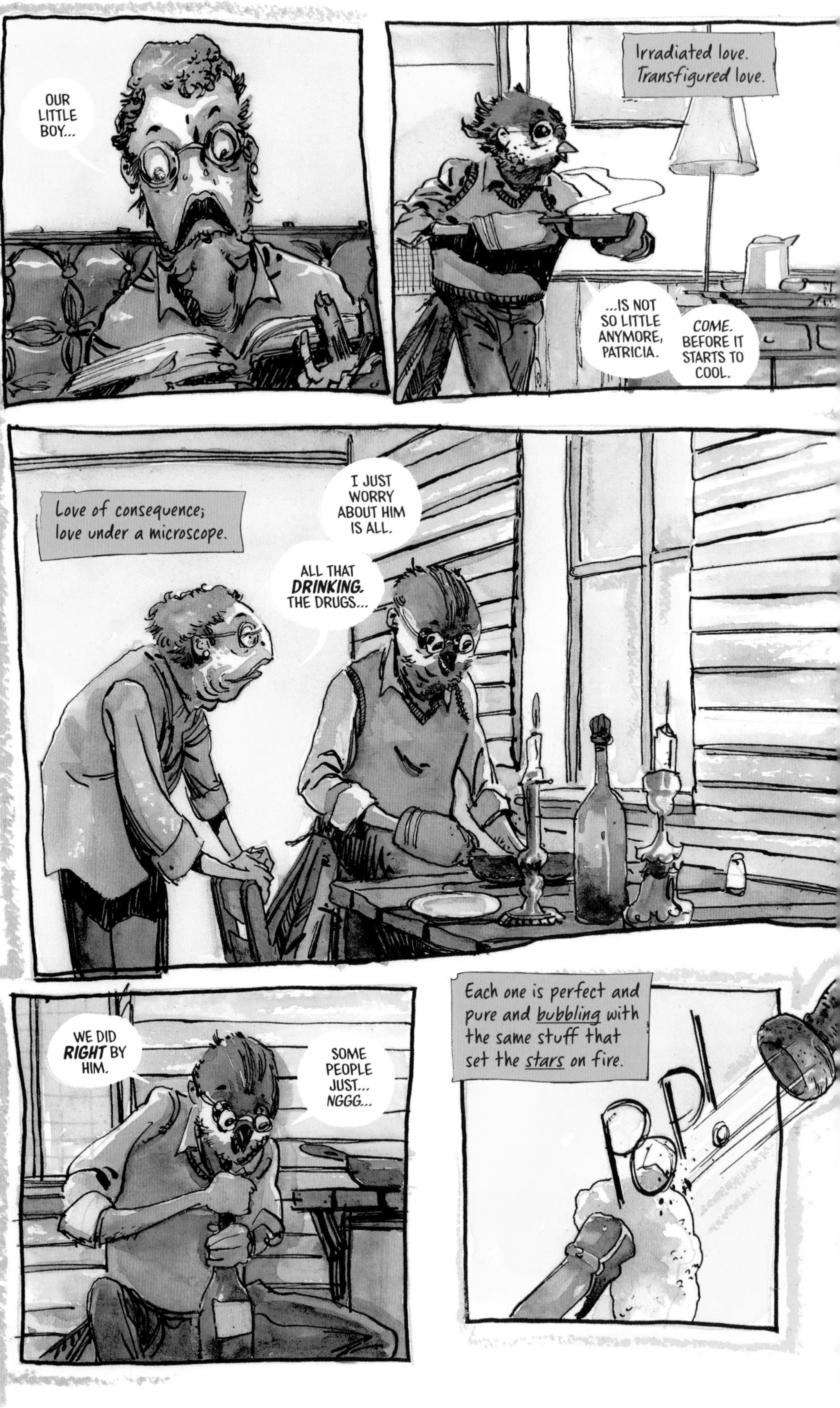
OUR LITTLE BOY...
Irradiated love. Transfigured love.
...IS NOT SO LITTLE ANYMORE, PATRICIA.
COME. BEFORE IT STARTS TO COOL.
Love of consequence; love under a microscope.
I JUST WORRY ABOUT HIM IS ALL.
ALL THAT **DRINKING.** THE DRUGS...
WE DID **RIGHT** BY HIM.
SOME PEOPLE JUST... NGGG...
Each one is perfect and pure and bubbling with the same stuff that set the stars on fire.
POP!

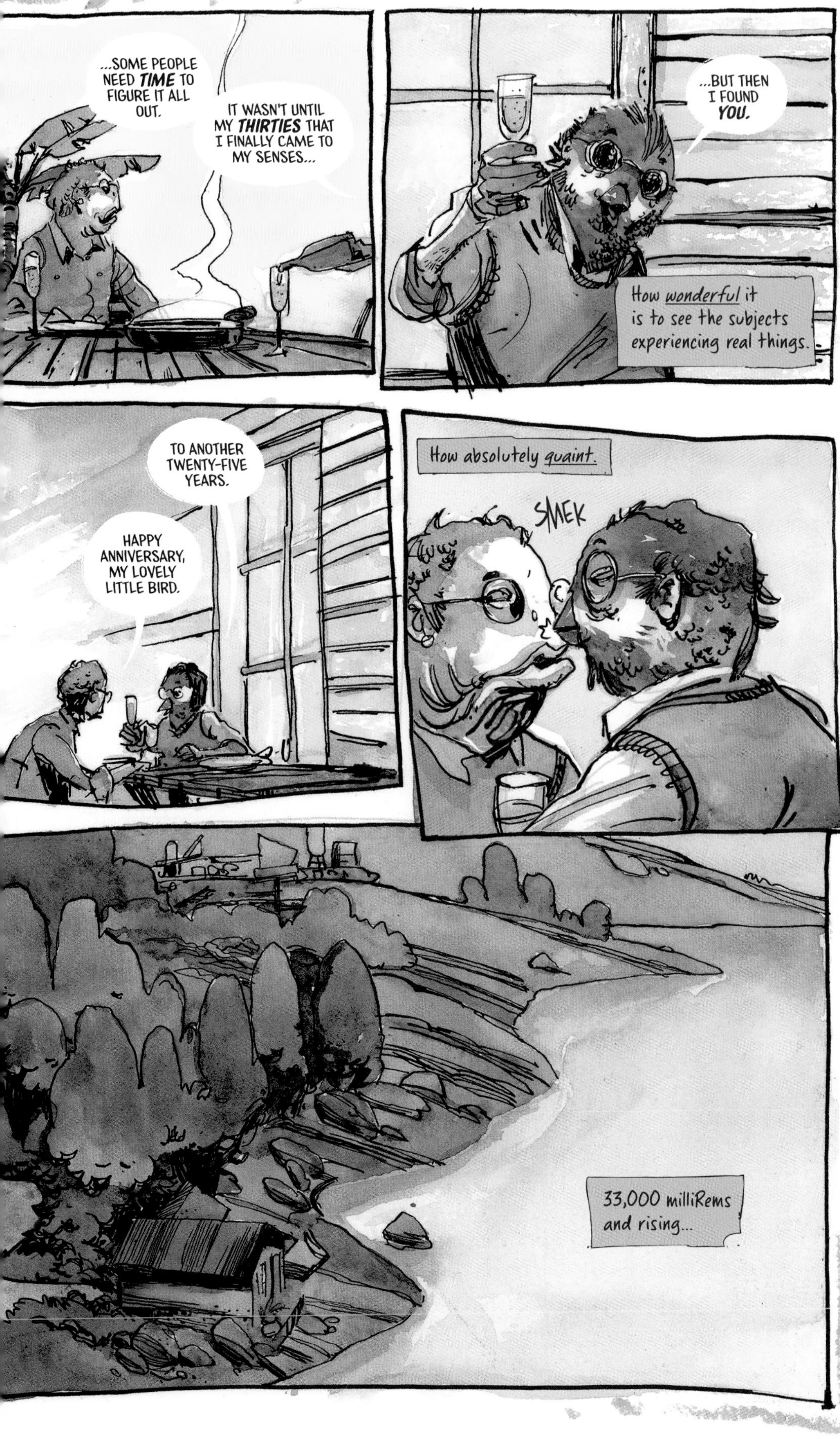
...SOME PEOPLE NEED TIME TO FIGURE IT ALL OUT.
IT WASN'T UNTIL MY THIRTIES THAT I FINALLY CAME TO MY SENSES...
...BUT THEN I FOUND YOU.
How wonderful it is to see the subjects experiencing real things.
HAPPY ANNIVERSARY, MY LOVELY LITTLE BIRD.
TO ANOTHER TWENTY-FIVE YEARS.
How absolutely quaint.
SMEK
33,000 milliRems and rising...

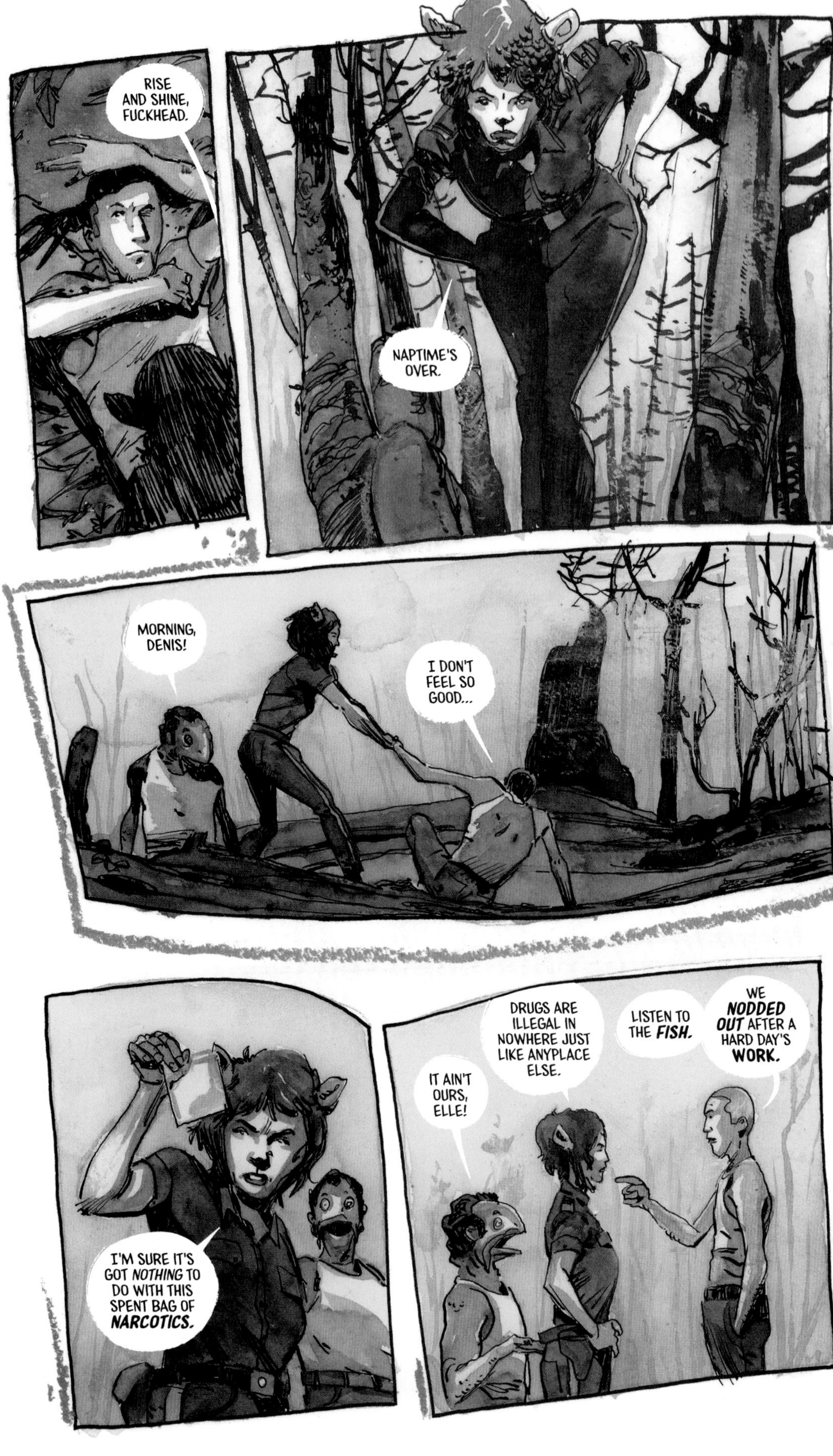
RISE AND SHINE, FUCKHEAD.
NAPTIME'S OVER.
MORNING, DENIS!
I DON'T FEEL SO GOOD...
I'M SURE IT'S GOT *NOTHING* TO DO WITH THIS SPENT BAG OF ***NARCOTICS.***
IT AIN'T OURS, ELLE!
DRUGS ARE ILLEGAL IN NOWHERE JUST LIKE ANYPLACE ELSE.
LISTEN TO THE ***FISH.***
WE ***NODDED OUT*** AFTER A HARD DAY'S **WORK.**

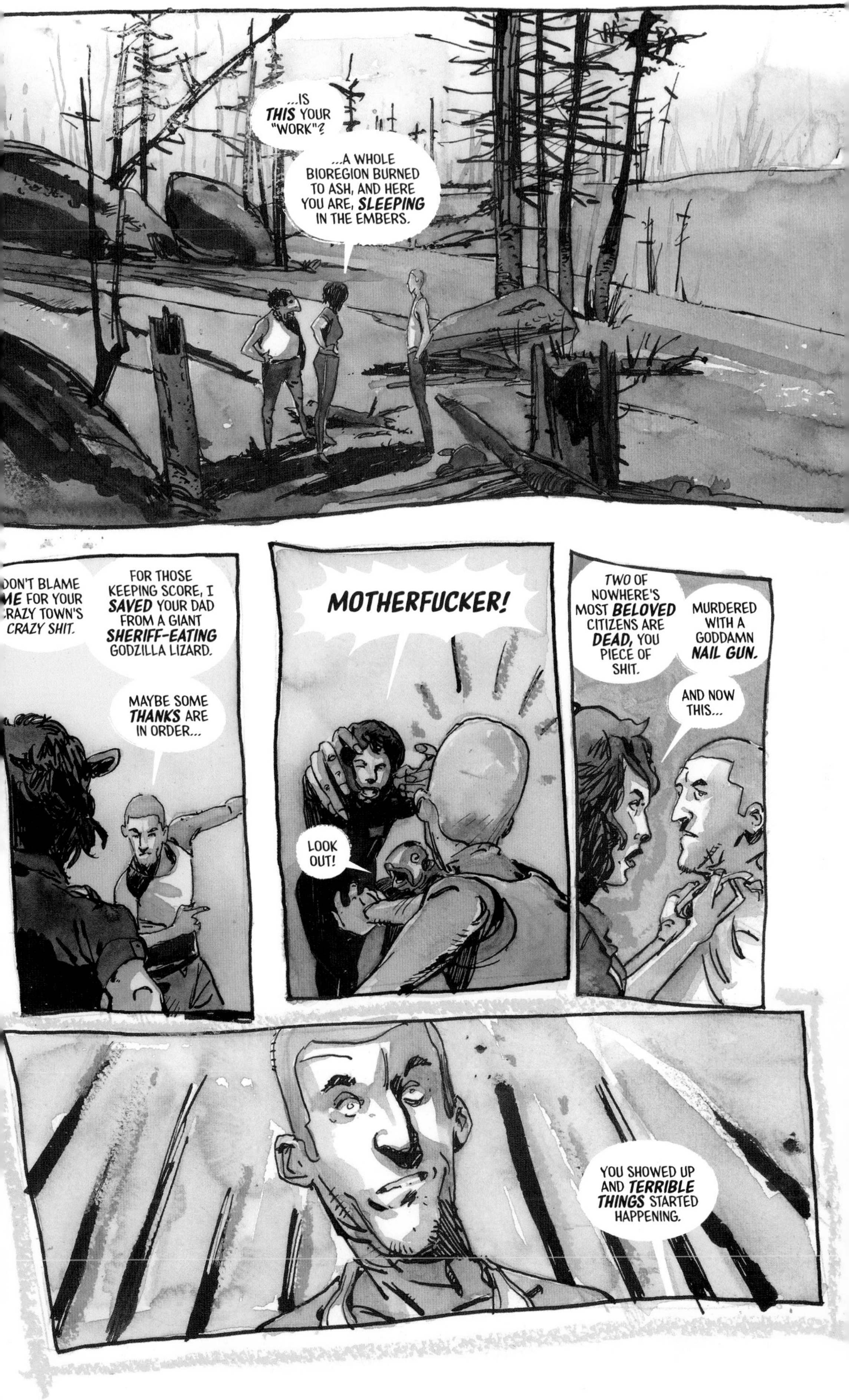
...IS THIS YOUR "WORK"?
...A WHOLE BIOREGION BURNED TO ASH, AND HERE YOU ARE, SLEEPING IN THE EMBERS.
DON'T BLAME ME FOR YOUR CRAZY TOWN'S CRAZY SHIT.
FOR THOSE KEEPING SCORE, I SAVED YOUR DAD FROM A GIANT SHERIFF-EATING GODZILLA LIZARD.
MAYBE SOME THANKS ARE IN ORDER...
MOTHERFUCKER!
LOOK OUT!
TWO OF NOWHERE'S MOST BELOVED CITIZENS ARE DEAD, YOU PIECE OF SHIT.
MURDERED WITH A GODDAMN NAIL GUN.
AND NOW THIS...
YOU SHOWED UP AND TERRIBLE THINGS STARTED HAPPENING.

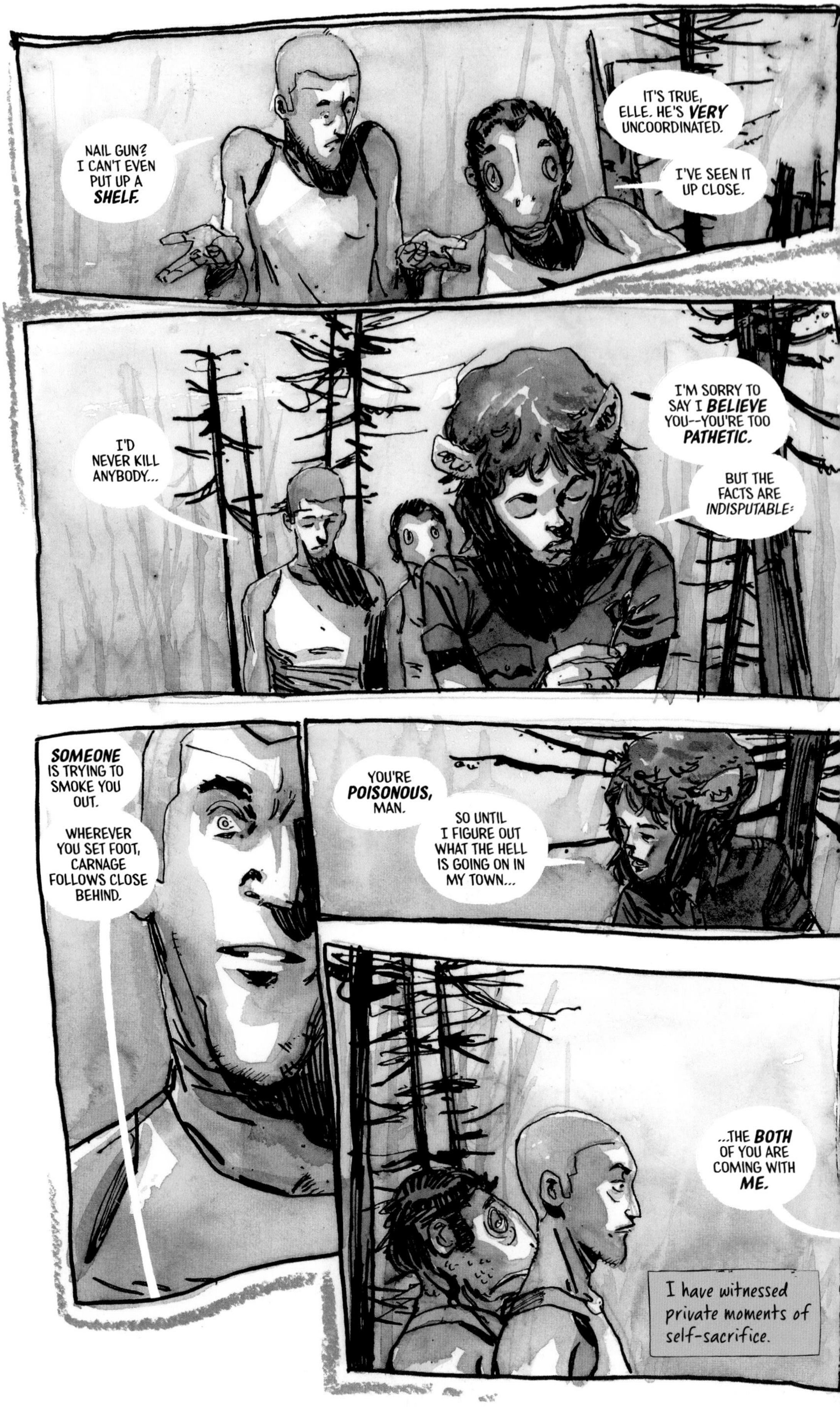
NAIL GUN? I CAN'T EVEN PUT UP A **SHELF.**
IT'S TRUE, ELLE. HE'S **VERY** UNCOORDINATED.
I'VE SEEN IT UP CLOSE.
I'D NEVER KILL ANYBODY...
I'M SORRY TO SAY I **BELIEVE** YOU--YOU'RE TOO **PATHETIC.**
BUT THE FACTS ARE *INDISPUTABLE:*
SOMEONE IS TRYING TO SMOKE YOU OUT.
WHEREVER YOU SET FOOT, CARNAGE FOLLOWS CLOSE BEHIND.
YOU'RE **POISONOUS,** MAN.
SO UNTIL I FIGURE OUT WHAT THE HELL IS GOING ON IN MY TOWN...
...THE **BOTH** OF YOU ARE COMING WITH **ME.**
I have witnessed private moments of self-sacrifice.

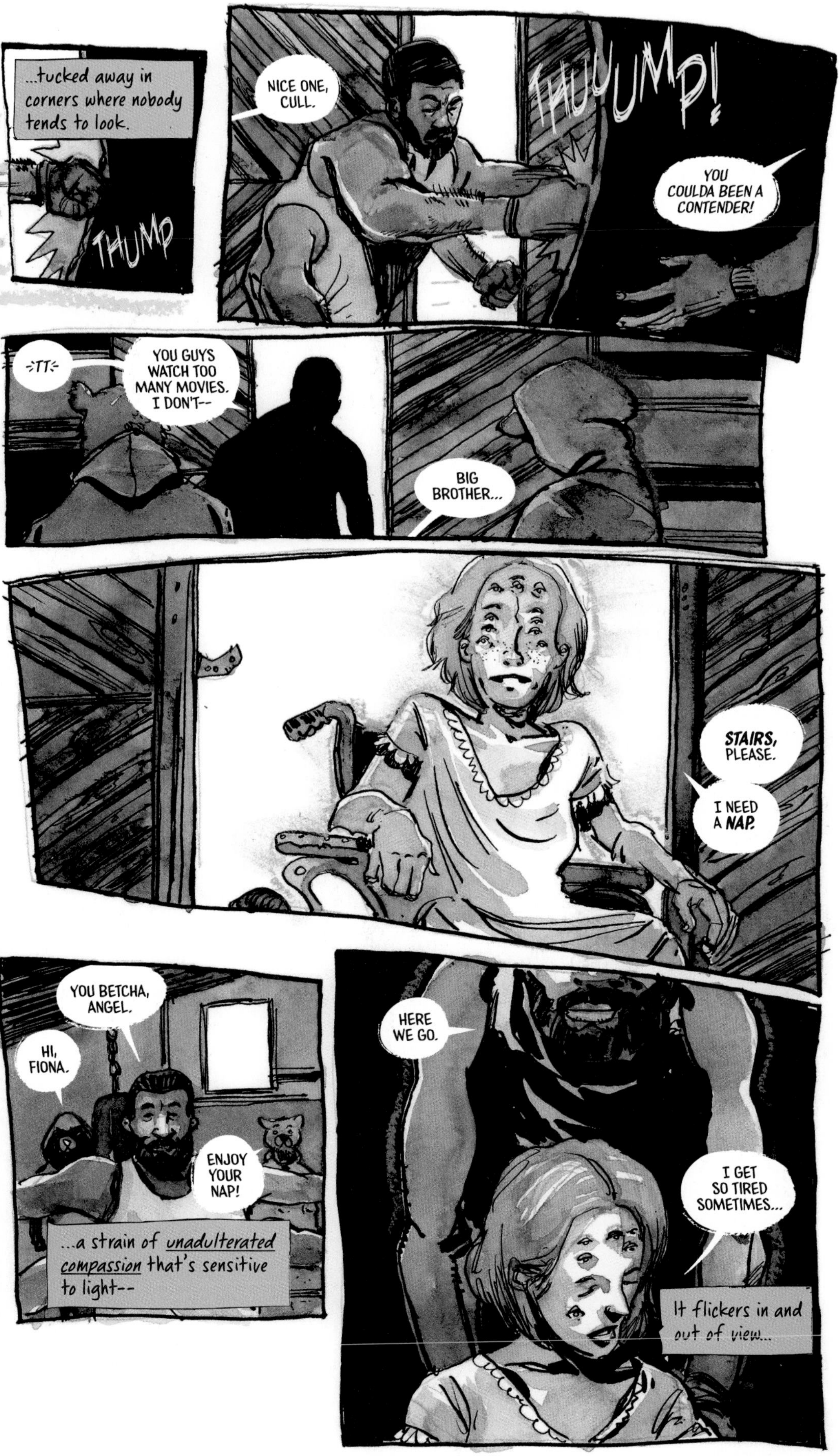
...tucked away in corners where nobody tends to look.
THUMP
NICE ONE, CULL.
THUUUMP!
YOU COULDA BEEN A CONTENDER!
TT
YOU GUYS WATCH TOO MANY MOVIES. I DON'T--
BIG BROTHER...
STAIRS, PLEASE.
I NEED A NAP.
YOU BETCHA, ANGEL.
HI, FIONA.
ENJOY YOUR NAP!
...a strain of unadulterated compassion that's sensitive to light--
HERE WE GO.
I GET SO TIRED SOMETIMES...
It flickers in and out of view...

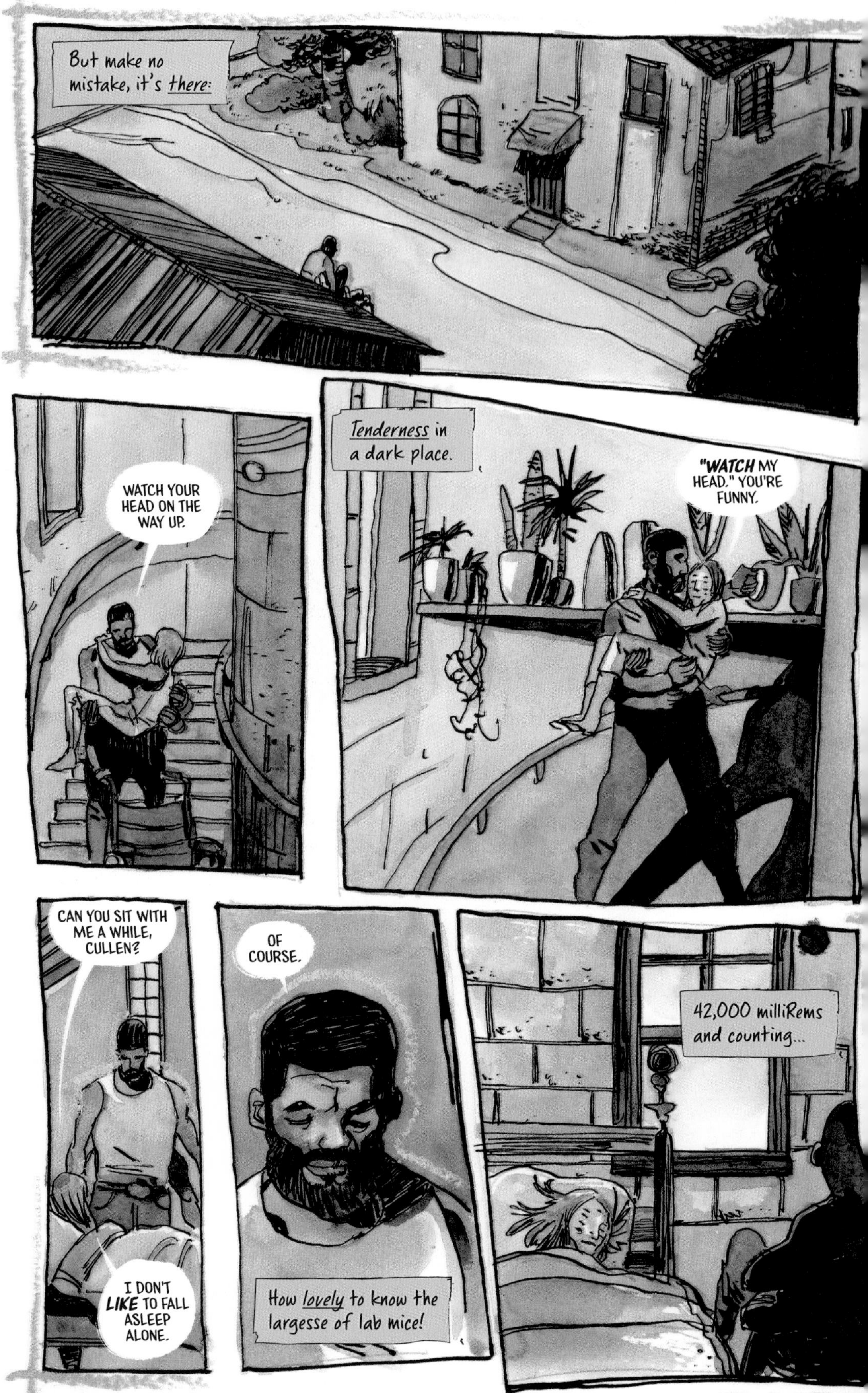
But make no mistake, it's there:
WATCH YOUR HEAD ON THE WAY UP.
Tenderness in a dark place.
"WATCH MY HEAD." YOU'RE FUNNY.
CAN YOU SIT WITH ME A WHILE, CULLEN?
I DON'T LIKE TO FALL ASLEEP ALONE.
OF COURSE.
How lovely to know the largesse of lab mice!
42,000 milliRems and counting...

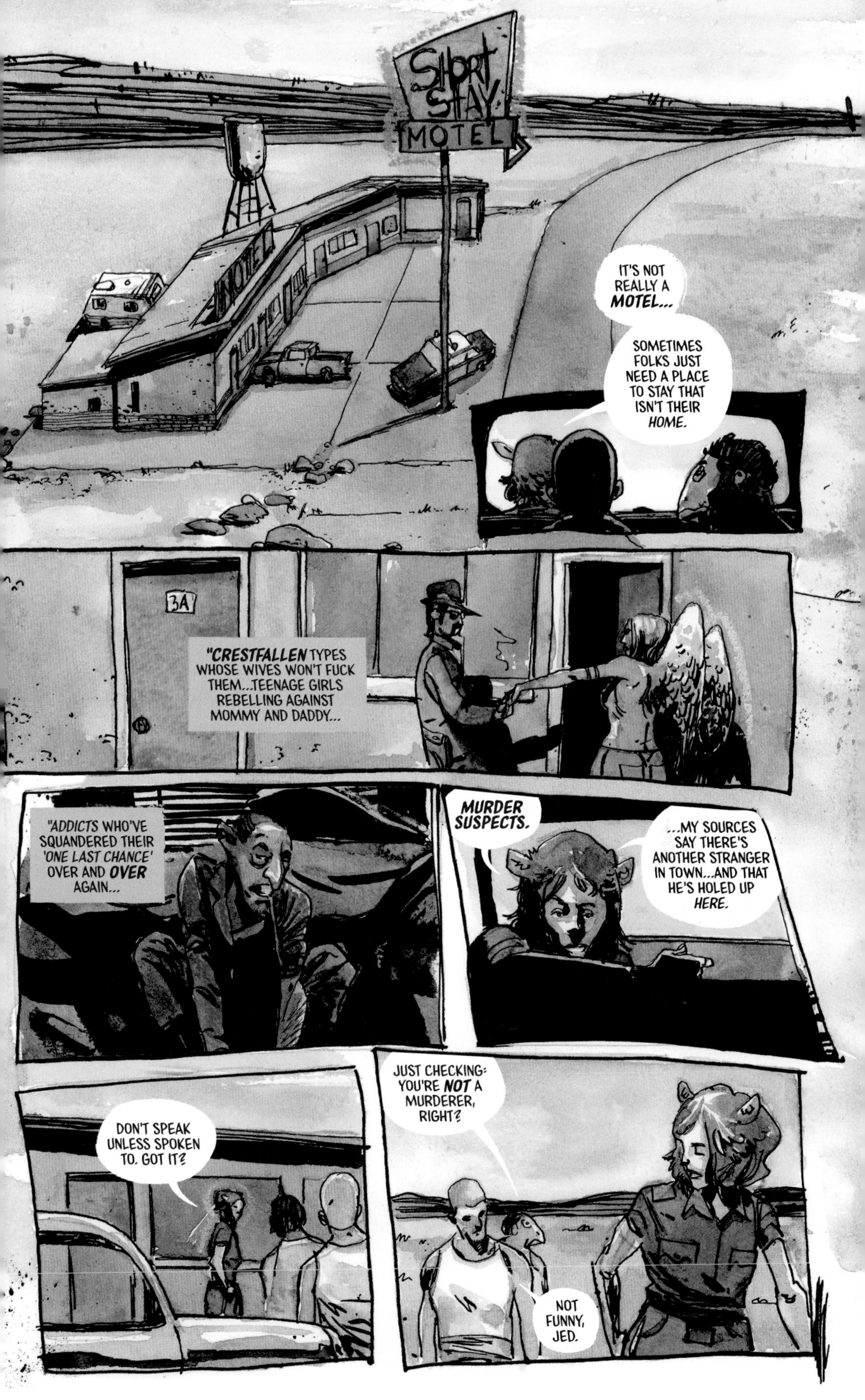
SHORT STAY MOTEL
MOTEL
IT'S NOT REALLY A MOTEL...
SOMETIMES FOLKS JUST NEED A PLACE TO STAY THAT ISN'T THEIR HOME.
3A
"CRESTFALLEN TYPES WHOSE WIVES WON'T FUCK THEM...TEENAGE GIRLS REBELLING AGAINST MOMMY AND DADDY...
"ADDICTS WHO'VE SQUANDERED THEIR 'ONE LAST CHANCE' OVER AND OVER AGAIN...
MURDER SUSPECTS.
...MY SOURCES SAY THERE'S ANOTHER STRANGER IN TOWN...AND THAT HE'S HOLED UP HERE.
DON'T SPEAK UNLESS SPOKEN TO. GOT IT?
JUST CHECKING: YOU'RE NOT A MURDERER, RIGHT?
NOT FUNNY, JED.

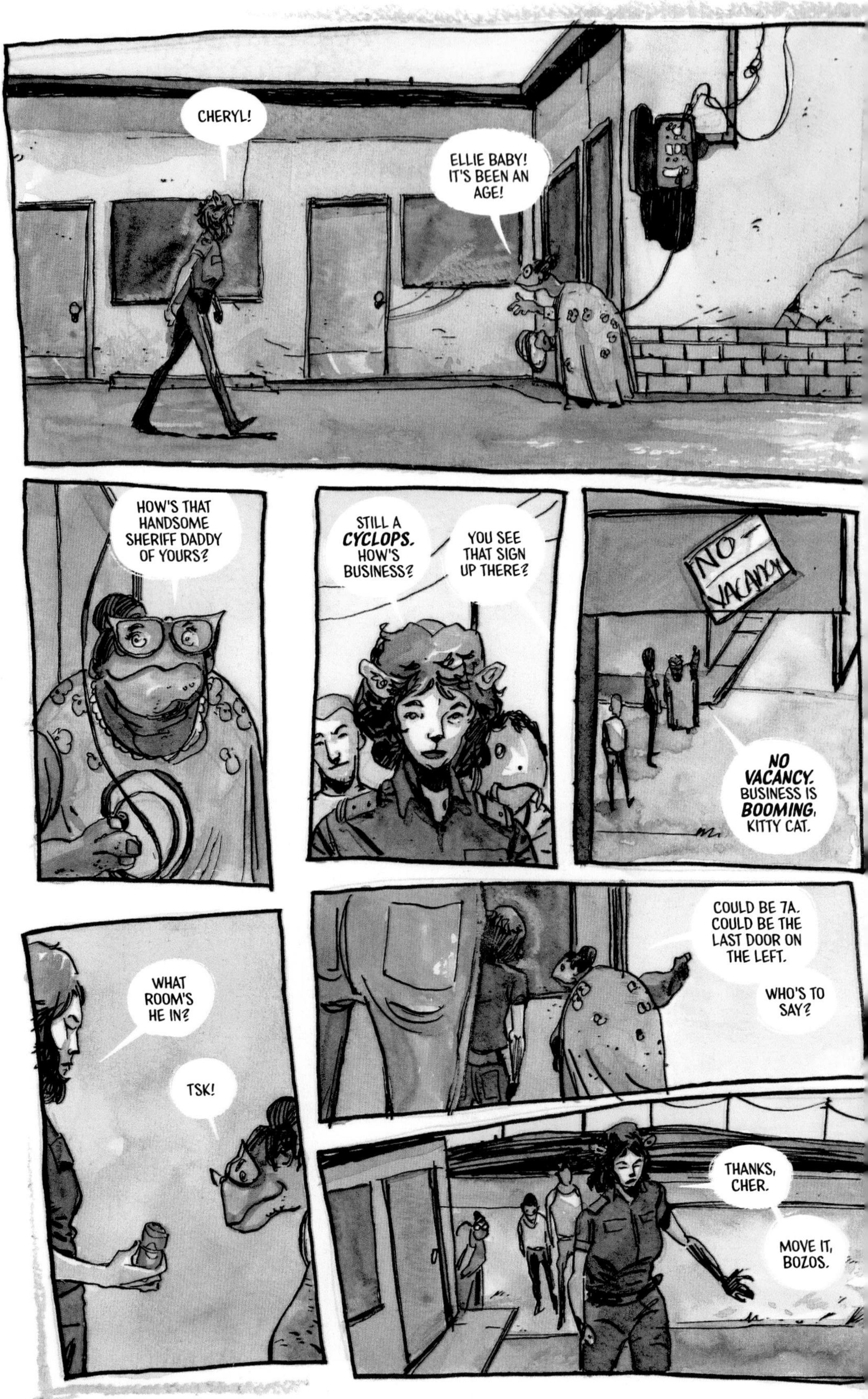

CHERYL!
ELLIE BABY! IT'S BEEN AN AGE!
HOW'S THAT HANDSOME SHERIFF DADDY OF YOURS?
STILL A **CYCLOPS.** HOW'S BUSINESS?
YOU SEE THAT SIGN UP THERE?
NO VACANCY
NO VACANCY. BUSINESS IS ***BOOMING,*** KITTY CAT.
WHAT ROOM'S HE IN?
TSK!
COULD BE 7A. COULD BE THE LAST DOOR ON THE LEFT.
WHO'S TO SAY?
THANKS, CHER.
MOVE IT, BOZOS.

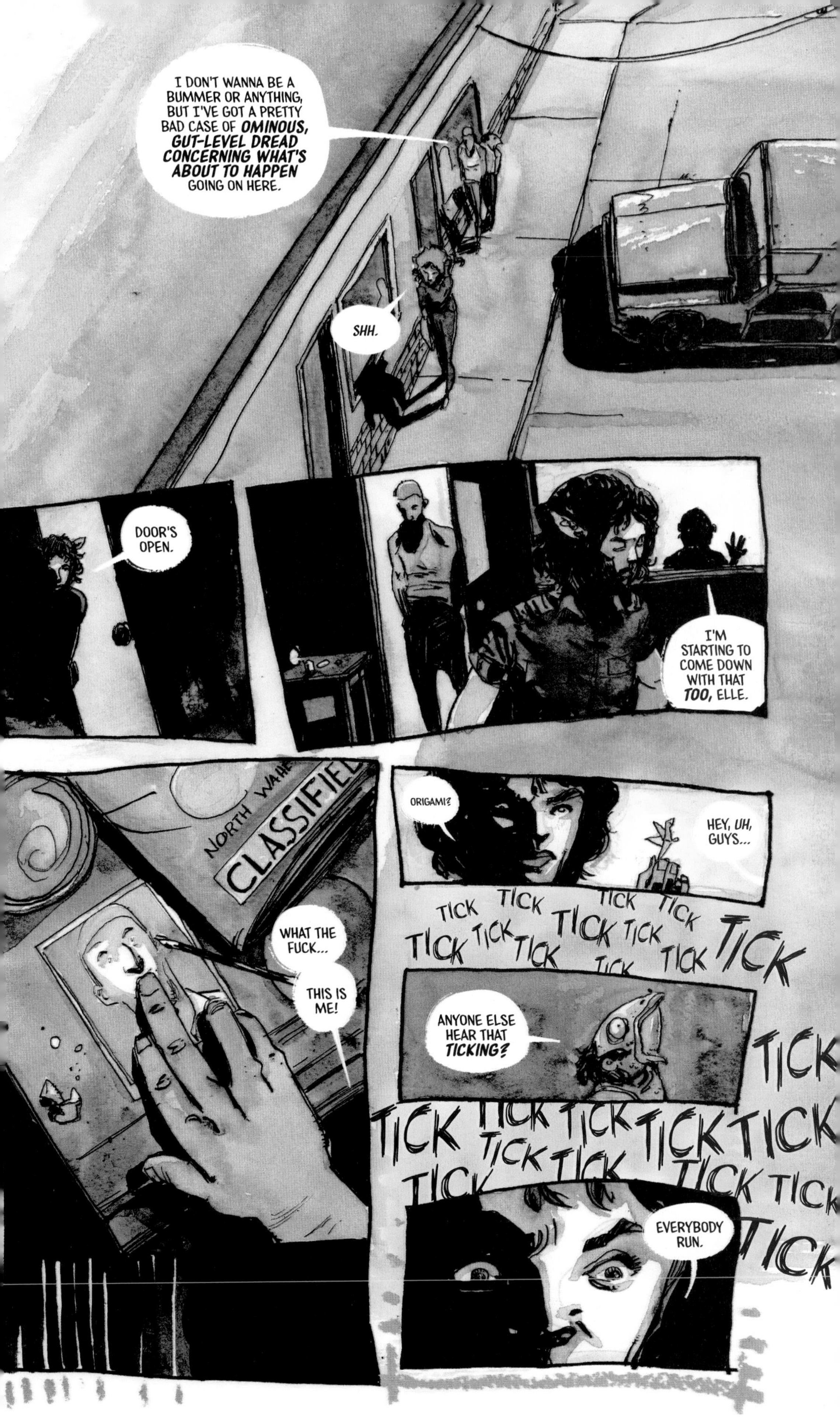
I DON'T WANNA BE A BUMMER OR ANYTHING, BUT I'VE GOT A PRETTY BAD CASE OF OMINOUS, GUT-LEVEL DREAD CONCERNING WHAT'S ABOUT TO HAPPEN GOING ON HERE.
SHH.
DOOR'S OPEN.
I'M STARTING TO COME DOWN WITH THAT TOO, ELLE.
NORTH WAH
CLASSIFIED
WHAT THE FUCK...
THIS IS ME!
ORIGAMI?
HEY, UH, GUYS...
TICK TICK TICK TICK TICK TICK TICK TICK TICK TICK TICK TICK
ANYONE ELSE HEAR THAT TICKING?
TICK
TICK TICK TICK TICK TICK TICK TICK TICK TICK TICK TICK TICK
EVERYBODY RUN.

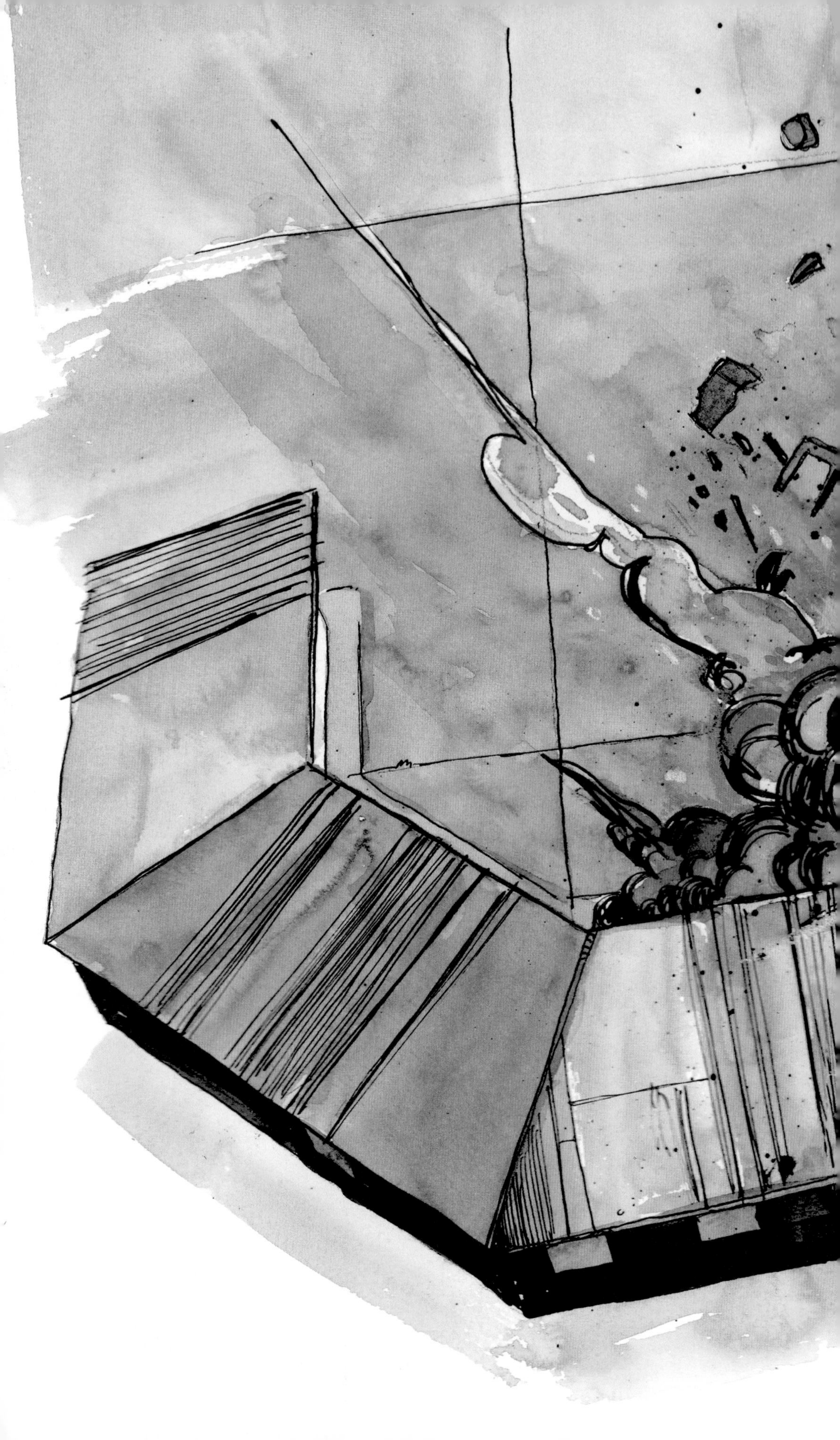

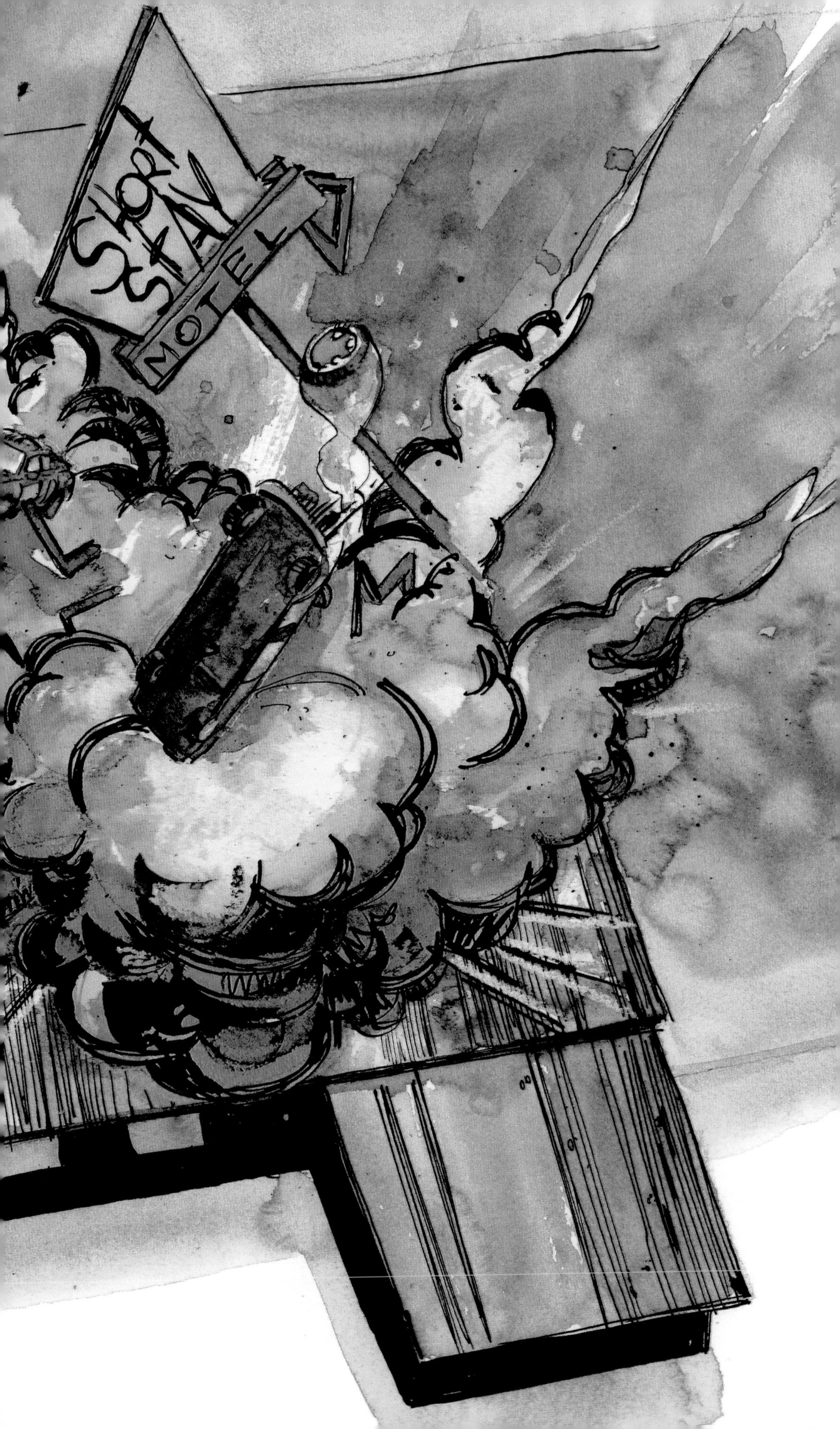
Short Stay
MOTEL

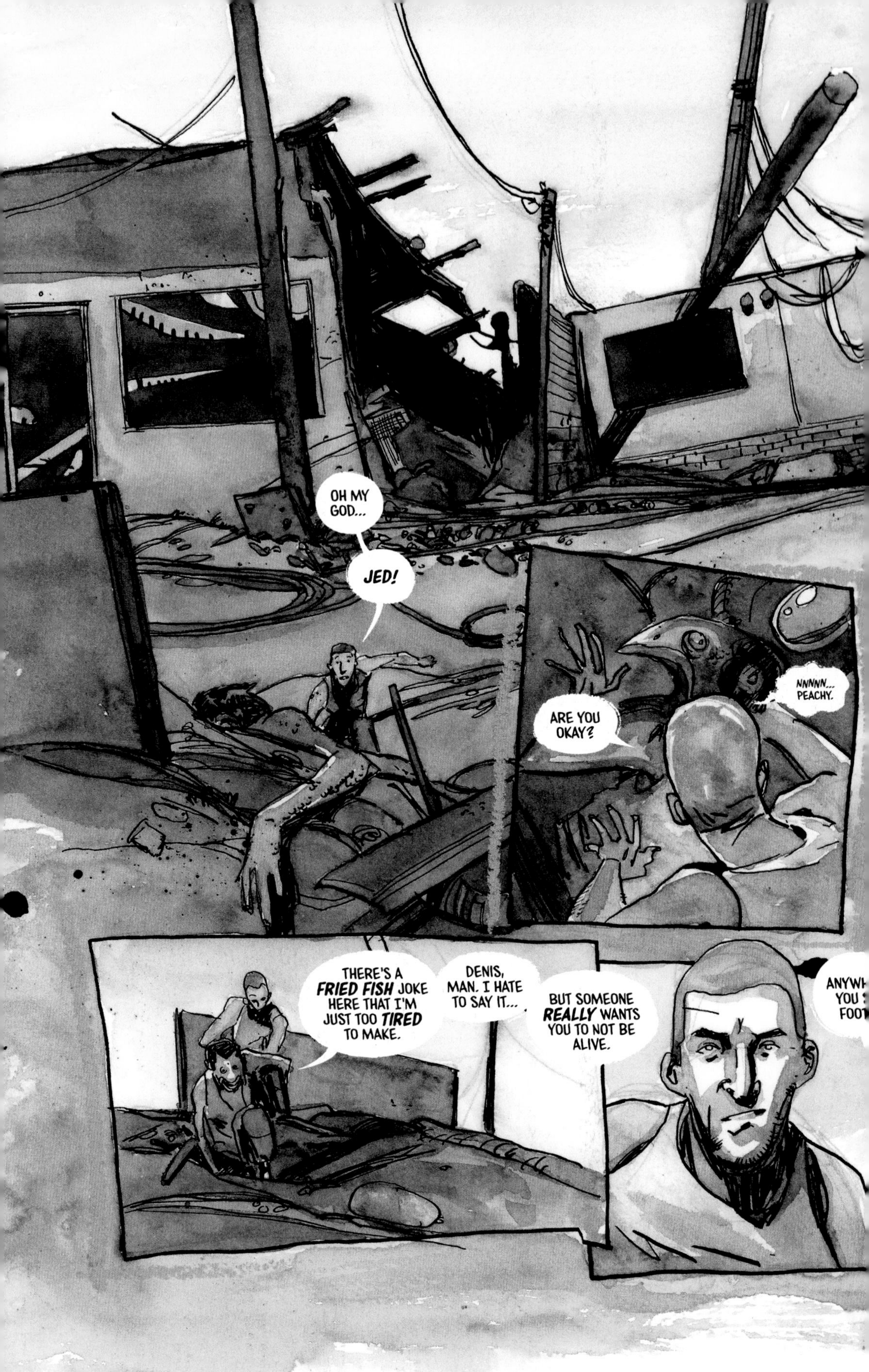
OH MY GOD...
JED!
ARE YOU OKAY?
NNNNN... PEACHY.
THERE'S A FRIED FISH JOKE HERE THAT I'M JUST TOO TIRED TO MAKE.
DENIS, MAN. I HATE TO SAY IT...
BUT SOMEONE REALLY WANTS YOU TO NOT BE ALIVE.

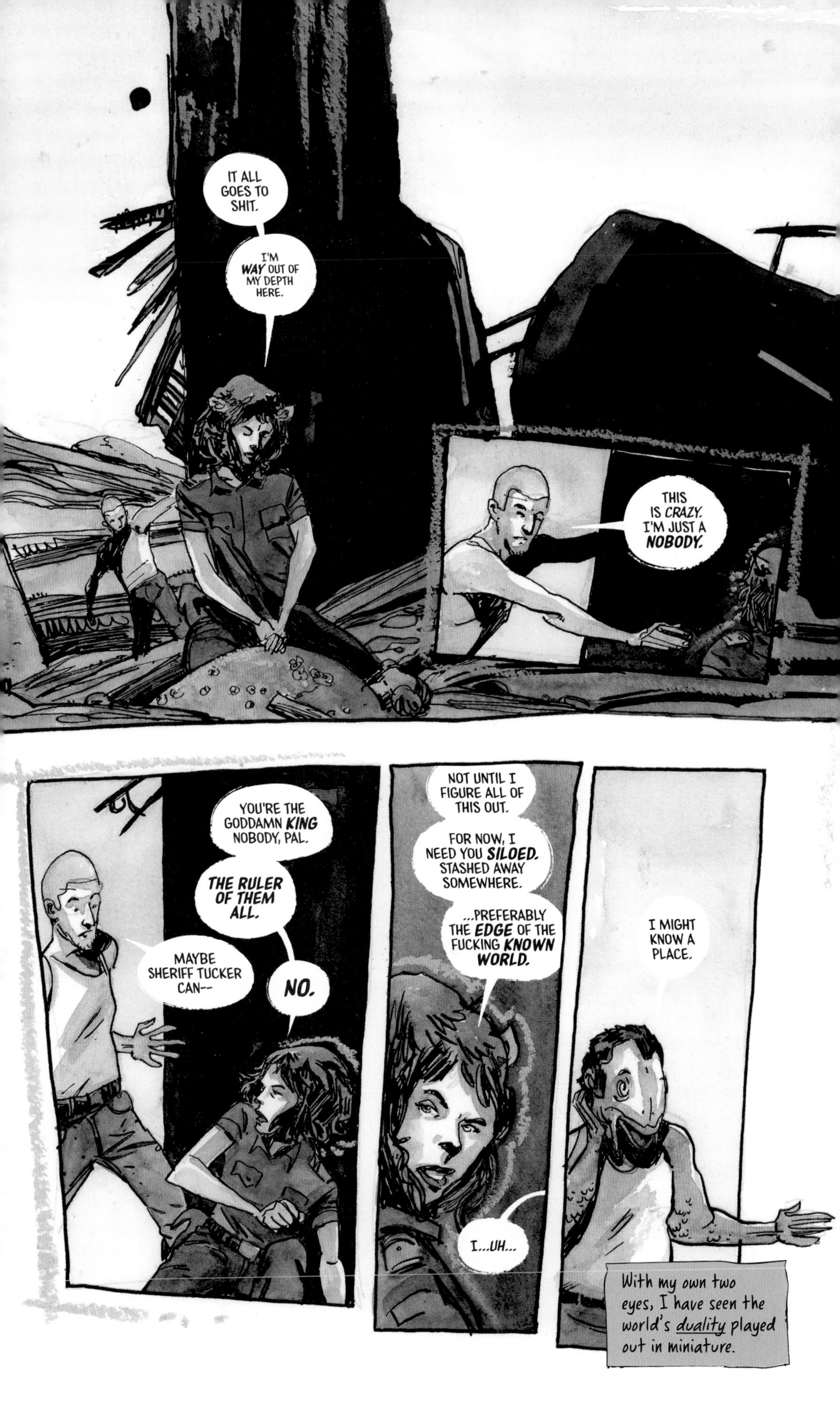
IT ALL GOES TO SHIT.
I'M WAY OUT OF MY DEPTH HERE.
THIS IS CRAZY. I'M JUST A NOBODY.
YOU'RE THE GODDAMN KING NOBODY, PAL.
THE RULER OF THEM ALL.
MAYBE SHERIFF TUCKER CAN--
NO.
NOT UNTIL I FIGURE ALL OF THIS OUT.
FOR NOW, I NEED YOU SILOED. STASHED AWAY SOMEWHERE.
...PREFERABLY THE EDGE OF THE FUCKING KNOWN WORLD.
I...UH...
I MIGHT KNOW A PLACE.
With my own two eyes, I have seen the world's duality played out in miniature.

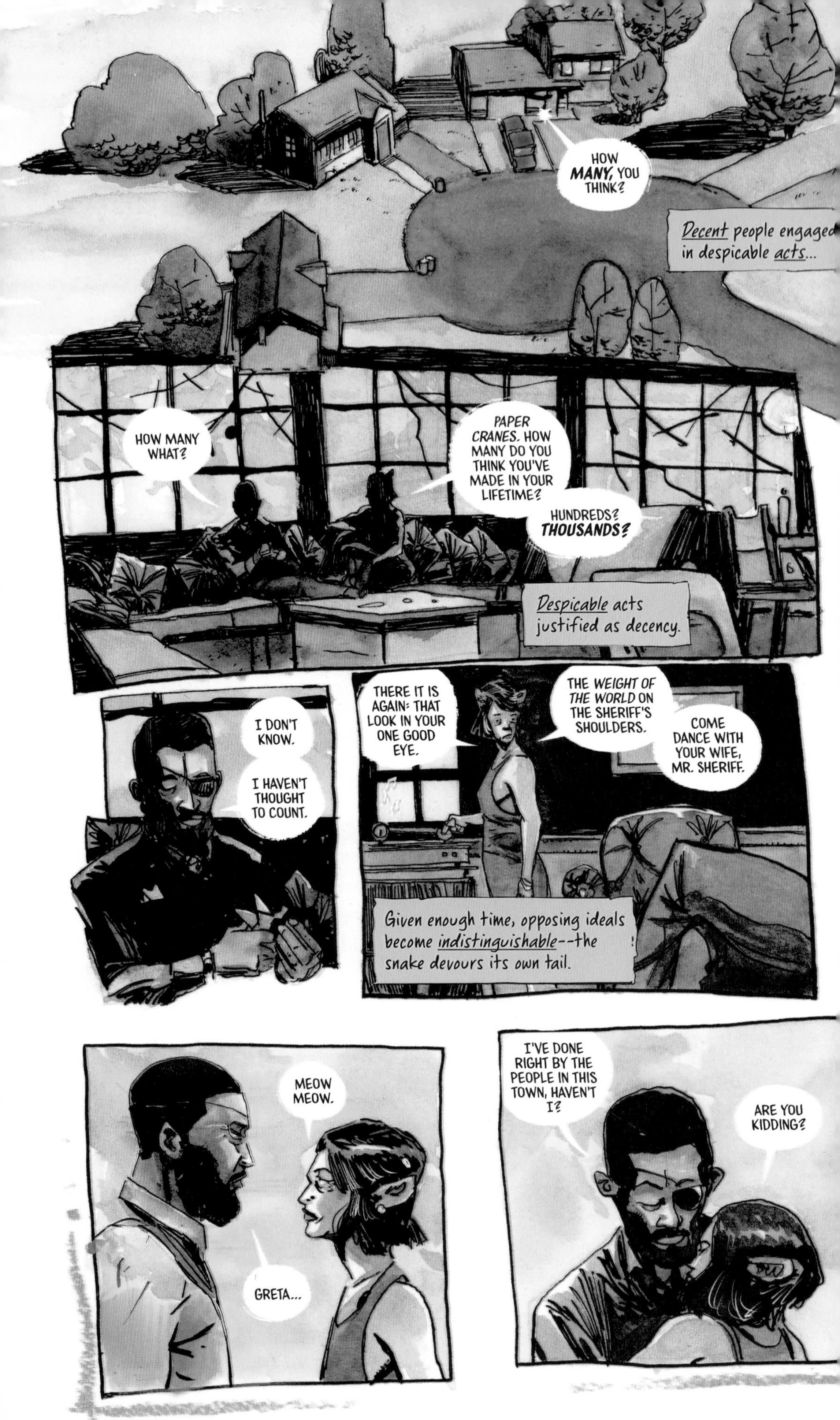

HOW MANY, YOU THINK?
Decent people engaged in despicable acts...
HOW MANY WHAT?
PAPER CRANES. HOW MANY DO YOU THINK YOU'VE MADE IN YOUR LIFETIME?
HUNDREDS? THOUSANDS?
Despicable acts justified as decency.
I DON'T KNOW.
I HAVEN'T THOUGHT TO COUNT.
THERE IT IS AGAIN: THAT LOOK IN YOUR ONE GOOD EYE.
THE WEIGHT OF THE WORLD ON THE SHERIFF'S SHOULDERS.
COME DANCE WITH YOUR WIFE, MR. SHERIFF.
Given enough time, opposing ideals become indistinguishable--the snake devours its own tail.
MEOW MEOW.
GRETA...
I'VE DONE RIGHT BY THE PEOPLE IN THIS TOWN, HAVEN'T I?
ARE YOU KIDDING?

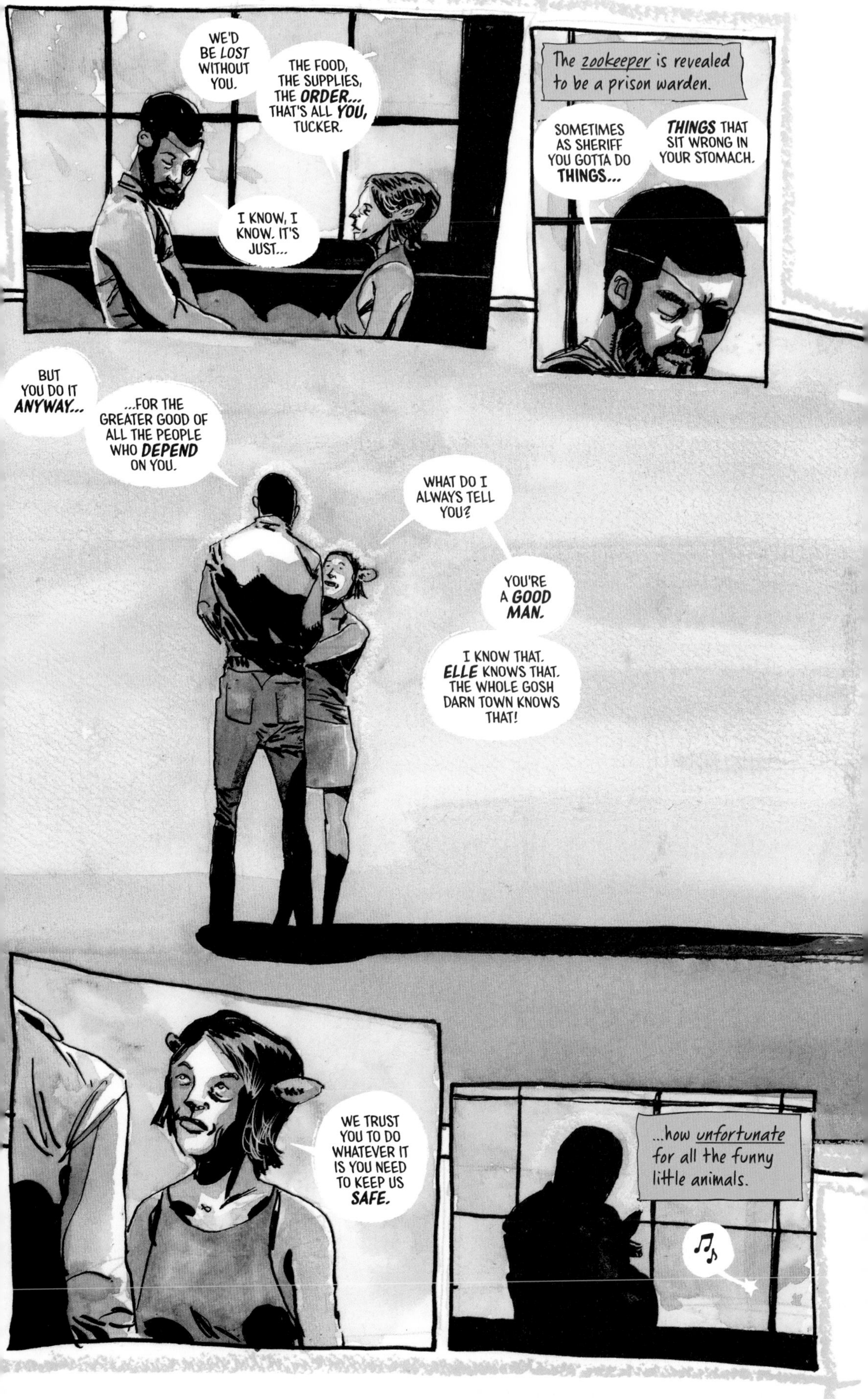
WE'D BE LOST WITHOUT YOU.
THE FOOD, THE SUPPLIES, THE ORDER... THAT'S ALL YOU, TUCKER.
I KNOW, I KNOW. IT'S JUST...
The zookeeper is revealed to be a prison warden.
SOMETIMES AS SHERIFF YOU GOTTA DO THINGS...
THINGS THAT SIT WRONG IN YOUR STOMACH.
BUT YOU DO IT ANYWAY...
...FOR THE GREATER GOOD OF ALL THE PEOPLE WHO DEPEND ON YOU.
WHAT DO I ALWAYS TELL YOU?
YOU'RE A GOOD MAN.
I KNOW THAT. ELLE KNOWS THAT. THE WHOLE GOSH DARN TOWN KNOWS THAT!
WE TRUST YOU TO DO WHATEVER IT IS YOU NEED TO KEEP US SAFE.
...how unfortunate for all the funny little animals.
♫

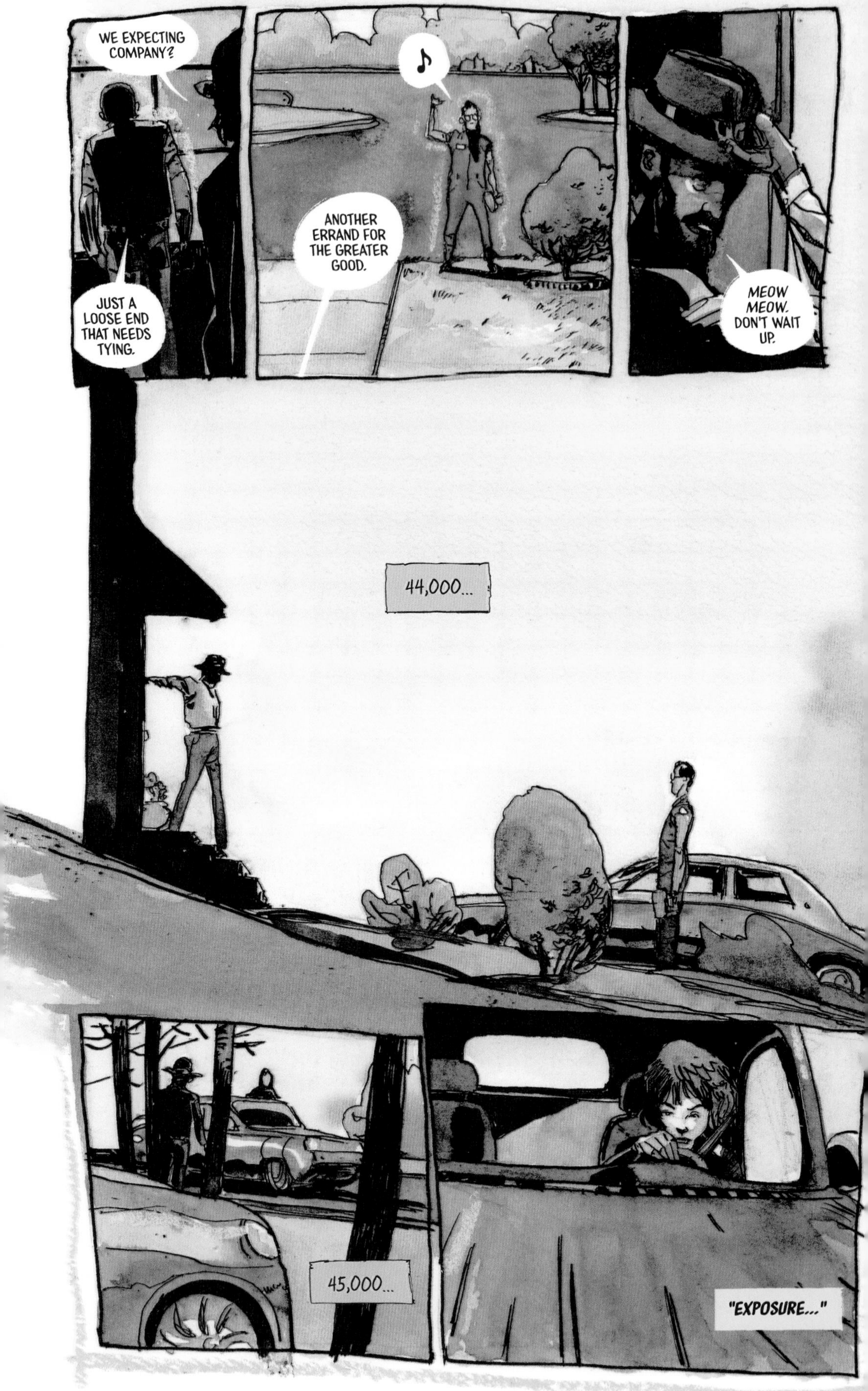
WE EXPECTING COMPANY?
JUST A LOOSE END THAT NEEDS TYING.
♪
ANOTHER ERRAND FOR THE GREATER GOOD.
MEOW MEOW. DON'T WAIT UP.
44,000...
45,000...
"EXPOSURE..."

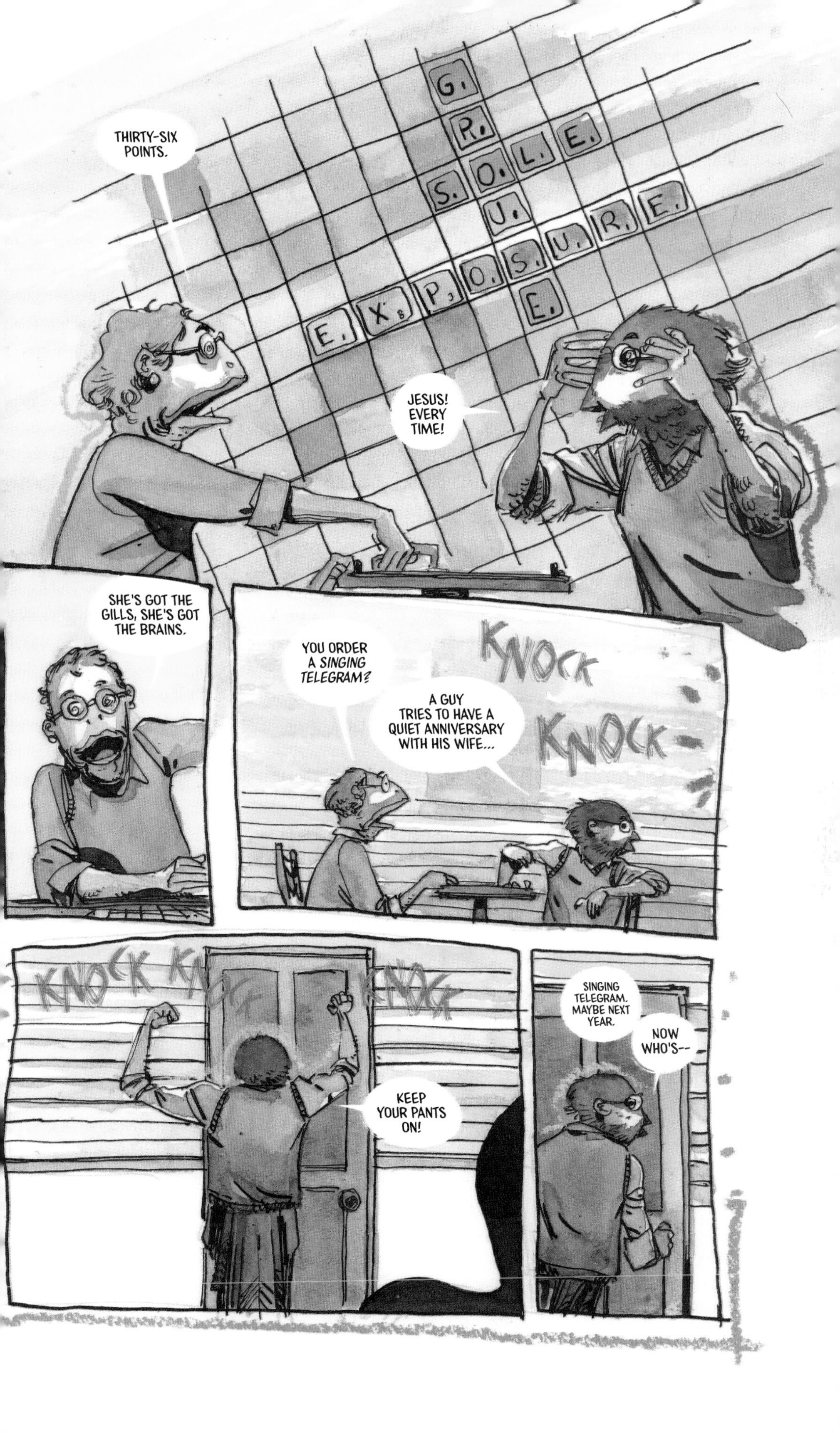
THIRTY-SIX POINTS.
G R O U S E
P O L E
S O L E
P U R E
E X P O S U R E
E X P O S E
JESUS! EVERY TIME!
SHE'S GOT THE GILLS, SHE'S GOT THE BRAINS.
KNOCK
KNOCK
YOU ORDER A *SINGING TELEGRAM*?
A GUY TRIES TO HAVE A QUIET ANNIVERSARY WITH HIS WIFE...
KNOCK KNOCK KNOCK
KEEP YOUR PANTS ON!
SINGING TELEGRAM. MAYBE NEXT YEAR.
NOW WHO'S--

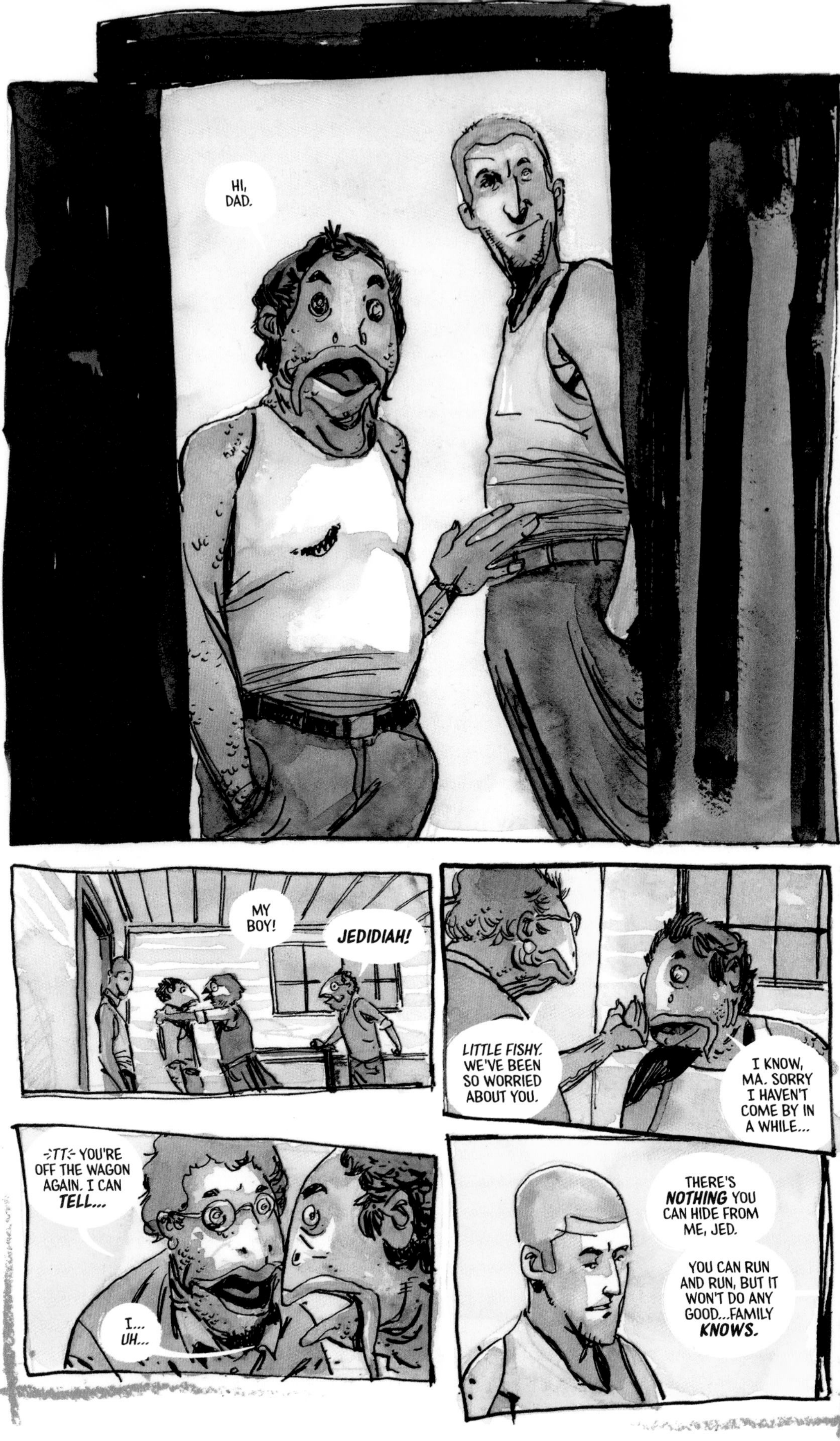
HI, DAD.
MY BOY!
JEDIDIAH!
LITTLE FISHY. WE'VE BEEN SO WORRIED ABOUT YOU.
I KNOW, MA. SORRY I HAVEN'T COME BY IN A WHILE...
TT YOU'RE OFF THE WAGON AGAIN. I CAN TELL...
I... UH...
THERE'S NOTHING YOU CAN HIDE FROM ME, JED.
YOU CAN RUN AND RUN, BUT IT WON'T DO ANY GOOD...FAMILY KNOWS.

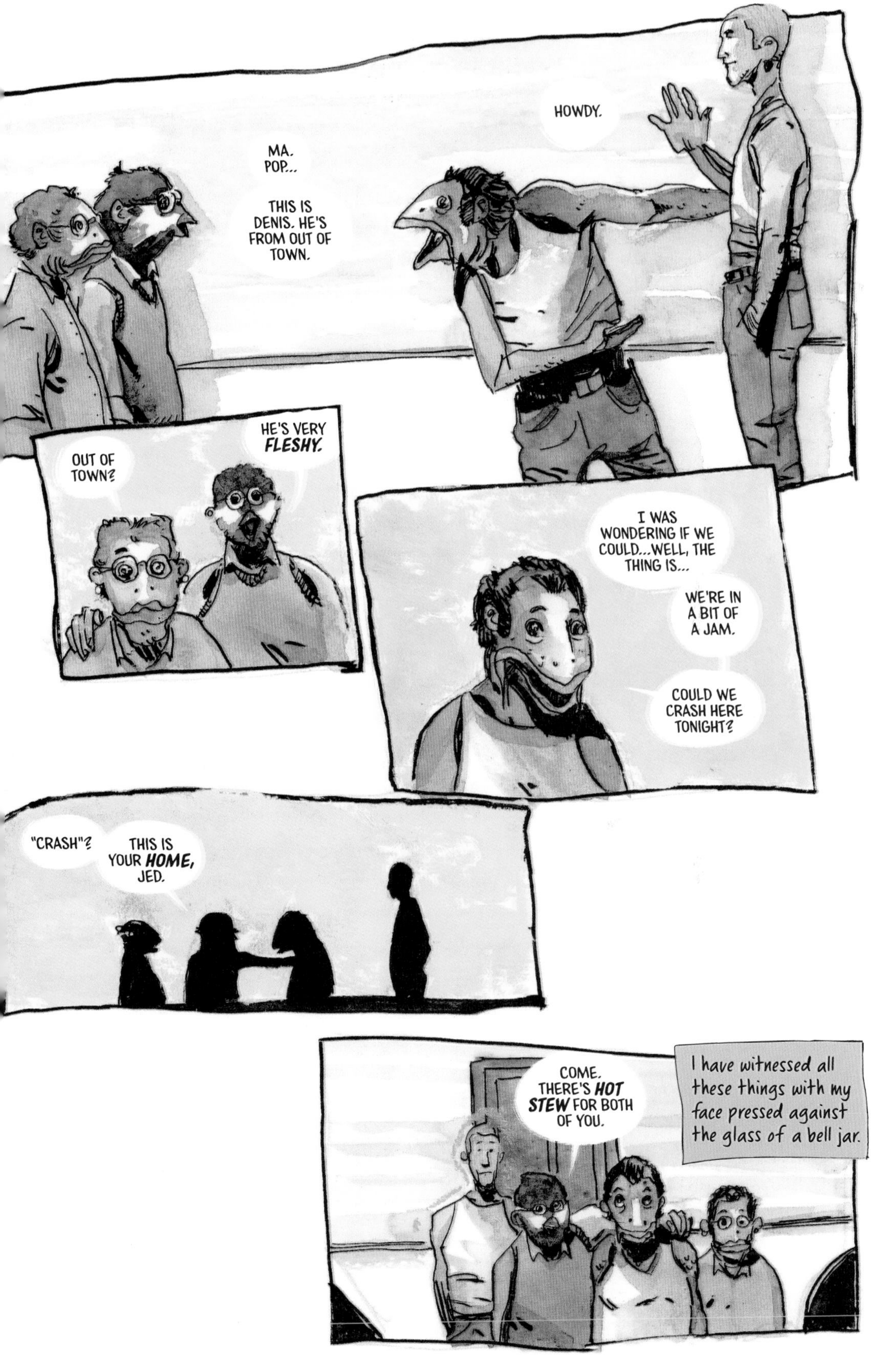
MA. POP...
THIS IS DENIS. HE'S FROM OUT OF TOWN.
HOWDY.
OUT OF TOWN?
HE'S VERY **FLESHY.**
I WAS WONDERING IF WE COULD...WELL, THE THING IS...
WE'RE IN A BIT OF A JAM.
COULD WE CRASH HERE TONIGHT?
"CRASH"?
THIS IS YOUR **HOME,** JED.
COME. THERE'S **HOT STEW** FOR BOTH OF YOU.
I have witnessed all these things with my face pressed against the glass of a bell jar.

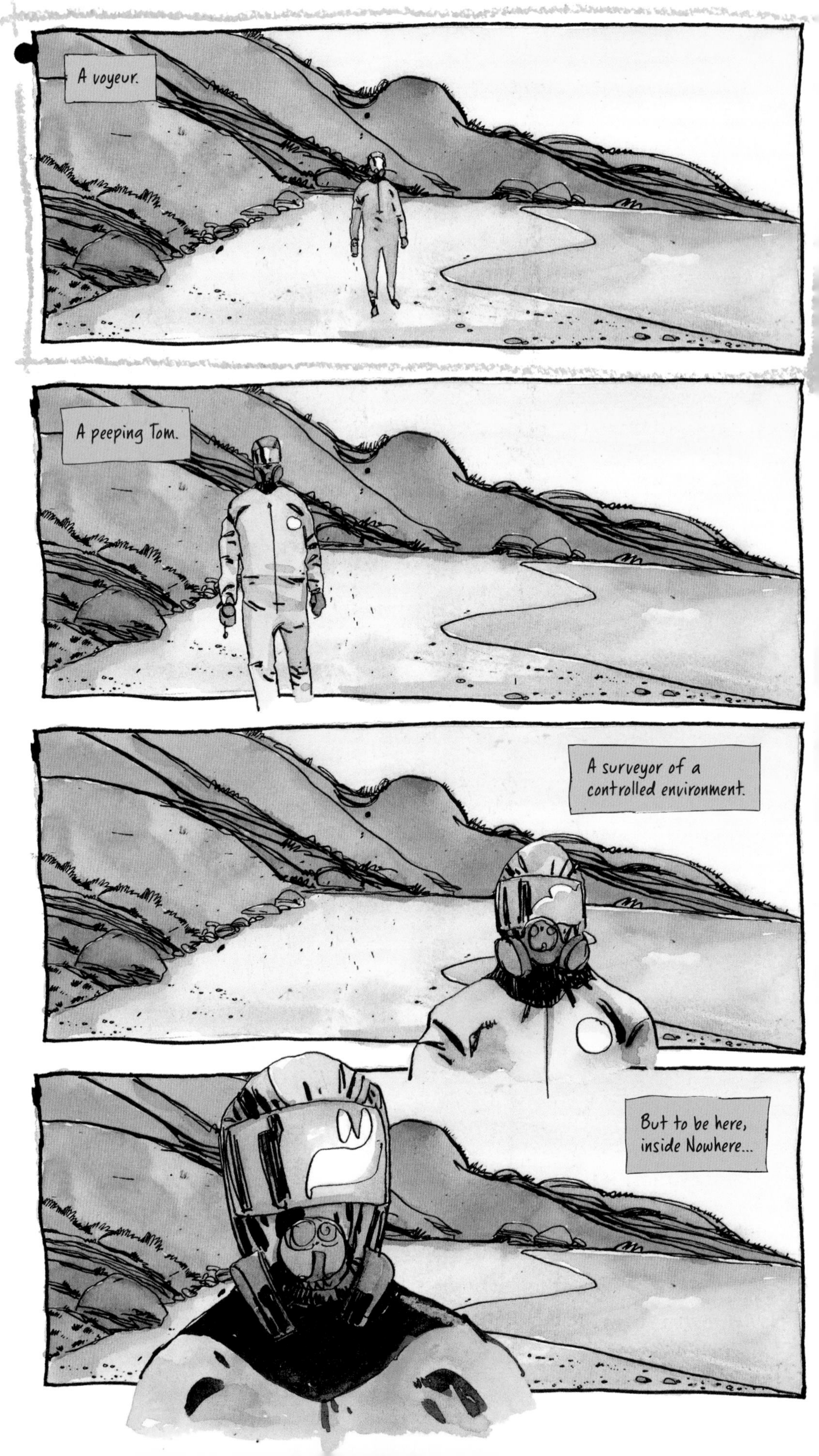
A voyeur.
A peeping Tom.
A surveyor of a controlled environment.
But to be here, inside Nowhere...

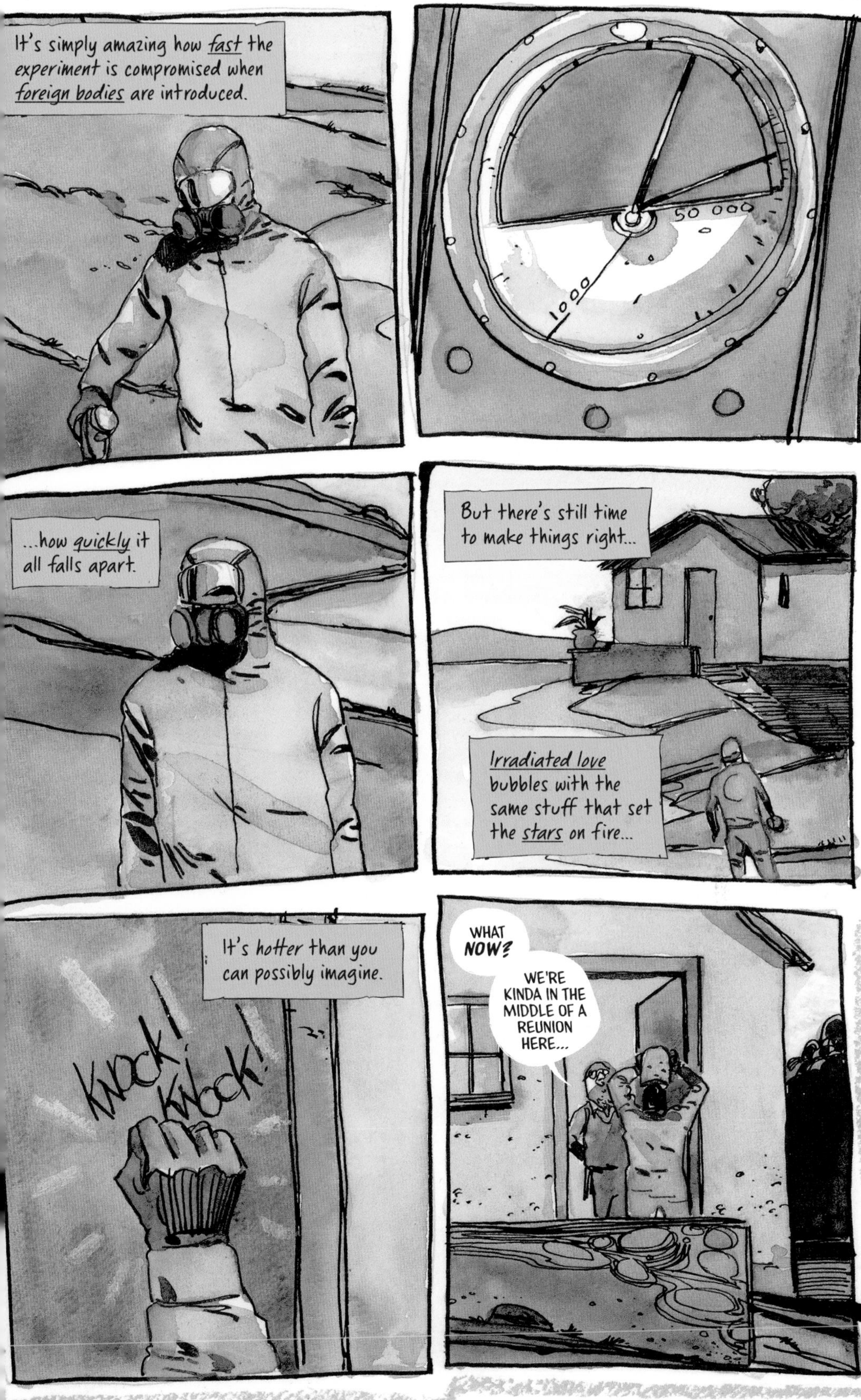
It's simply amazing how fast the experiment is compromised when foreign bodies are introduced.
50 000
1000
...how quickly it all falls apart.
But there's still time to make things right...
Irradiated love bubbles with the same stuff that set the stars on fire...
It's hotter than you can possibly imagine.
KNOCK! KNOCK!
WHAT NOW?
WE'RE KINDA IN THE MIDDLE OF A REUNION HERE...

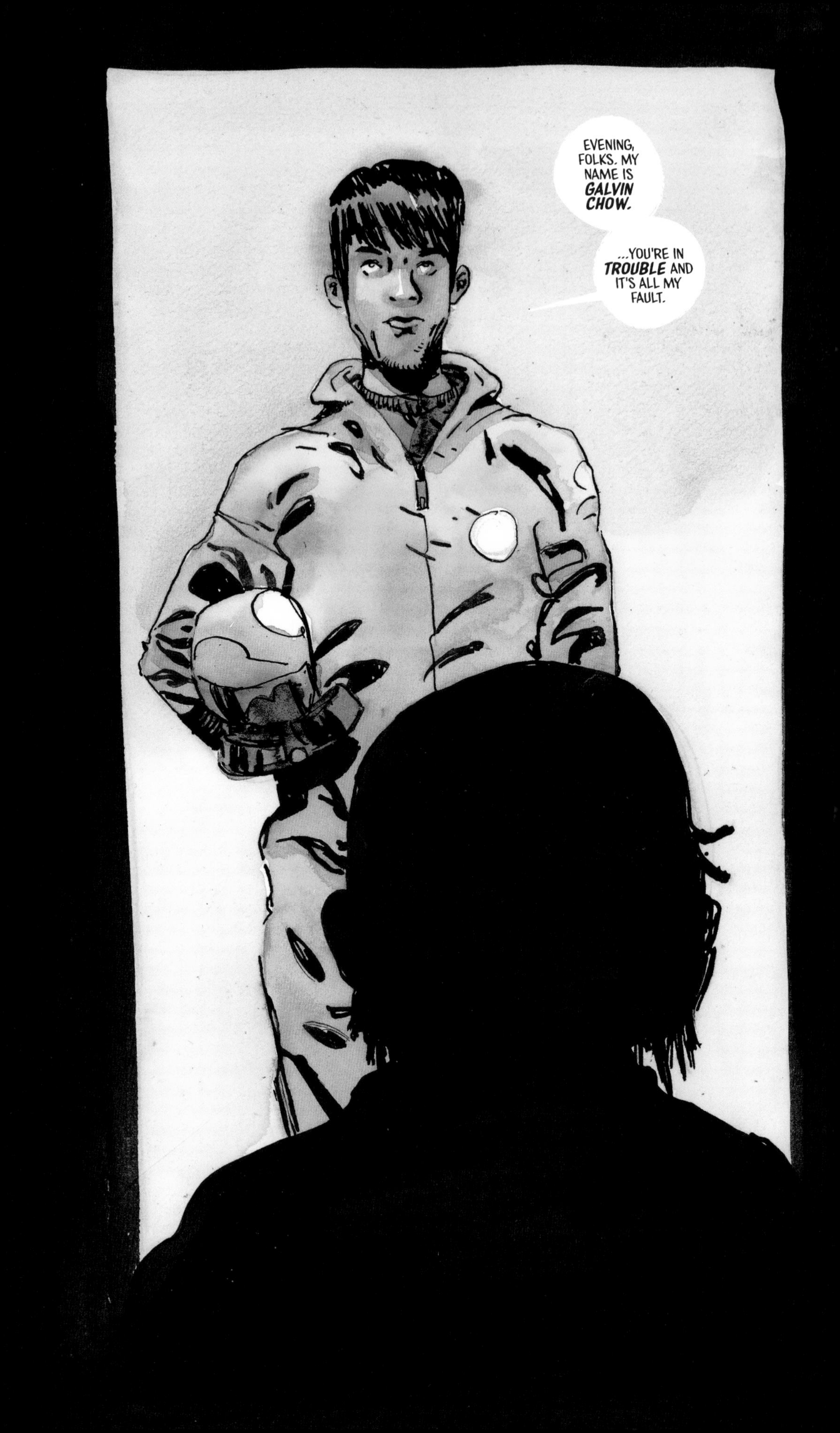
EVENING, FOLKS. MY NAME IS GALVIN CHOW.
...YOU'RE IN TROUBLE AND IT'S ALL MY FAULT.

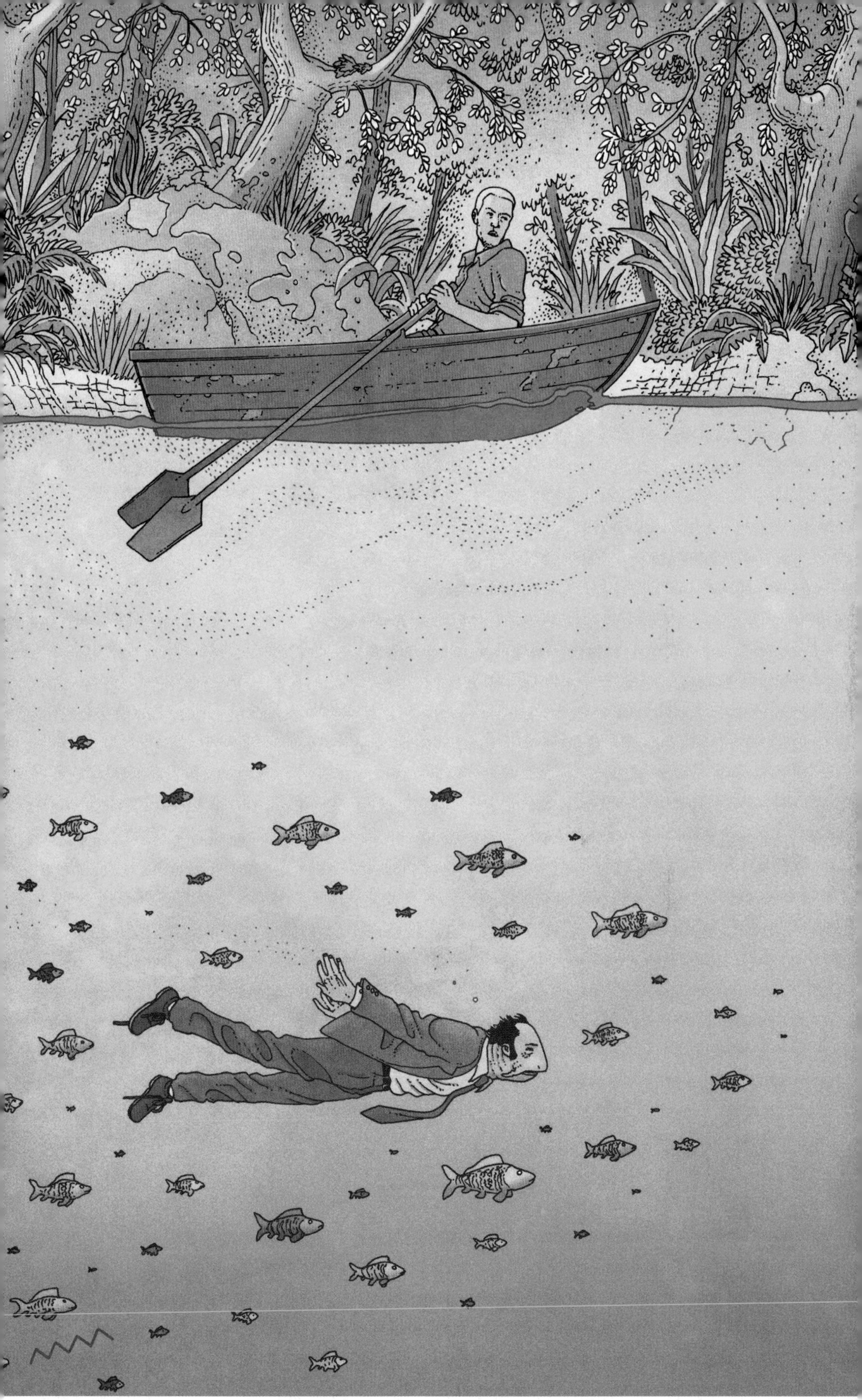

ISSUE THREE COVER BY **MARTÍN MORAZZO** WITH COLORS BY **CHRIS O'HALLORAN**

CHAPTER FOUR

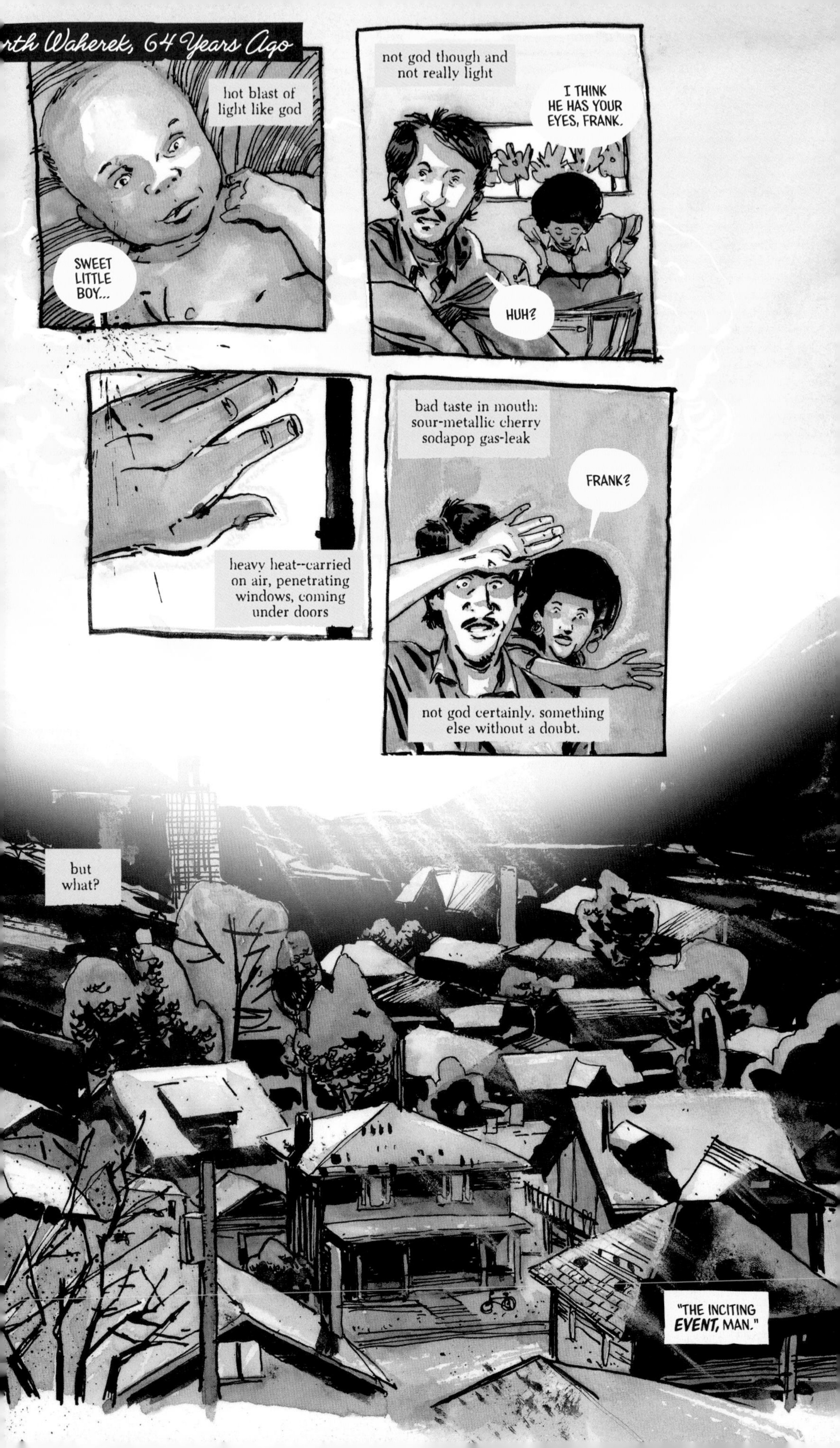
rth Waherek, 64 Years Ago
hot blast of light like god
SWEET LITTLE BOY...
not god though and not really light
I THINK HE HAS YOUR EYES, FRANK.
HUH?
heavy heat--carried on air, penetrating windows, coming under doors
bad taste in mouth: sour-metallic cherry sodapop gas-leak
FRANK?
not god certainly. something else without a doubt.
but what?
"THE INCITING EVENT, MAN."

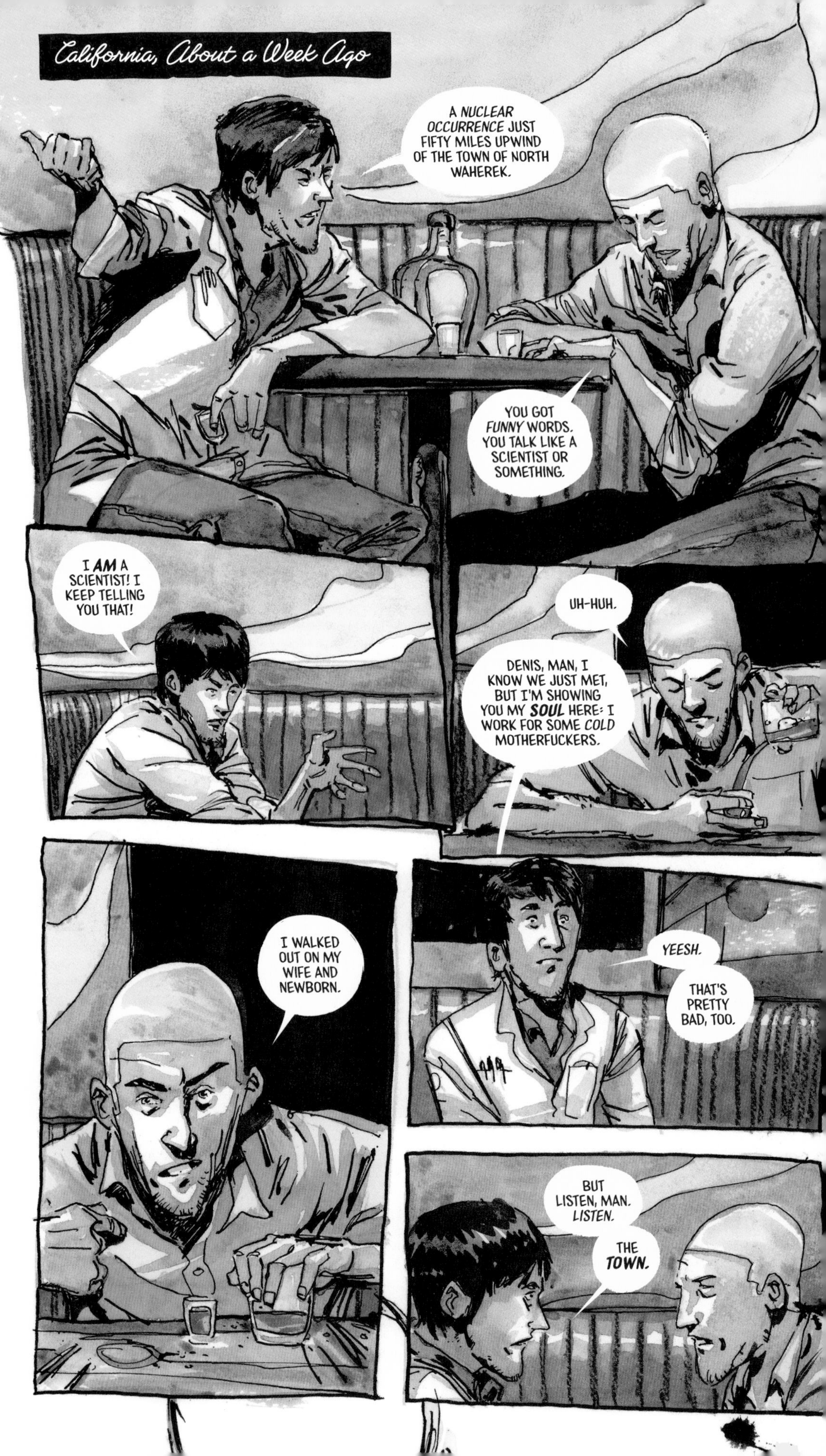
California, About a Week Ago
A NUCLEAR OCCURRENCE JUST FIFTY MILES UPWIND OF THE TOWN OF NORTH WAHEREK.
YOU GOT FUNNY WORDS. YOU TALK LIKE A SCIENTIST OR SOMETHING.
I AM A SCIENTIST! I KEEP TELLING YOU THAT!
UH-HUH.
DENIS, MAN, I KNOW WE JUST MET, BUT I'M SHOWING YOU MY SOUL HERE: I WORK FOR SOME COLD MOTHERFUCKERS.
I WALKED OUT ON MY WIFE AND NEWBORN.
YEESH.
THAT'S PRETTY BAD, TOO.
BUT LISTEN, MAN. LISTEN.
THE TOWN.

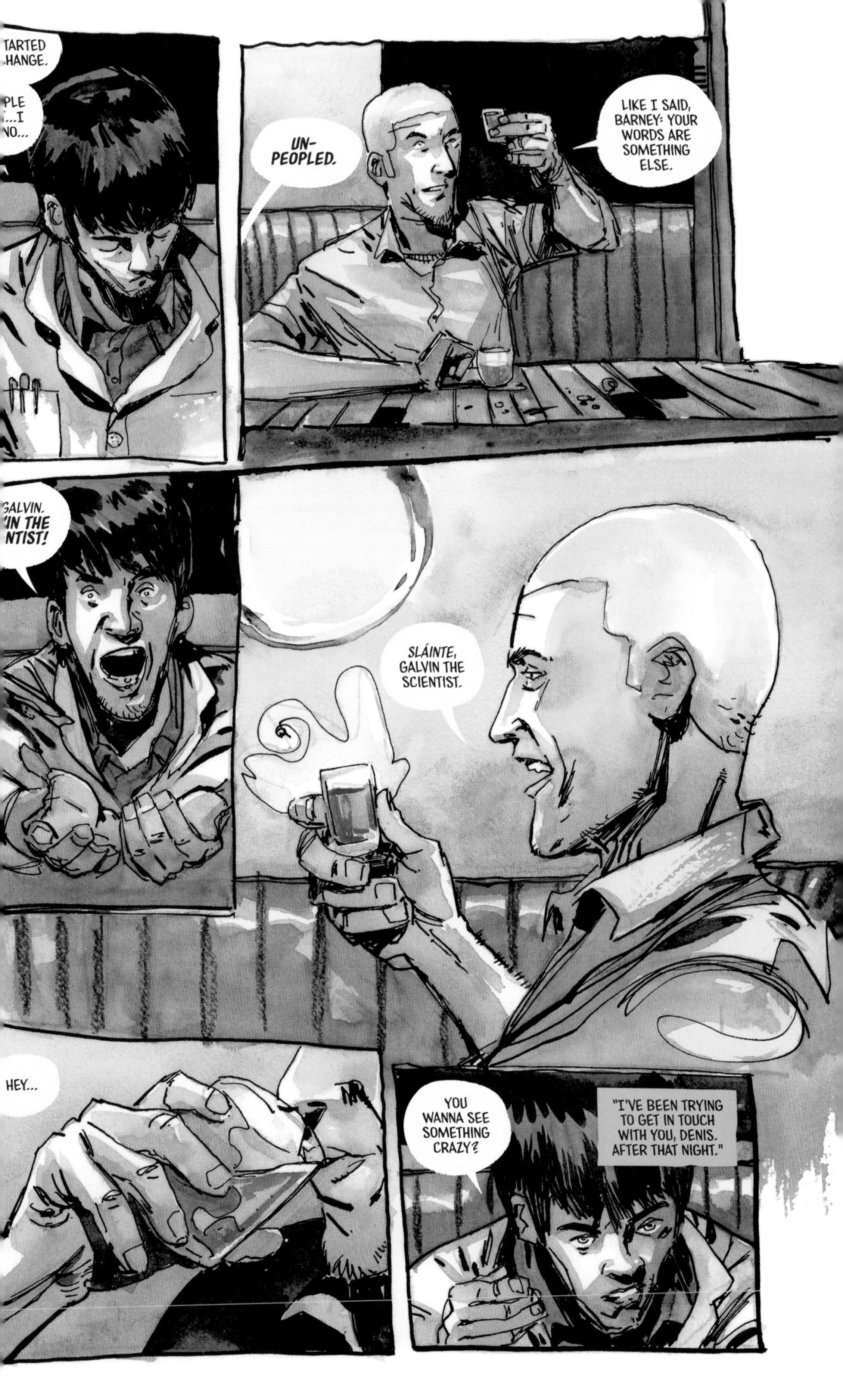
TARTED
HANGE.
PLE
...I
NO...
UN-PEOPLED.
LIKE I SAID, BARNEY: YOUR WORDS ARE SOMETHING ELSE.
GALVIN.
IN THE
NTIST!
SLÁINTE, GALVIN THE SCIENTIST.
HEY...
YOU WANNA SEE SOMETHING CRAZY?
"I'VE BEEN TRYING TO GET IN TOUCH WITH YOU, DENIS. AFTER THAT NIGHT."

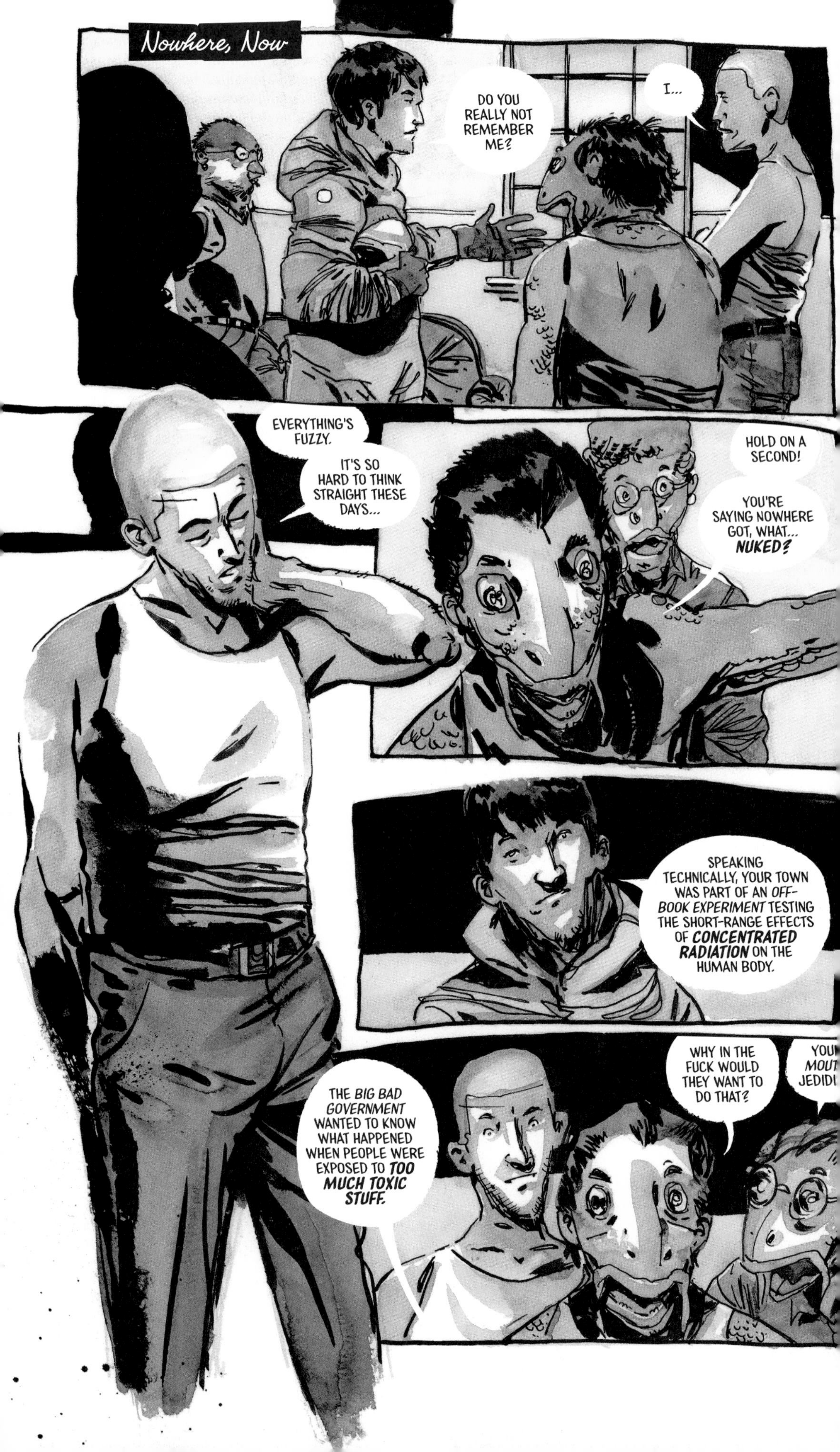
Nowhere, Now
DO YOU REALLY NOT REMEMBER ME?
I...
EVERYTHING'S FUZZY.
IT'S SO HARD TO THINK STRAIGHT THESE DAYS...
HOLD ON A SECOND!
YOU'RE SAYING NOWHERE GOT, WHAT... NUKED?
SPEAKING TECHNICALLY, YOUR TOWN WAS PART OF AN OFF-BOOK EXPERIMENT TESTING THE SHORT-RANGE EFFECTS OF CONCENTRATED RADIATION ON THE HUMAN BODY.
THE BIG BAD GOVERNMENT WANTED TO KNOW WHAT HAPPENED WHEN PEOPLE WERE EXPOSED TO TOO MUCH TOXIC STUFF.
WHY IN THE FUCK WOULD THEY WANT TO DO THAT?

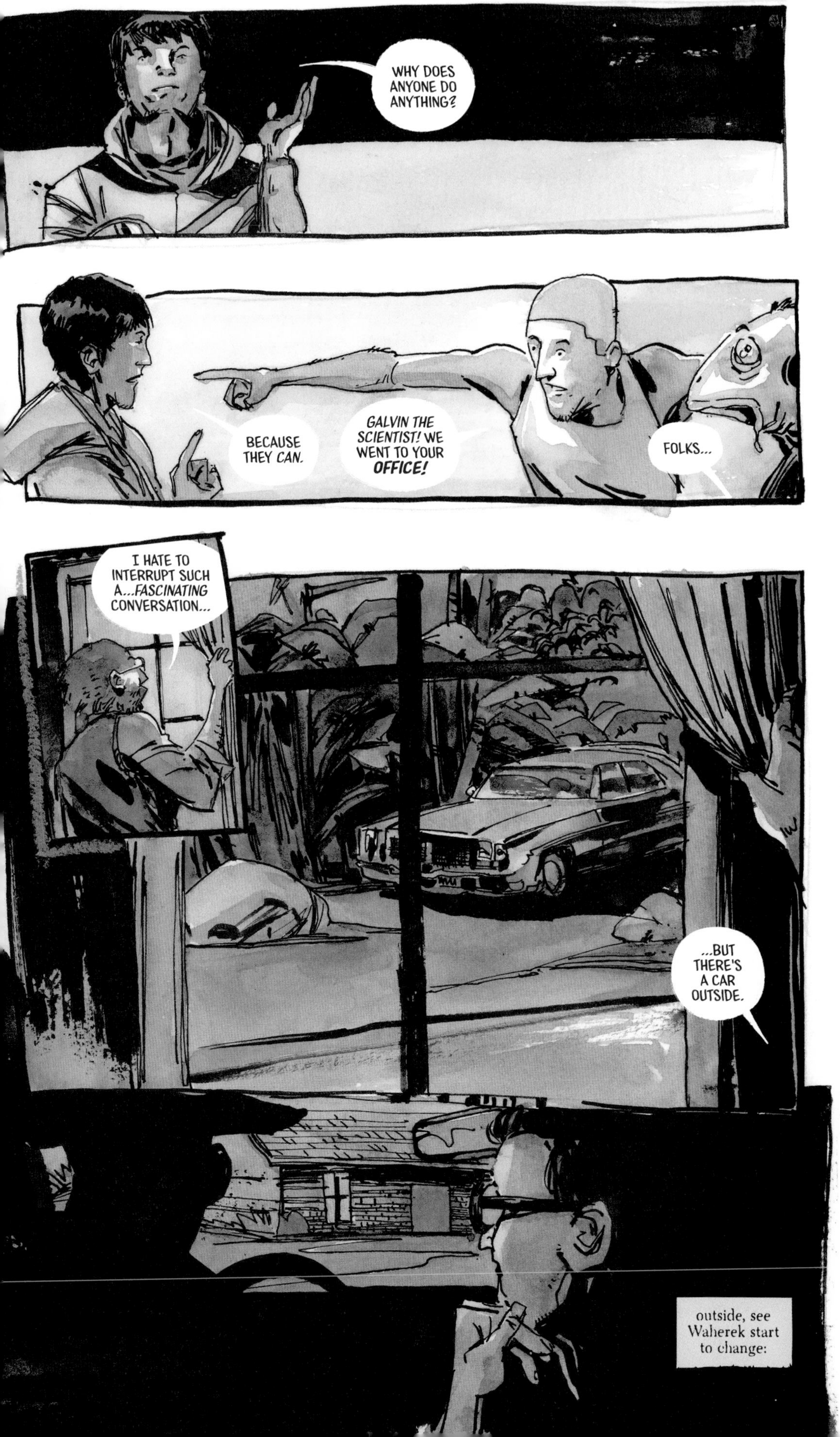
WHY DOES ANYONE DO ANYTHING?
BECAUSE THEY CAN.
GALVIN THE SCIENTIST! WE WENT TO YOUR OFFICE!
FOLKS...
I HATE TO INTERRUPT SUCH A...FASCINATING CONVERSATION...
...BUT THERE'S A CAR OUTSIDE.
outside, see Waherek start to change:

everything is post-light now

all life is life after Glare

life full of wonder, life full of strangeness:

...grocer's fingers have grown very long

MORNING, FRANK!

Joan, head of PTA...

skin is deep blue

Jim from down by the beach has started to resemble his pet parrot

scared feelin scared for n town.

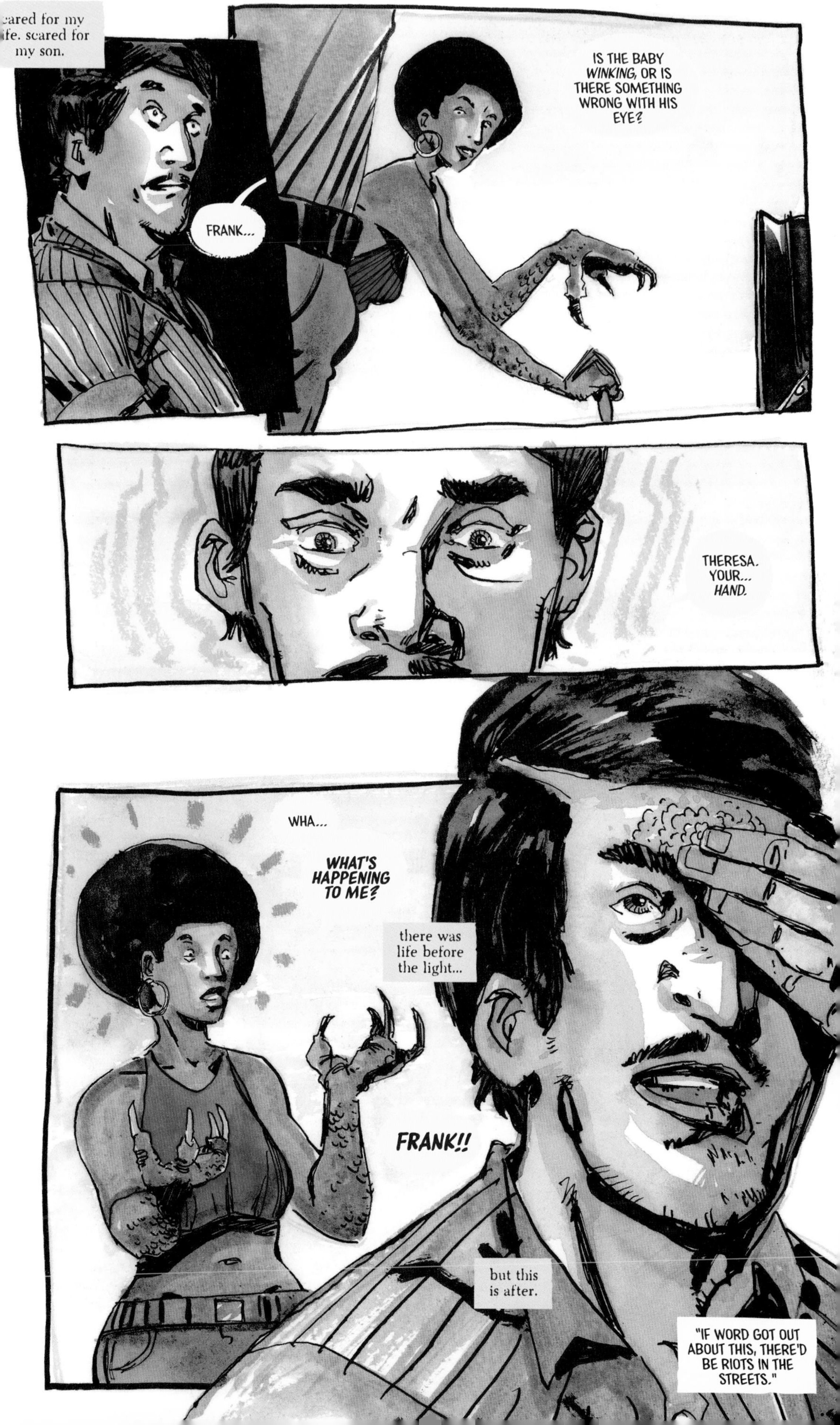

cared for my
ife. scared for
my son.
IS THE BABY WINKING, OR IS THERE SOMETHING WRONG WITH HIS EYE?
FRANK...
THERESA. YOUR... HAND.
WHA...
WHAT'S HAPPENING TO ME?
there was life before the light...
FRANK!!
but this is after.
"IF WORD GOT OUT ABOUT THIS, THERE'D BE RIOTS IN THE STREETS."

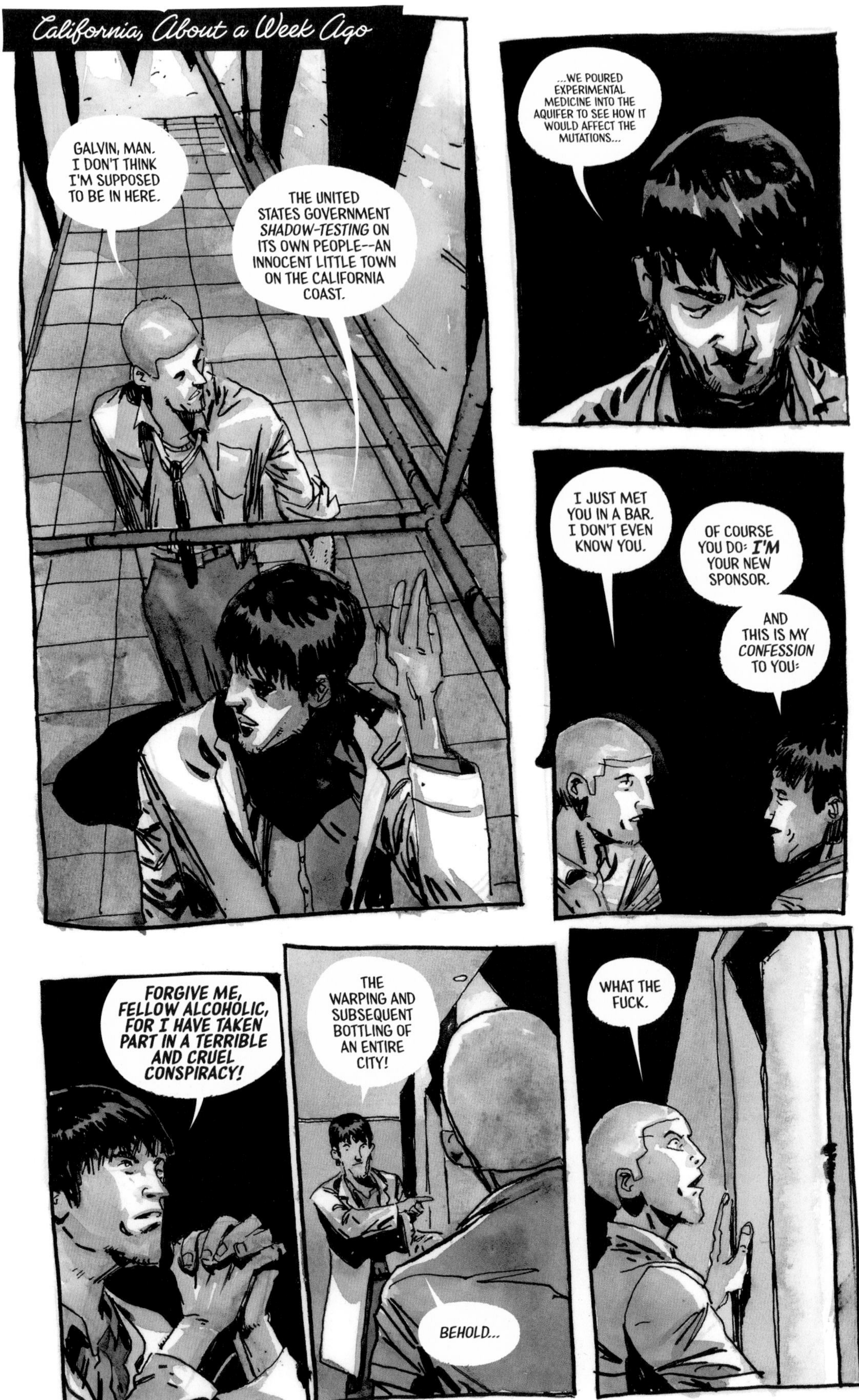
California, About a Week Ago
GALVIN, MAN. I DON'T THINK I'M SUPPOSED TO BE IN HERE.
THE UNITED STATES GOVERNMENT SHADOW-TESTING ON ITS OWN PEOPLE--AN INNOCENT LITTLE TOWN ON THE CALIFORNIA COAST.
...WE POURED EXPERIMENTAL MEDICINE INTO THE AQUIFER TO SEE HOW IT WOULD AFFECT THE MUTATIONS...
I JUST MET YOU IN A BAR. I DON'T EVEN KNOW YOU.
OF COURSE YOU DO: I'M YOUR NEW SPONSOR.
AND THIS IS MY CONFESSION TO YOU:
FORGIVE ME, FELLOW ALCOHOLIC, FOR I HAVE TAKEN PART IN A TERRIBLE AND CRUEL CONSPIRACY!
THE WARPING AND SUBSEQUENT BOTTLING OF AN ENTIRE CITY!
BEHOLD...
WHAT THE FUCK.

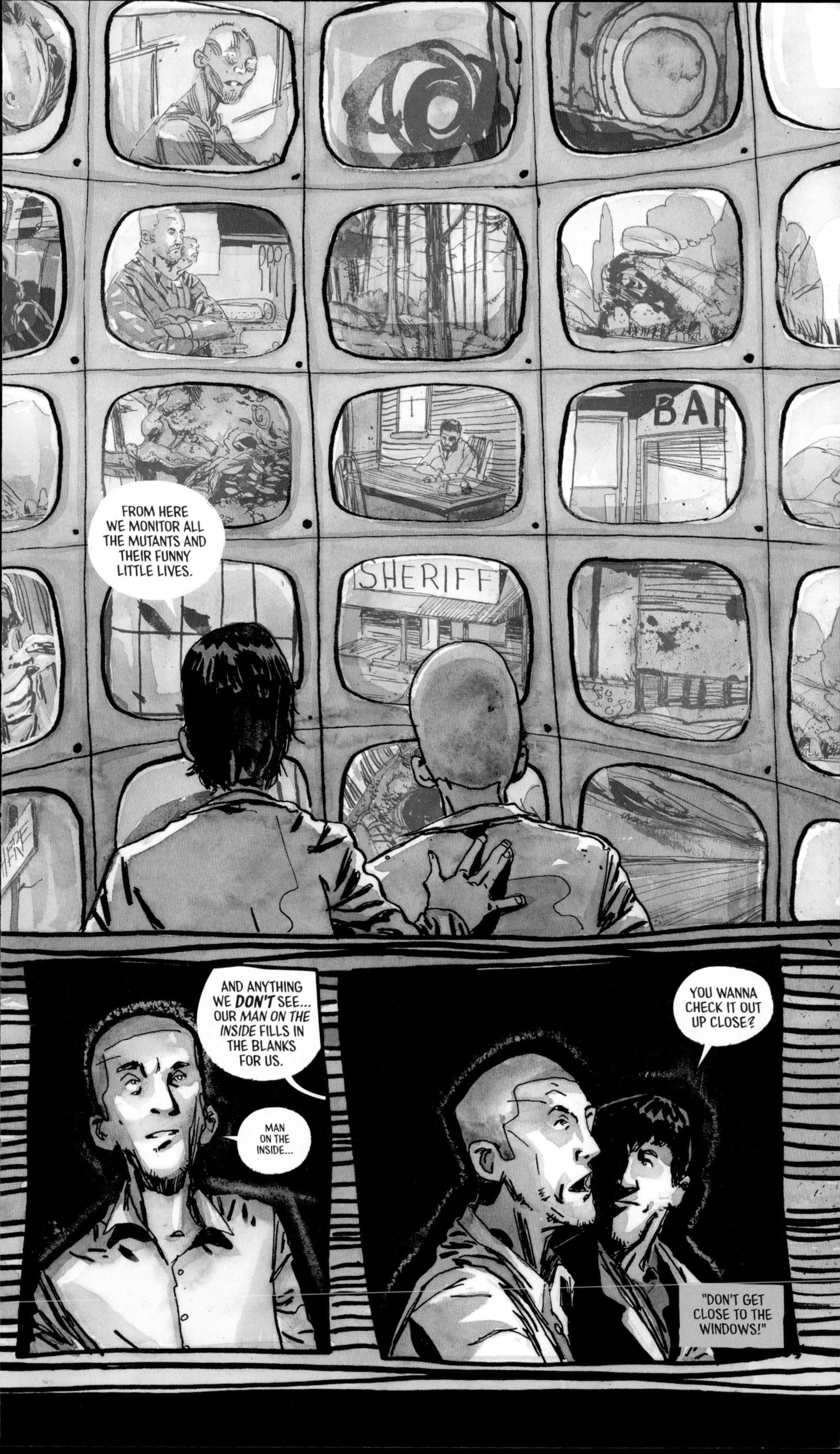

BAR
FROM HERE WE MONITOR ALL THE MUTANTS AND THEIR FUNNY LITTLE LIVES.
SHERIFF
AND ANYTHING WE **DON'T** SEE... OUR *MAN ON THE INSIDE* FILLS IN THE BLANKS FOR US.
MAN ON THE INSIDE...
YOU WANNA CHECK IT OUT UP CLOSE?
"DON'T GET CLOSE TO THE WINDOWS!"

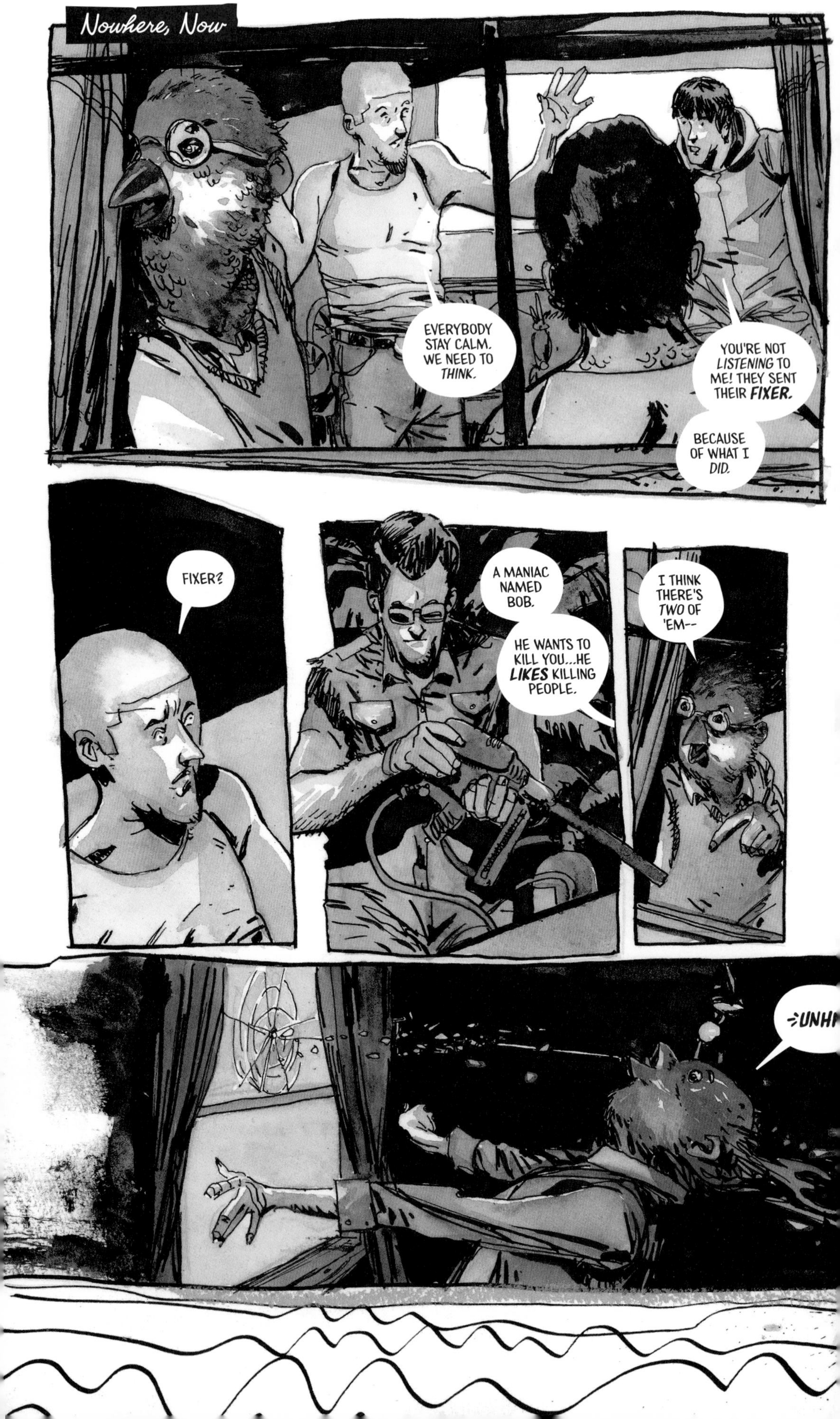
Nowhere, Now
EVERYBODY STAY CALM. WE NEED TO THINK.
YOU'RE NOT LISTENING TO ME! THEY SENT THEIR FIXER.
BECAUSE OF WHAT I DID.
FIXER?
A MANIAC NAMED BOB.
HE WANTS TO KILL YOU...HE LIKES KILLING PEOPLE.
I THINK THERE'S TWO OF 'EM--
UNH

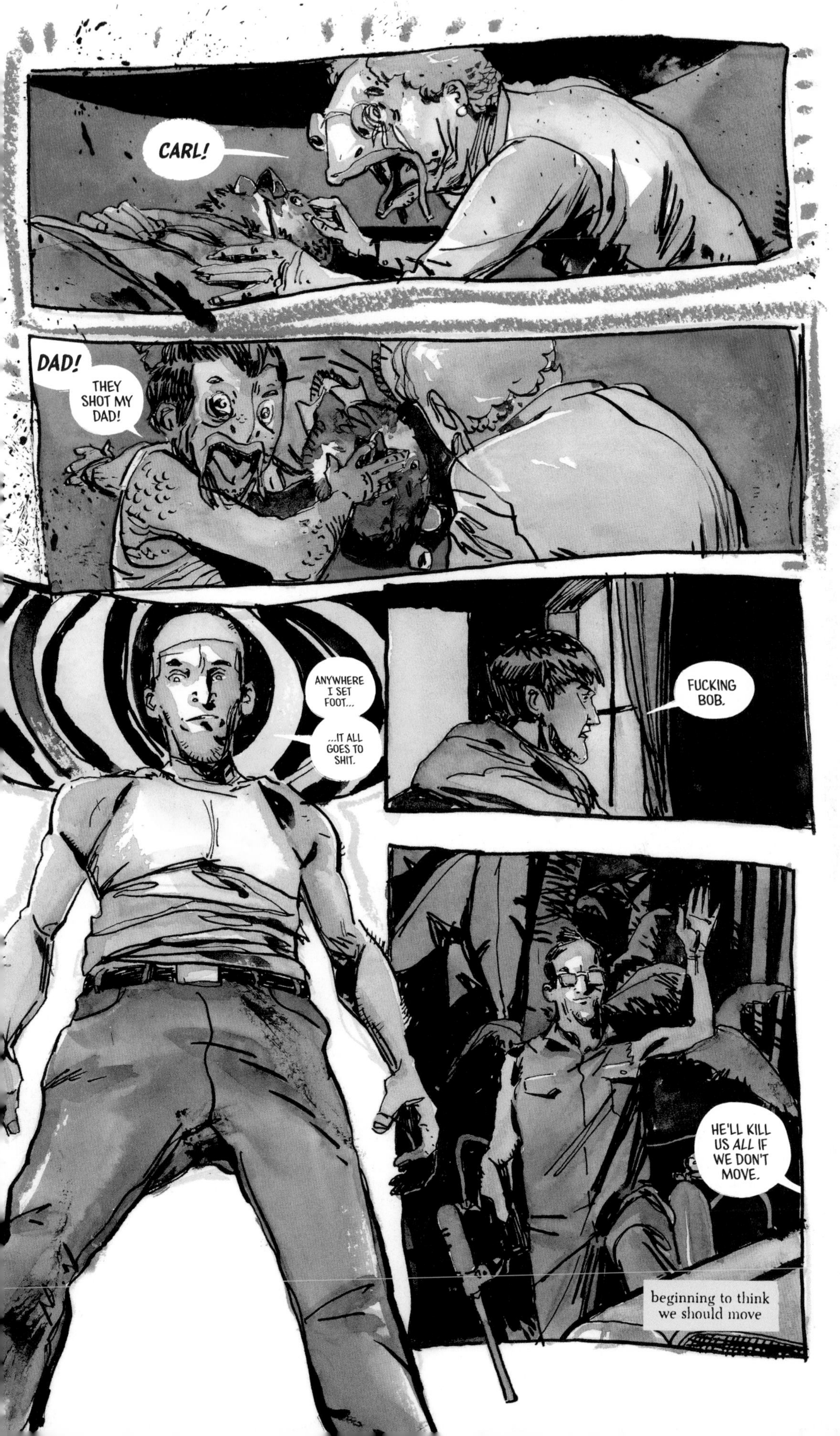
CARL!
DAD!
THEY SHOT MY DAD!
ANYWHERE I SET FOOT...
...IT ALL GOES TO SHIT.
FUCKING BOB.
HE'LL KILL US *ALL* IF WE DON'T MOVE.
beginning to think we should move

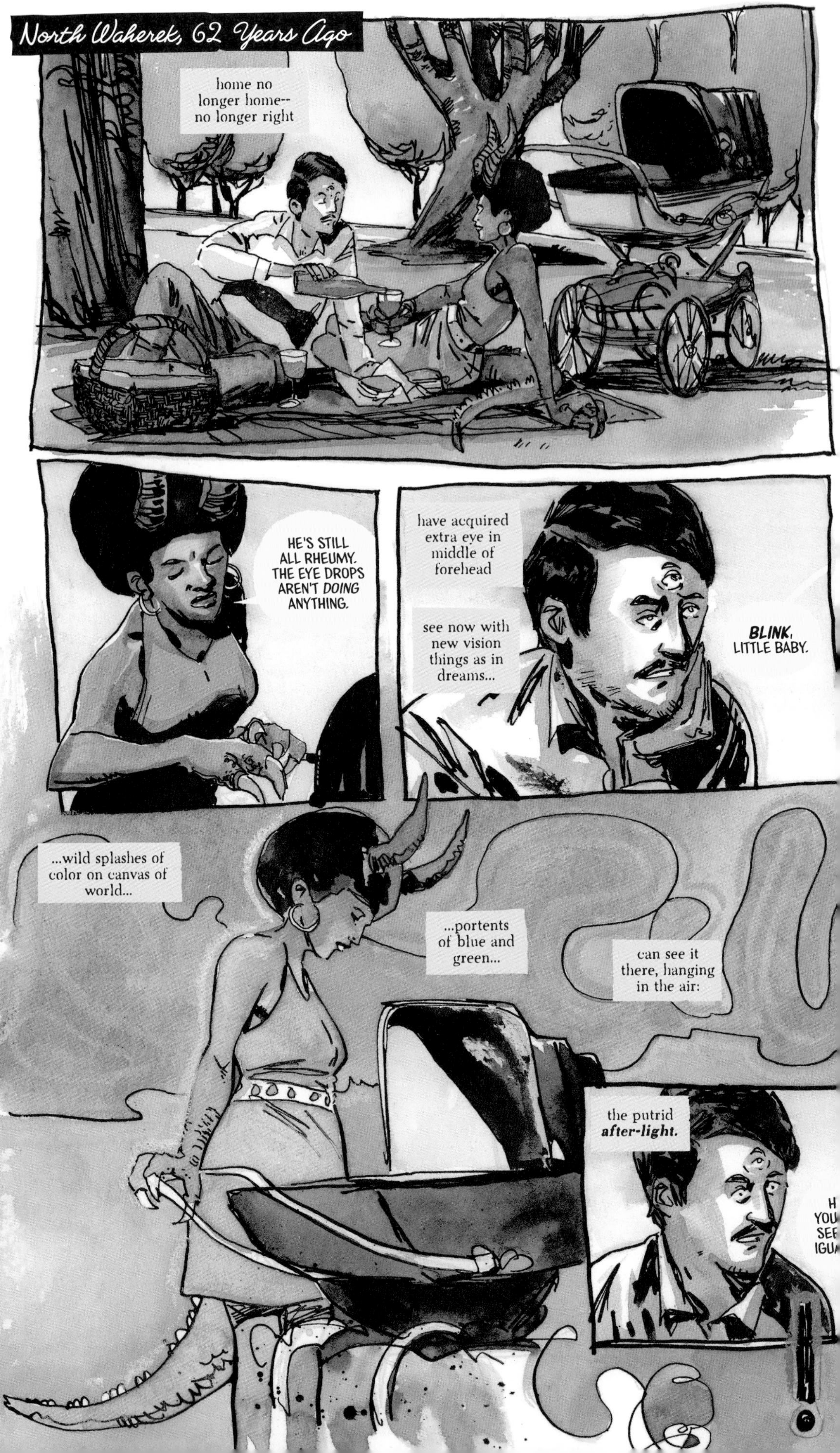
North Waherek, 62 Years Ago
home no longer home-- no longer right
HE'S STILL ALL RHEUMY. THE EYE DROPS AREN'T *DOING* ANYTHING.
have acquired extra eye in middle of forehead
see now with new vision things as in dreams...
BLINK, LITTLE BABY.
...wild splashes of color on canvas of world...
...portents of blue and green...
can see it there, hanging in the air:
the putrid ***after-light.***

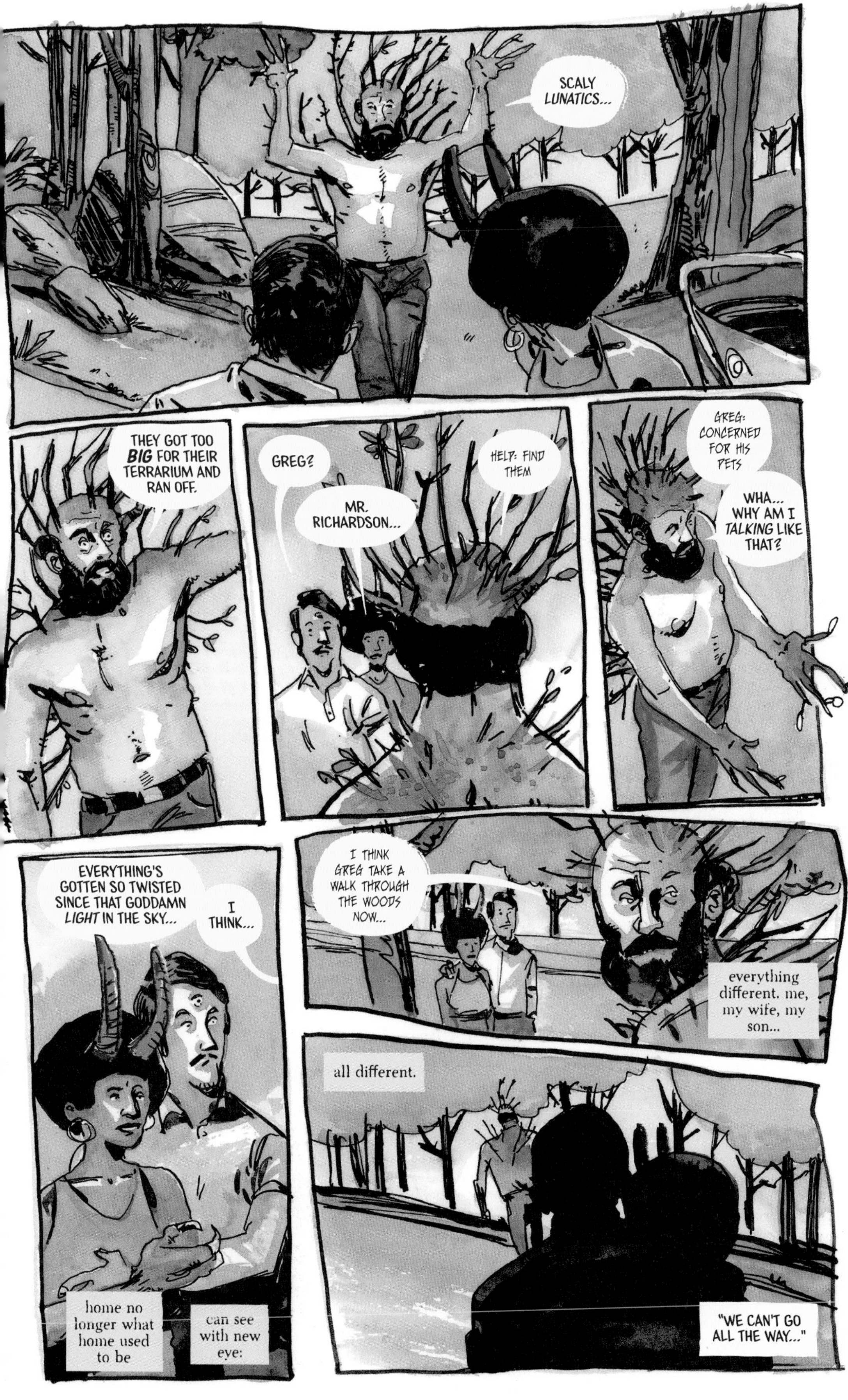
SCALY LUNATICS...
THEY GOT TOO BIG FOR THEIR TERRARIUM AND RAN OFF.
GREG?
MR. RICHARDSON...
HELP: FIND THEM
GREG: CONCERNED FOR HIS PETS
WHA... WHY AM I TALKING LIKE THAT?
EVERYTHING'S GOTTEN SO TWISTED SINCE THAT GODDAMN LIGHT IN THE SKY...
I THINK...
home no longer what home used to be
can see with new eye:
I THINK GREG TAKE A WALK THROUGH THE WOODS NOW...
everything different. me, my wife, my son...
all different.
"WE CAN'T GO ALL THE WAY..."

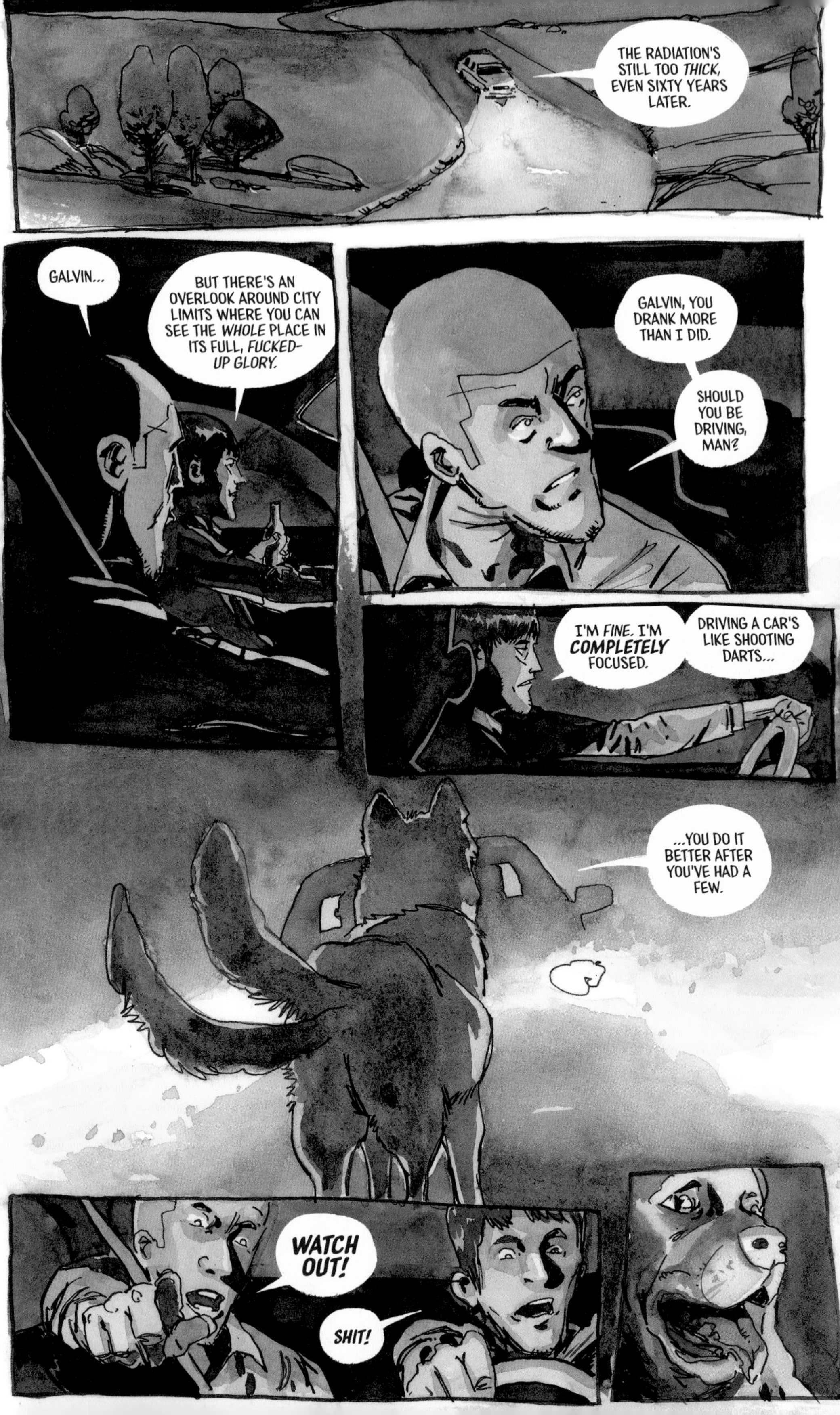
THE RADIATION'S STILL TOO THICK, EVEN SIXTY YEARS LATER.
GALVIN...
BUT THERE'S AN OVERLOOK AROUND CITY LIMITS WHERE YOU CAN SEE THE WHOLE PLACE IN ITS FULL, FUCKED-UP GLORY.
GALVIN, YOU DRANK MORE THAN I DID.
SHOULD YOU BE DRIVING, MAN?
I'M FINE. I'M COMPLETELY FOCUSED.
DRIVING A CAR'S LIKE SHOOTING DARTS...
...YOU DO IT BETTER AFTER YOU'VE HAD A FEW.
WATCH OUT!
SHIT!

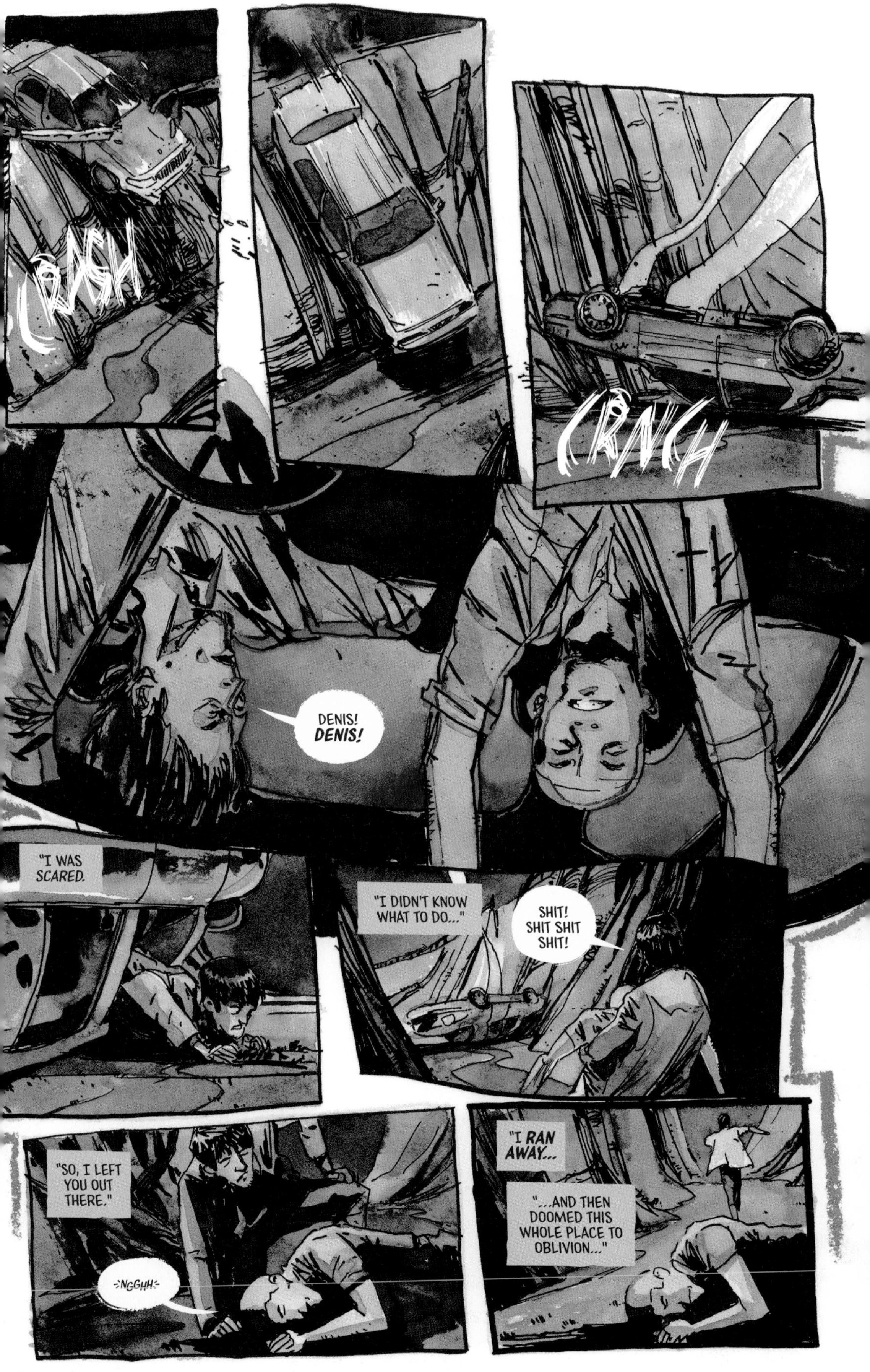
CRASH
CRNCH
DENIS! DENIS!
"I WAS SCARED.
"I DIDN'T KNOW WHAT TO DO..."
SHIT! SHIT SHIT SHIT!
"SO, I LEFT YOU OUT THERE."
NGGHH
"I RAN AWAY...
"...AND THEN DOOMED THIS WHOLE PLACE TO OBLIVION..."

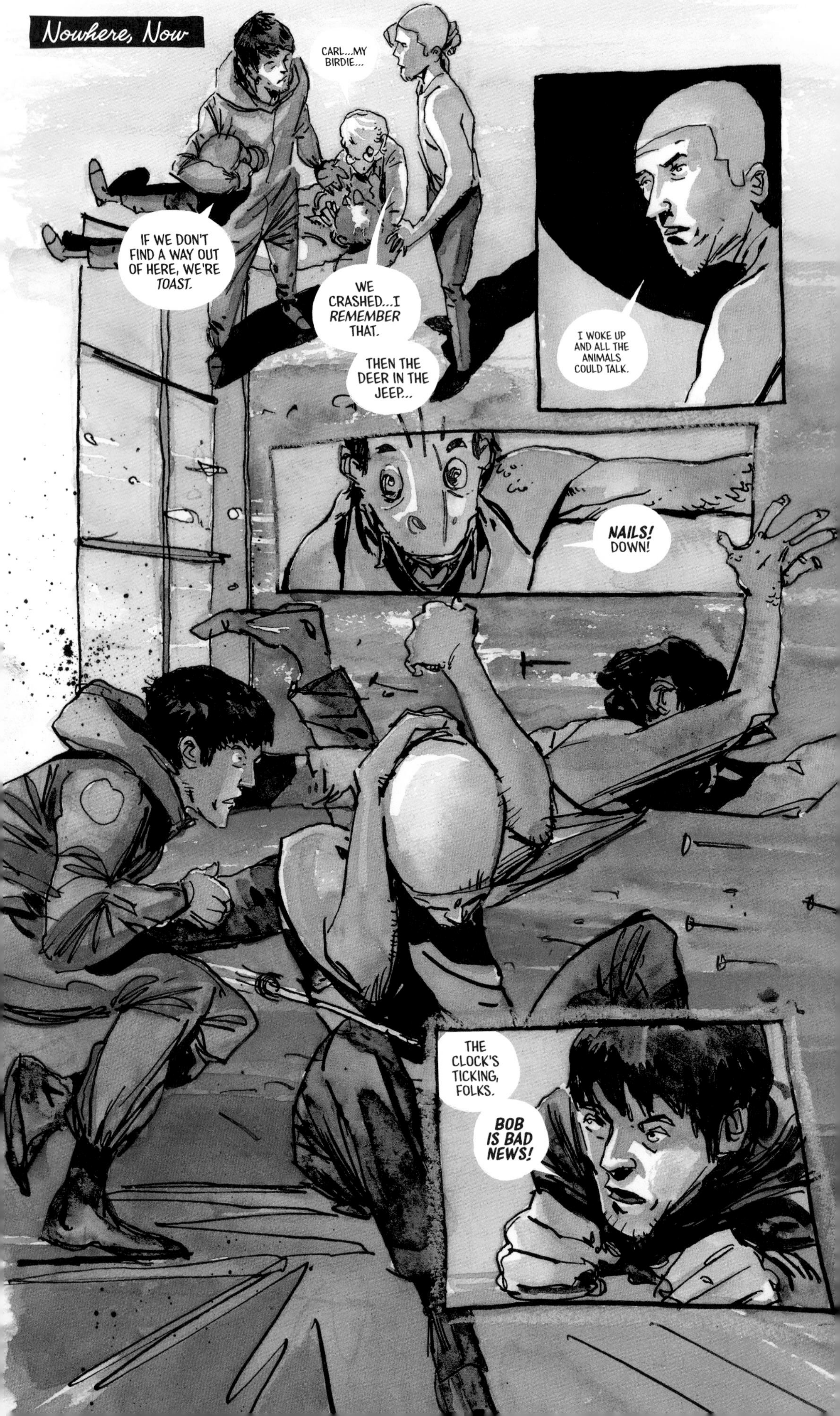
Nowhere, Now
CARL...MY BIRDIE...
IF WE DON'T FIND A WAY OUT OF HERE, WE'RE *TOAST.*
WE CRASHED...I *REMEMBER* THAT.
THEN THE DEER IN THE JEEP...
I WOKE UP AND ALL THE ANIMALS COULD TALK.
NAILS! DOWN!
THE CLOCK'S TICKING, FOLKS.
BOB IS BAD NEWS!

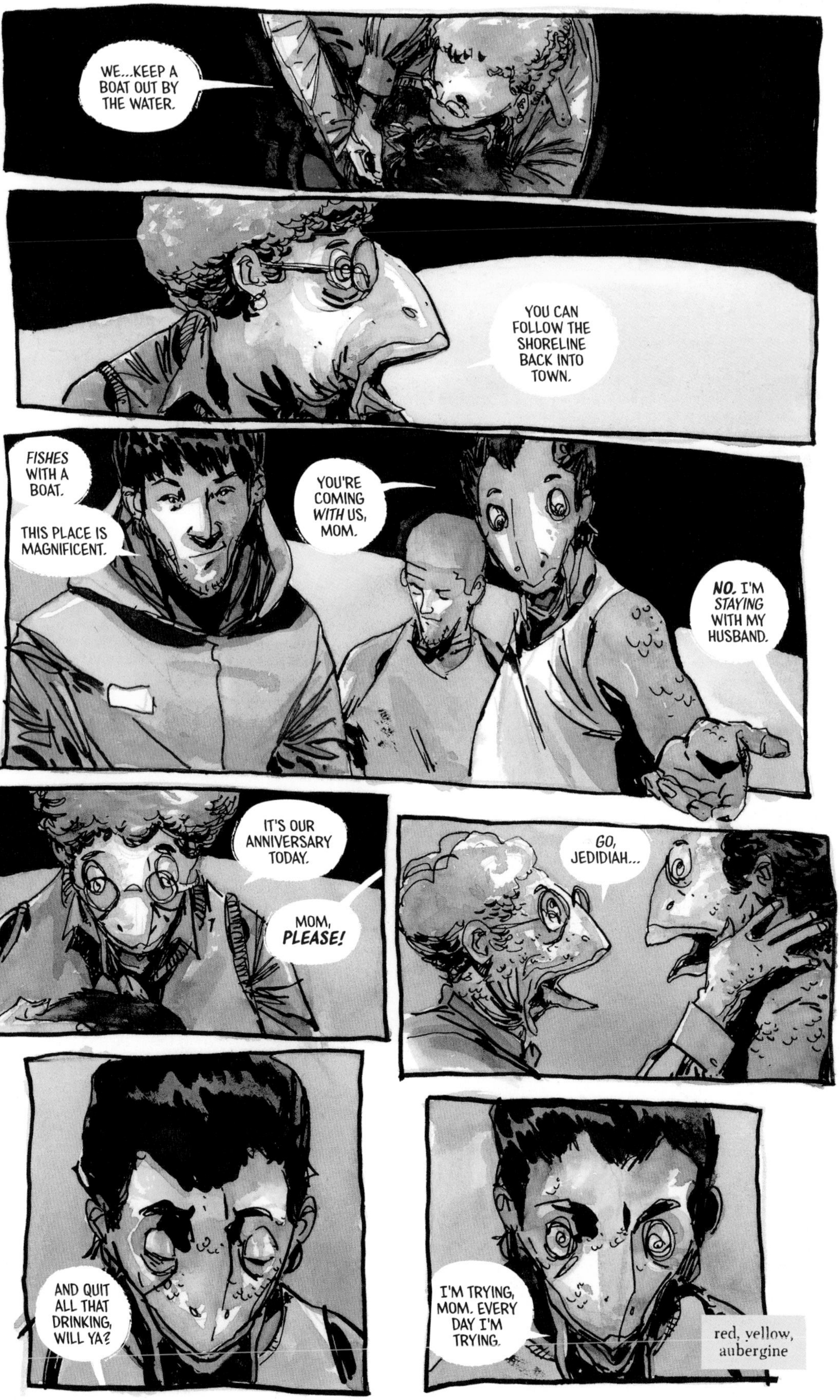
WE...KEEP A BOAT OUT BY THE WATER.
YOU CAN FOLLOW THE SHORELINE BACK INTO TOWN.
FISHES WITH A BOAT.
THIS PLACE IS MAGNIFICENT.
YOU'RE COMING WITH US, MOM.
NO. I'M STAYING WITH MY HUSBAND.
IT'S OUR ANNIVERSARY TODAY.
MOM, PLEASE!
GO, JEDIDIAH...
AND QUIT ALL THAT DRINKING, WILL YA?
I'M TRYING, MOM. EVERY DAY I'M TRYING.

red, yellow, aubergine

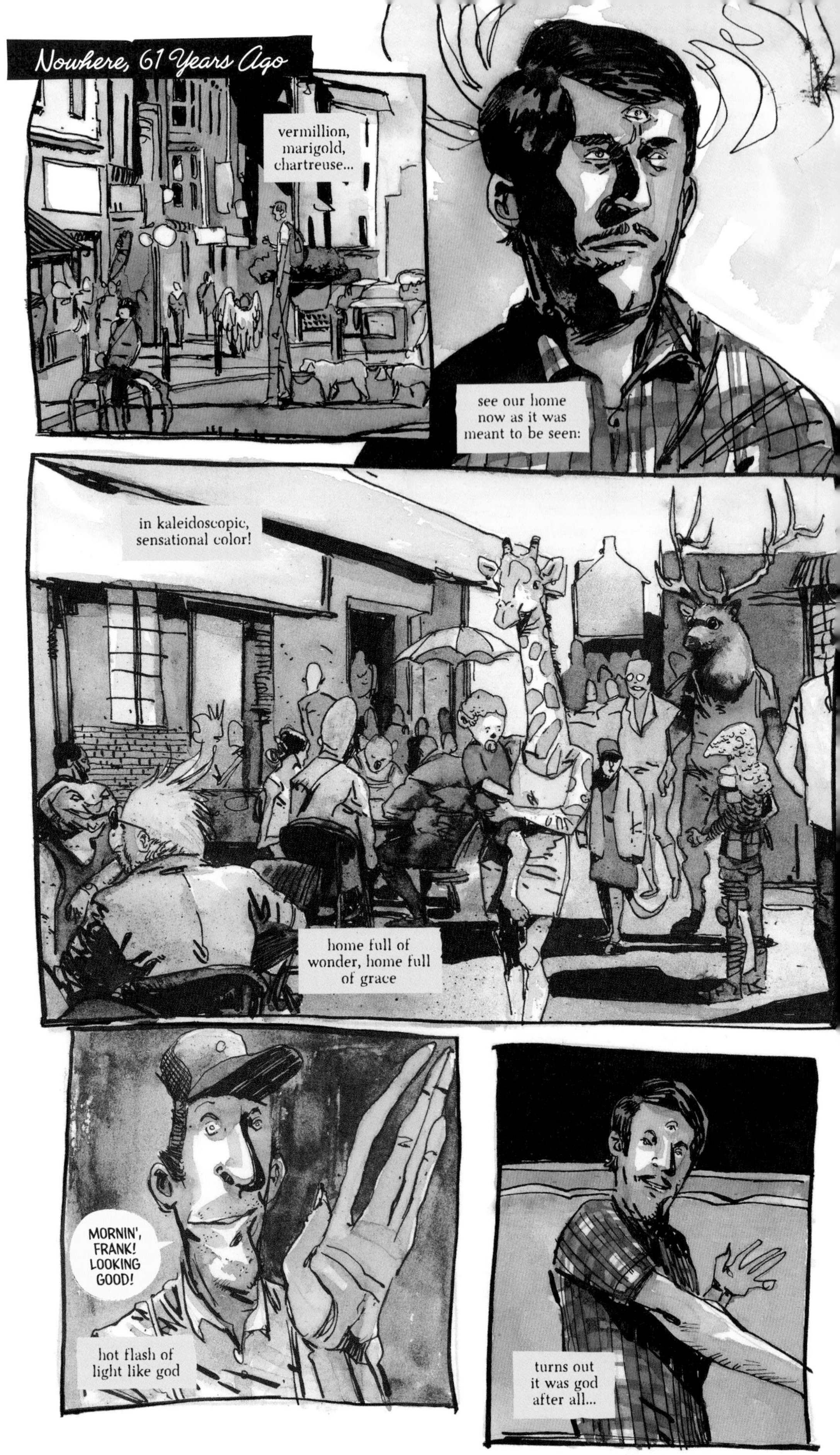

Nowhere, 61 Years Ago
vermillion, marigold, chartreuse...
see our home now as it was meant to be seen:
in kaleidoscopic, sensational color!
home full of wonder, home full of grace
MORNIN', FRANK! LOOKING GOOD!
hot flash of light like god
turns out it was god after all...

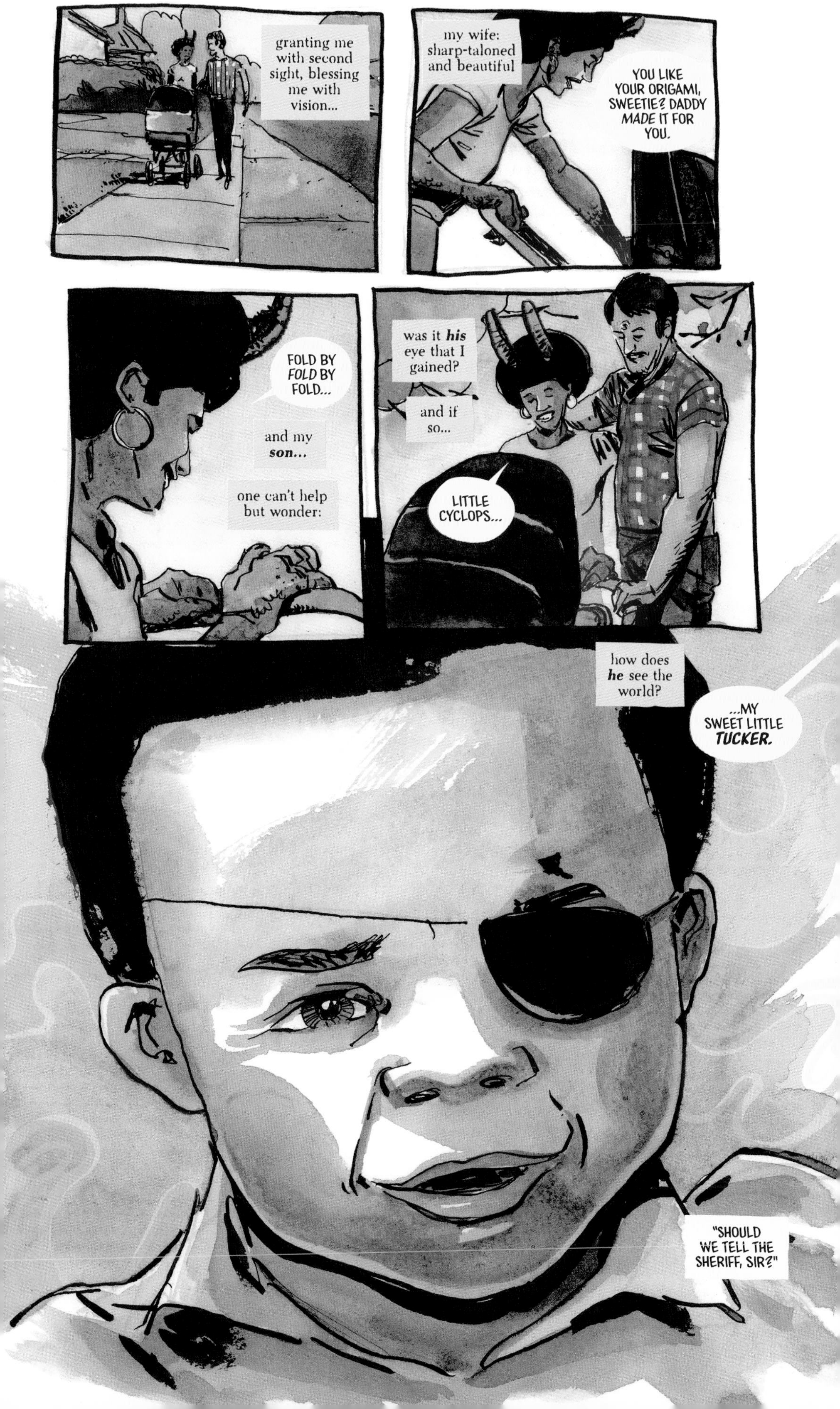
granting me with second sight, blessing me with vision...
my wife: sharp-taloned and beautiful
YOU LIKE YOUR ORIGAMI, SWEETIE? DADDY MADE IT FOR YOU.
FOLD BY FOLD BY FOLD...
and my son...
one can't help but wonder:
was it his eye that I gained?
and if so...
LITTLE CYCLOPS...
how does he see the world?
...MY SWEET LITTLE TUCKER.
"SHOULD WE TELL THE SHERIFF, SIR?"

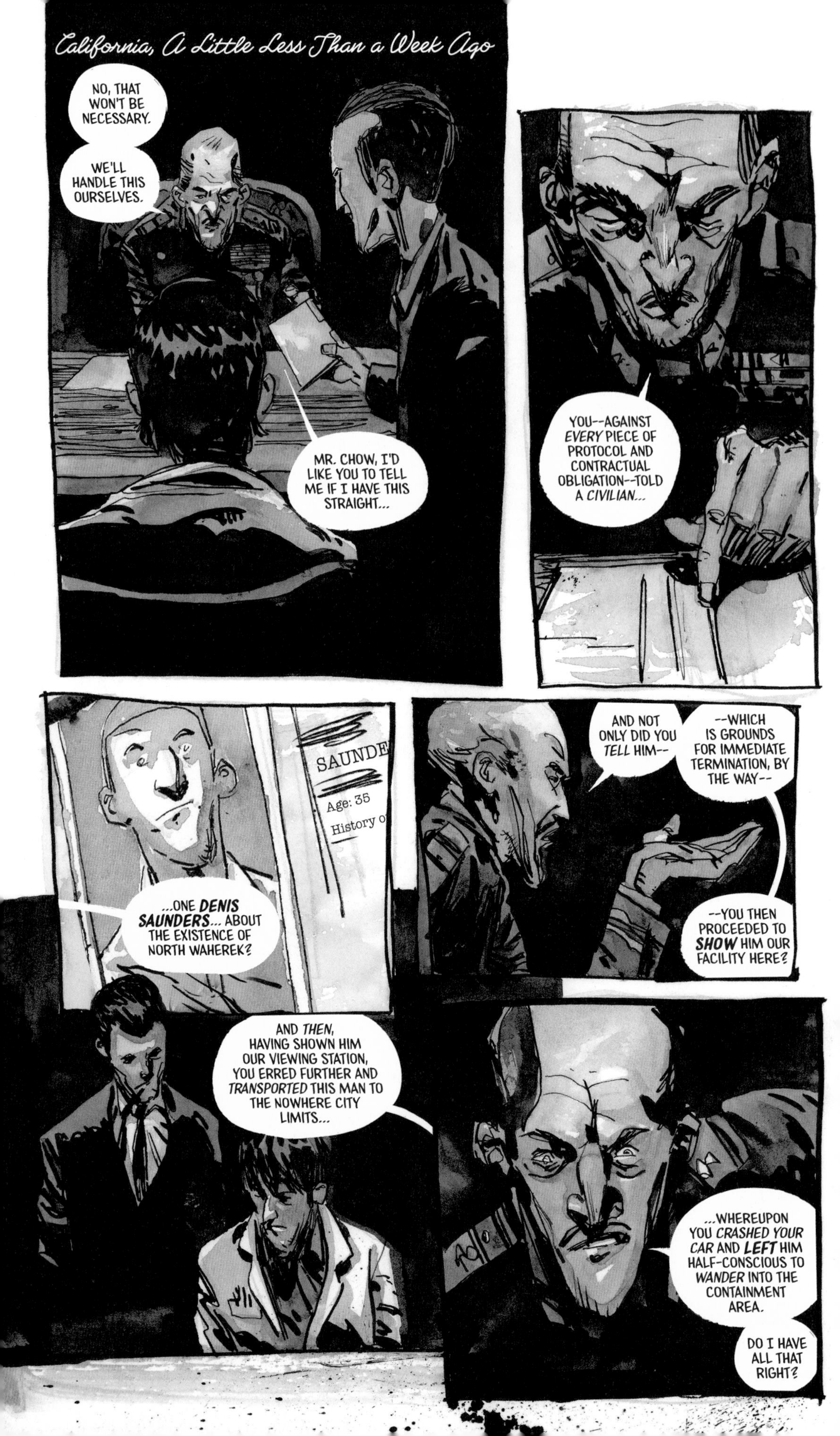
California, A Little Less Than a Week Ago
NO, THAT WON'T BE NECESSARY.
WE'LL HANDLE THIS OURSELVES.
MR. CHOW, I'D LIKE YOU TO TELL ME IF I HAVE THIS STRAIGHT...
YOU--AGAINST *EVERY* PIECE OF PROTOCOL AND CONTRACTUAL OBLIGATION--TOLD A *CIVILIAN*...
SAUNDE
Age: 35
History o
...ONE **DENIS SAUNDERS**... ABOUT THE EXISTENCE OF NORTH WAHEREK?
AND NOT ONLY DID YOU *TELL* HIM--
--WHICH IS GROUNDS FOR IMMEDIATE TERMINATION, BY THE WAY--
--YOU THEN PROCEEDED TO ***SHOW*** HIM OUR FACILITY HERE?
AND *THEN*, HAVING SHOWN HIM OUR VIEWING STATION, YOU ERRED FURTHER AND *TRANSPORTED* THIS MAN TO THE NOWHERE CITY LIMITS...
...WHEREUPON YOU *CRASHED YOUR CAR* AND ***LEFT*** HIM HALF-CONSCIOUS TO *WANDER* INTO THE CONTAINMENT AREA.
DO I HAVE ALL THAT RIGHT?

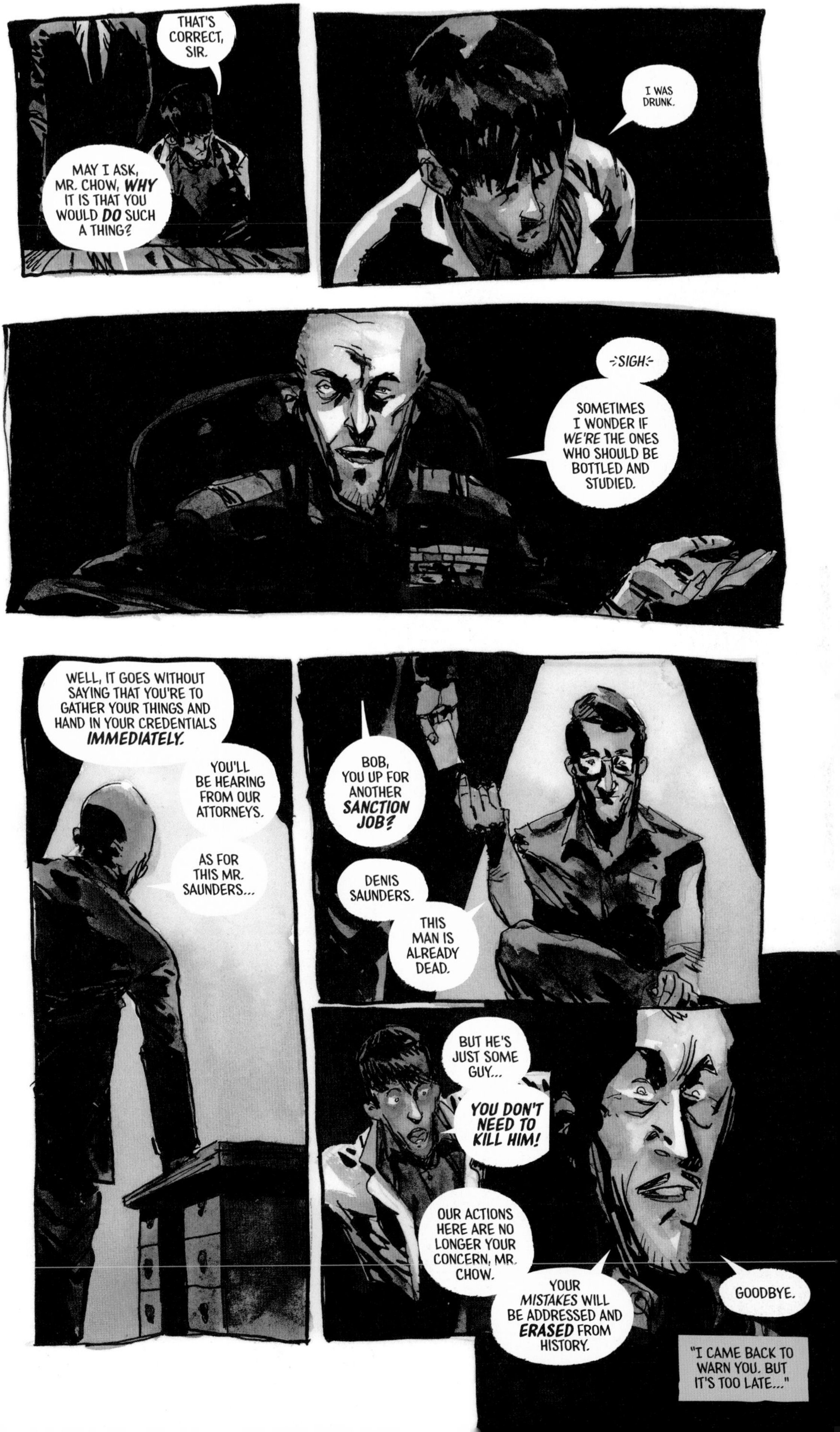
THAT'S CORRECT, SIR.
MAY I ASK, MR. CHOW, WHY IT IS THAT YOU WOULD DO SUCH A THING?
I WAS DRUNK.
-SIGH-
SOMETIMES I WONDER IF WE'RE THE ONES WHO SHOULD BE BOTTLED AND STUDIED.
WELL, IT GOES WITHOUT SAYING THAT YOU'RE TO GATHER YOUR THINGS AND HAND IN YOUR CREDENTIALS IMMEDIATELY.
YOU'LL BE HEARING FROM OUR ATTORNEYS.
AS FOR THIS MR. SAUNDERS...
BOB, YOU UP FOR ANOTHER SANCTION JOB?
DENIS SAUNDERS.
THIS MAN IS ALREADY DEAD.
BUT HE'S JUST SOME GUY...
YOU DON'T NEED TO KILL HIM!
OUR ACTIONS HERE ARE NO LONGER YOUR CONCERN, MR. CHOW.
YOUR MISTAKES WILL BE ADDRESSED AND ERASED FROM HISTORY.
GOODBYE.
"I CAME BACK TO WARN YOU. BUT IT'S TOO LATE..."

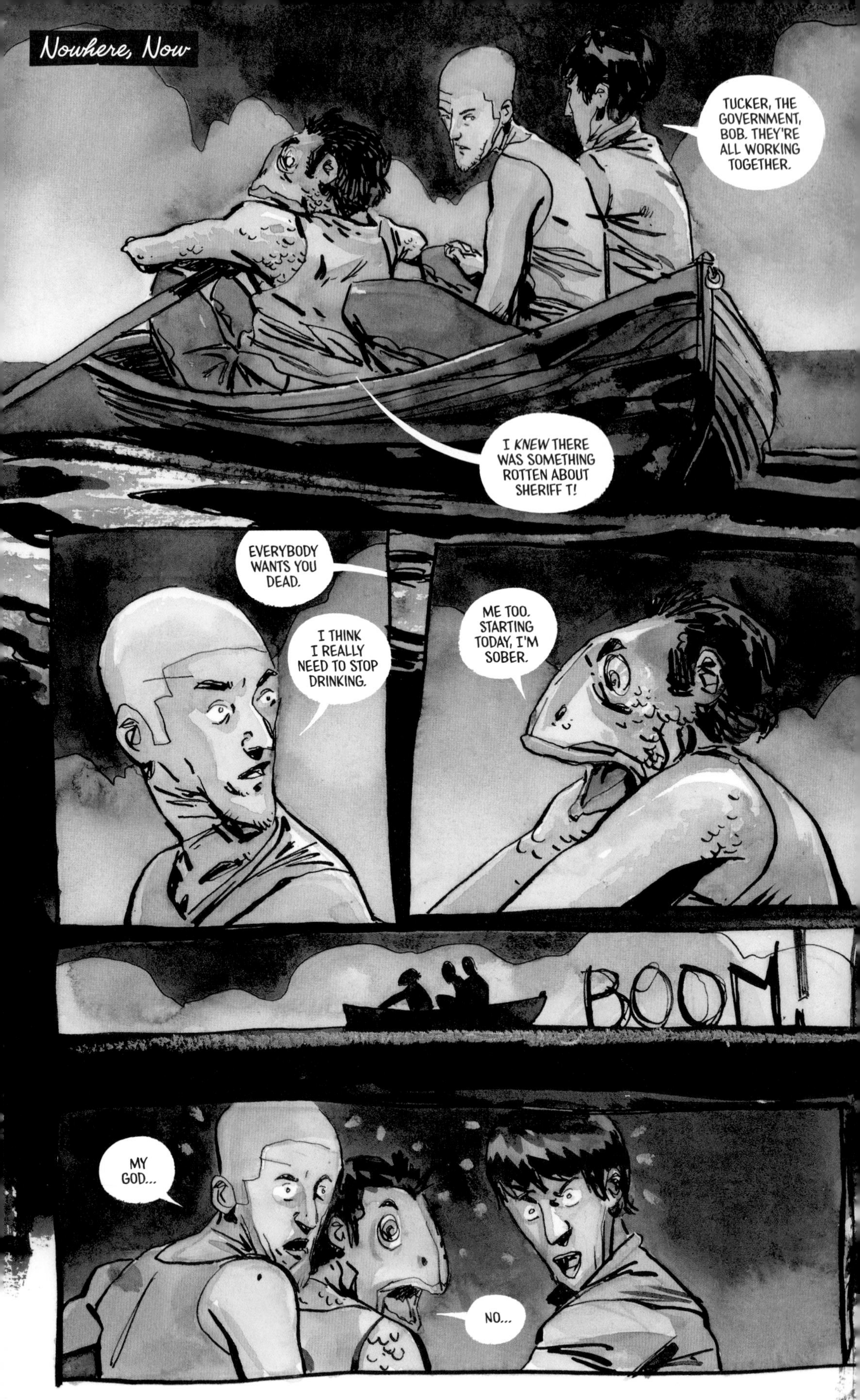
Nowhere, Now
TUCKER, THE GOVERNMENT, BOB. THEY'RE ALL WORKING TOGETHER.
I *KNEW* THERE WAS SOMETHING ROTTEN ABOUT SHERIFF T!
EVERYBODY WANTS YOU DEAD.
I THINK I REALLY NEED TO STOP DRINKING.
ME TOO. STARTING TODAY, I'M SOBER.
BOOM!
MY GOD...
NO...

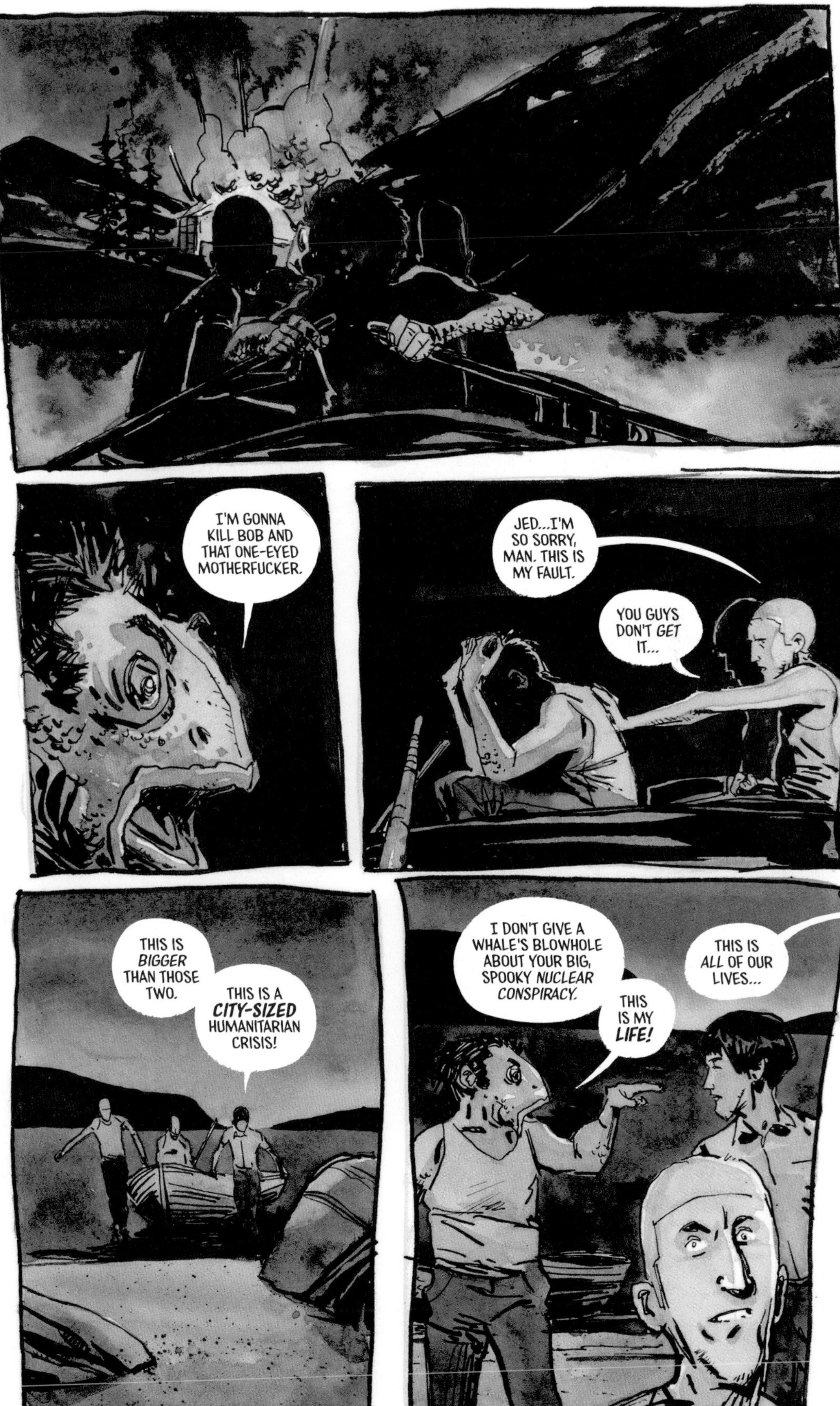
I'M GONNA KILL BOB AND THAT ONE-EYED MOTHERFUCKER.
JED...I'M SO SORRY, MAN. THIS IS MY FAULT.
YOU GUYS DON'T *GET* IT...
THIS IS *BIGGER* THAN THOSE TWO.
THIS IS A **CITY-SIZED** HUMANITARIAN CRISIS!
I DON'T GIVE A WHALE'S BLOWHOLE ABOUT YOUR BIG, SPOOKY *NUCLEAR CONSPIRACY*.
THIS IS MY **LIFE!**
THIS IS *ALL* OF OUR LIVES...

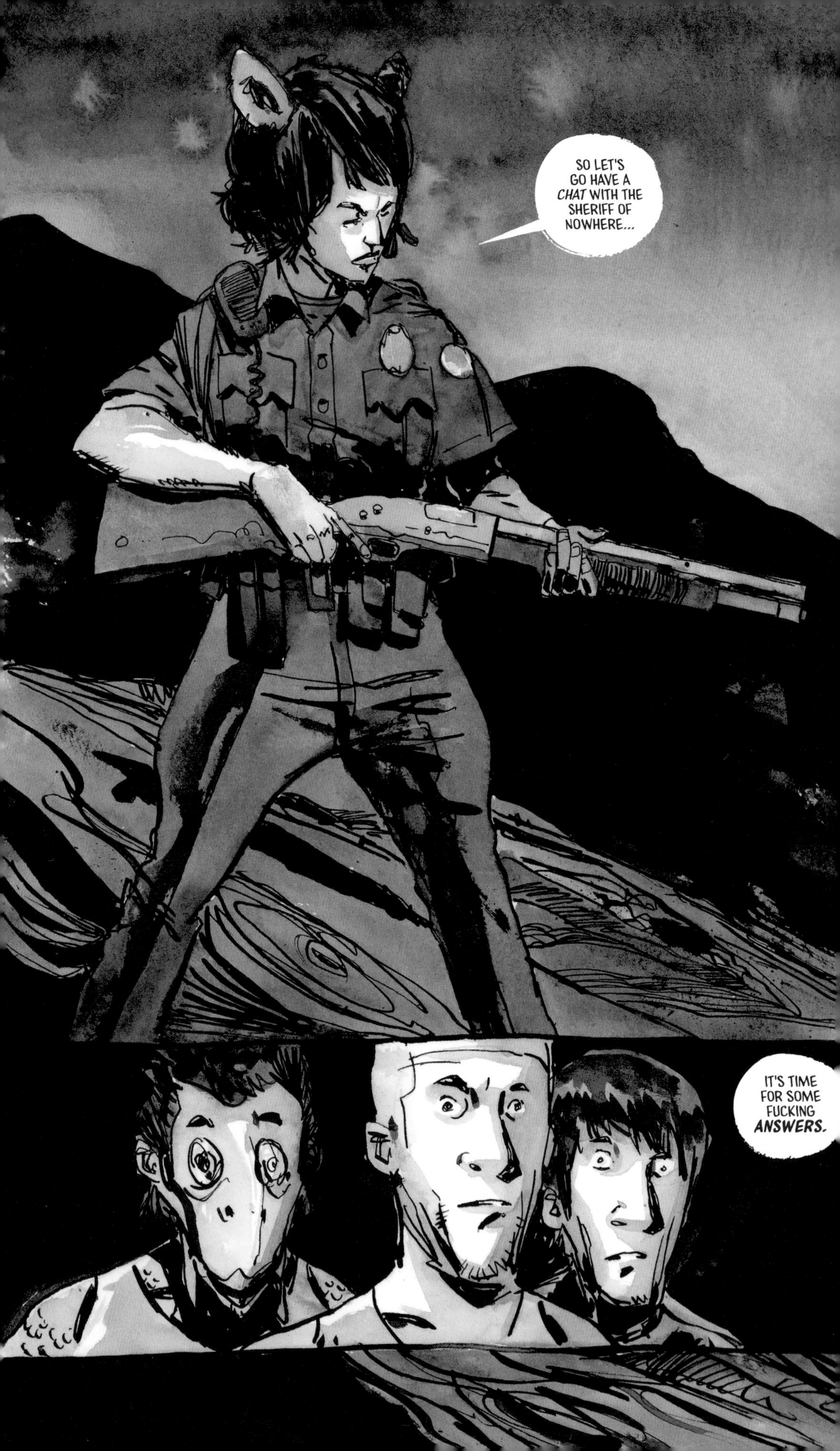
SO LET'S GO HAVE A *CHAT* WITH THE SHERIFF OF NOWHERE...
IT'S TIME FOR SOME FUCKING ***ANSWERS.***

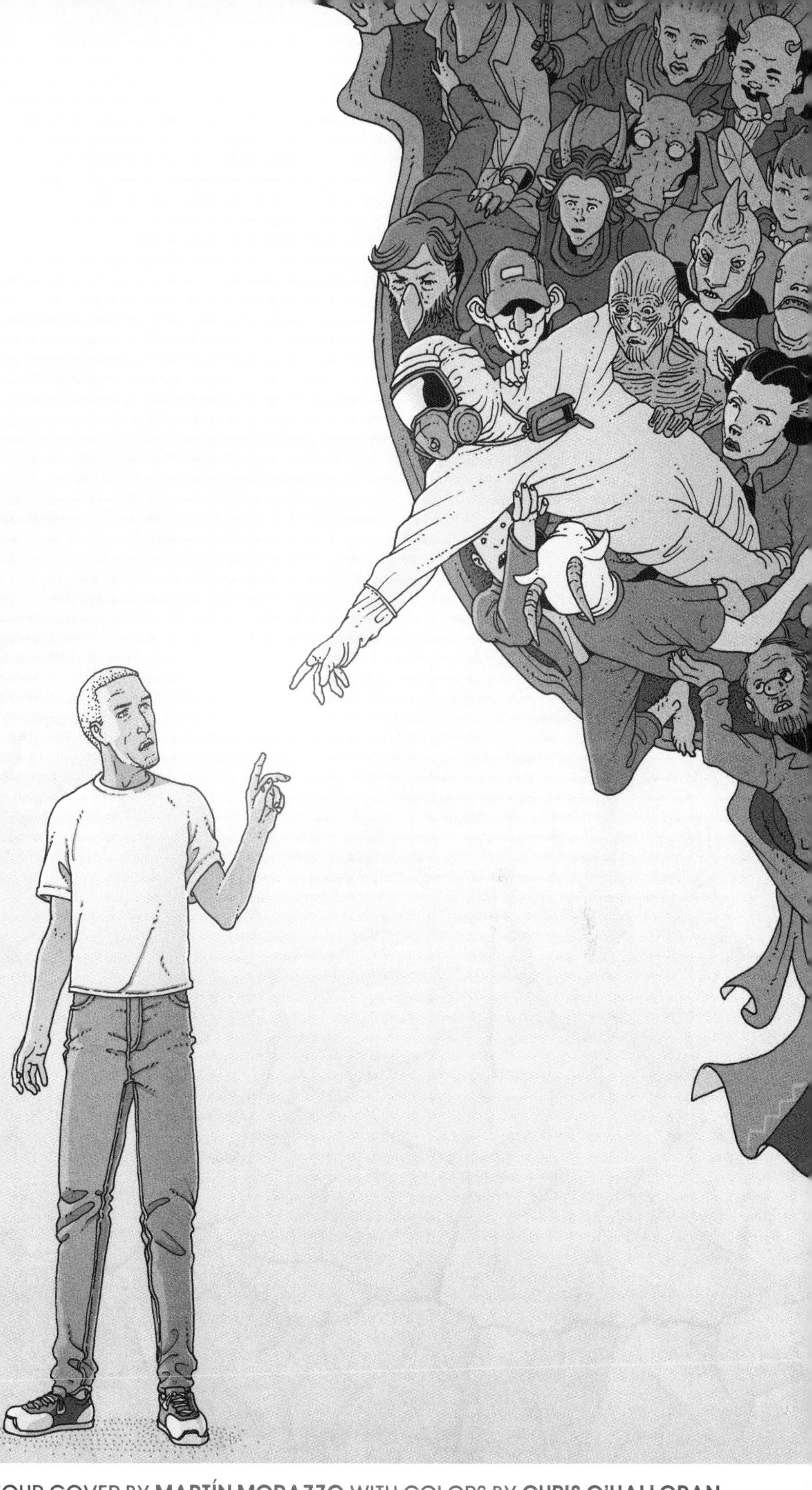

ISSUE FOUR COVER BY **MARTÍN MORAZZO** WITH COLORS BY **CHRIS O'HALLORAN**

CHAPTER FIVE

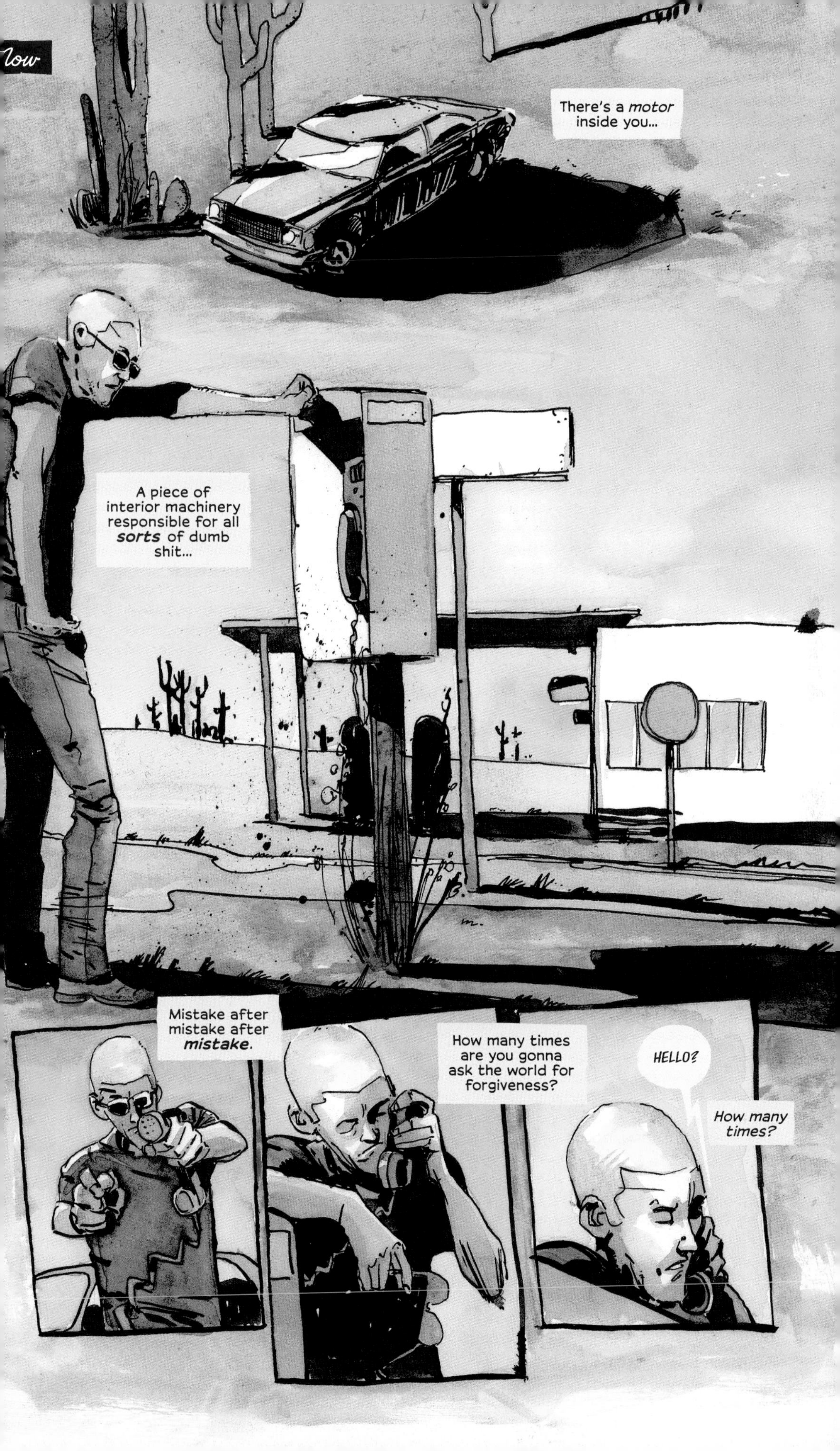
There's a *motor* inside you...
A piece of interior machinery responsible for all ***sorts*** of dumb shit...
Mistake after mistake after ***mistake***.
How many times are you gonna ask the world for forgiveness?
HELLO?
How many times?

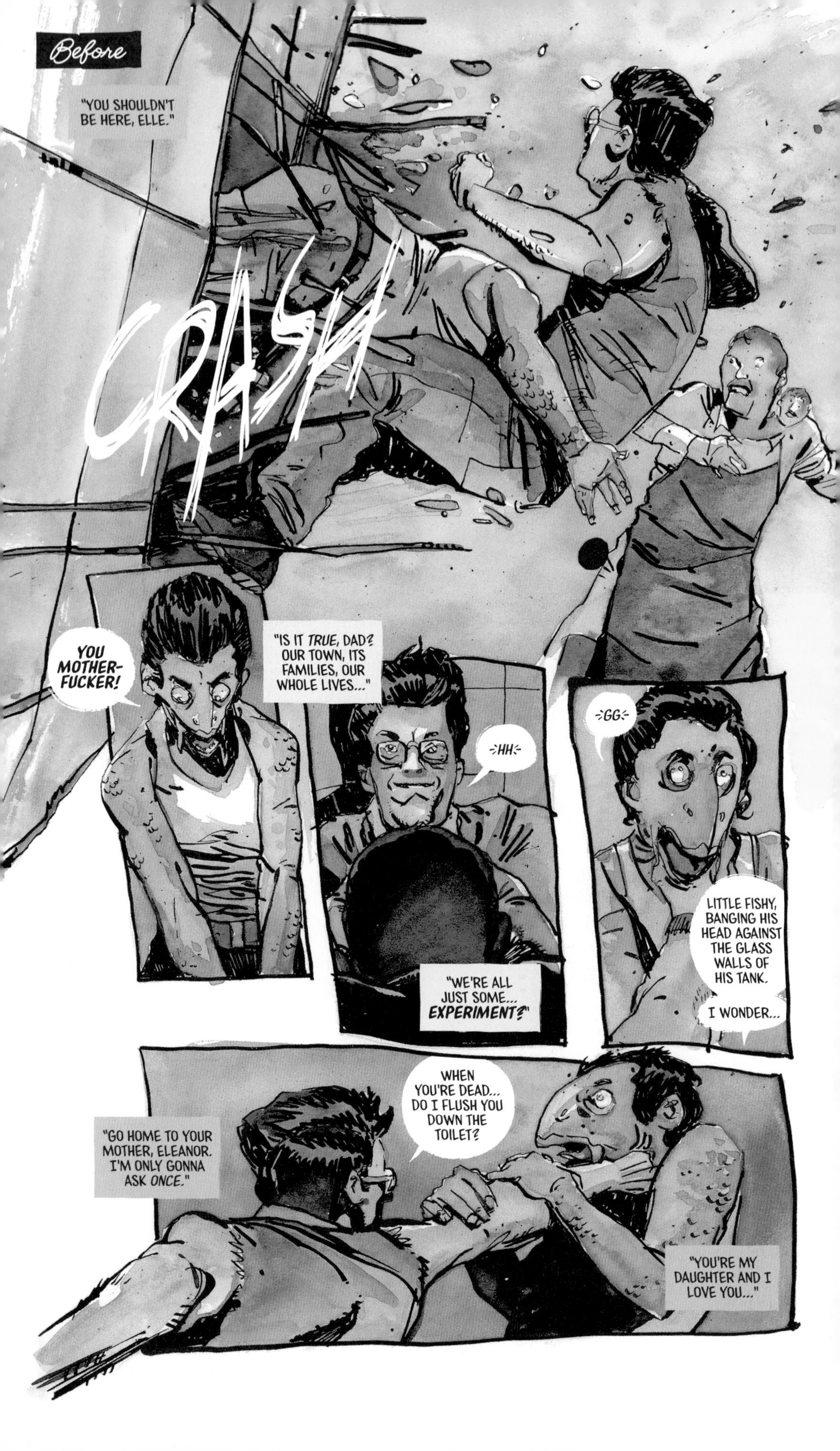
Before
"YOU SHOULDN'T BE HERE, ELLE."
CRASH
YOU MOTHER-FUCKER!
"IS IT TRUE, DAD? OUR TOWN, ITS FAMILIES, OUR WHOLE LIVES..."
HH
"WE'RE ALL JUST SOME... EXPERIMENT?"
GG
LITTLE FISHY, BANGING HIS HEAD AGAINST THE GLASS WALLS OF HIS TANK.
I WONDER...
"GO HOME TO YOUR MOTHER, ELEANOR. I'M ONLY GONNA ASK ONCE."
WHEN YOU'RE DEAD... DO I FLUSH YOU DOWN THE TOILET?
"YOU'RE MY DAUGHTER AND I LOVE YOU..."

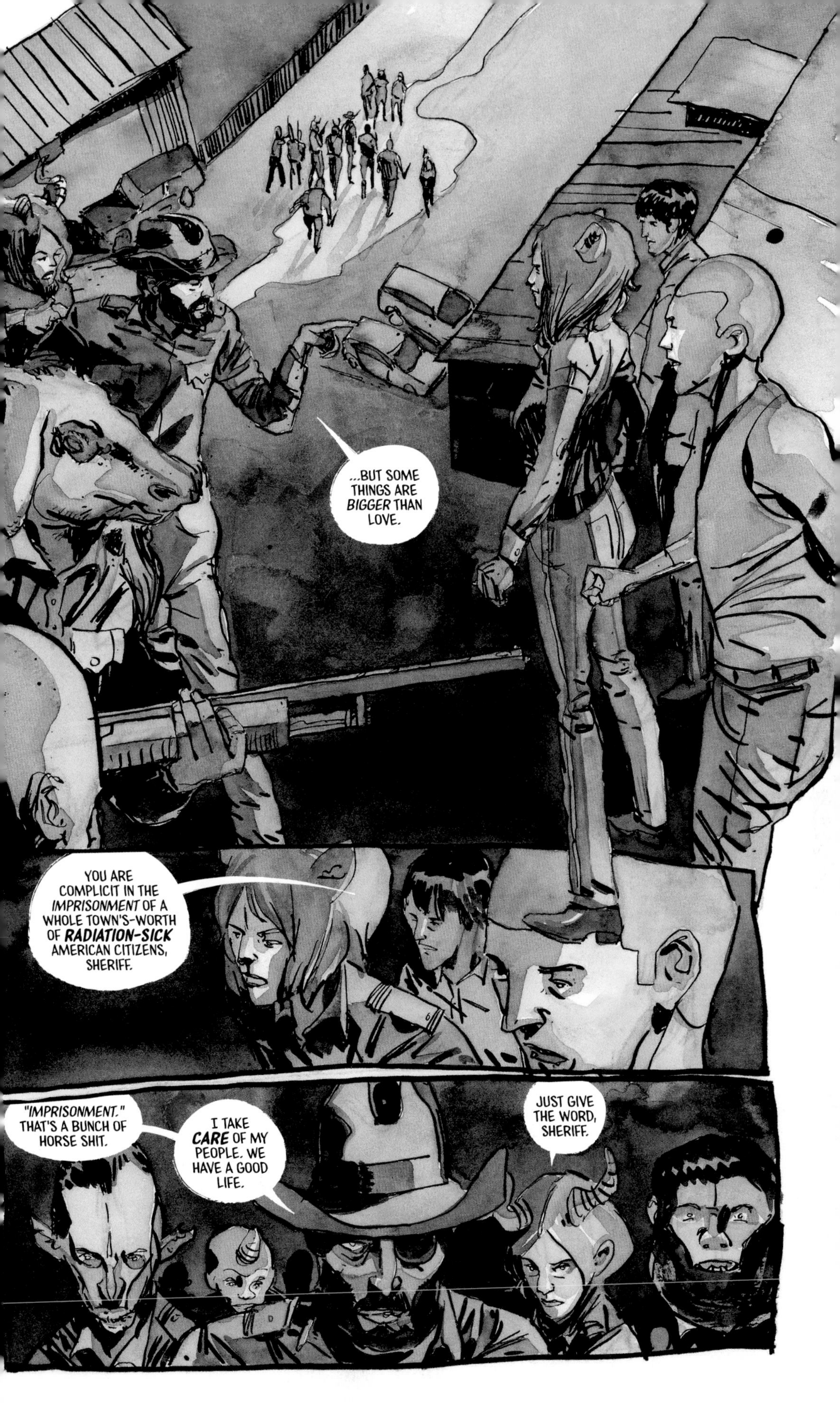
...BUT SOME THINGS ARE BIGGER THAN LOVE.
YOU ARE COMPLICIT IN THE IMPRISONMENT OF A WHOLE TOWN'S-WORTH OF RADIATION-SICK AMERICAN CITIZENS, SHERIFF.
"IMPRISONMENT." THAT'S A BUNCH OF HORSE SHIT.
I TAKE CARE OF MY PEOPLE. WE HAVE A GOOD LIFE.
JUST GIVE THE WORD, SHERIFF.

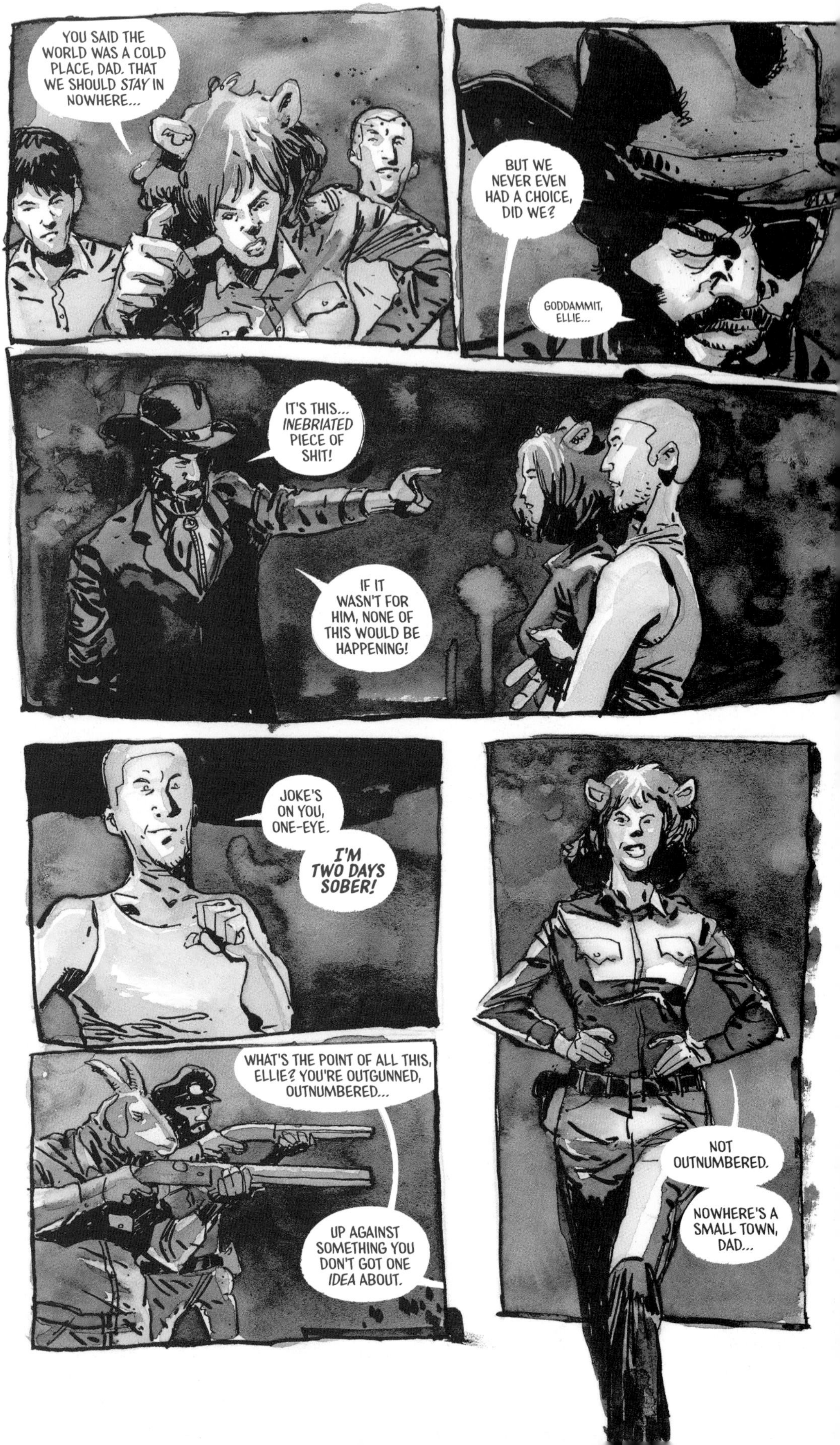
YOU SAID THE WORLD WAS A COLD PLACE, DAD. THAT WE SHOULD *STAY* IN NOWHERE...
BUT WE NEVER EVEN HAD A CHOICE, DID WE?
GODDAMMIT, ELLIE...
IT'S THIS... *INEBRIATED* PIECE OF SHIT!
IF IT WASN'T FOR HIM, NONE OF THIS WOULD BE HAPPENING!
JOKE'S ON YOU, ONE-EYE.
I'M TWO DAYS SOBER!
WHAT'S THE POINT OF ALL THIS, ELLIE? YOU'RE OUTGUNNED, OUTNUMBERED...
UP AGAINST SOMETHING YOU DON'T GOT ONE *IDEA* ABOUT.
NOT OUTNUMBERED.
NOWHERE'S A SMALL TOWN, DAD...

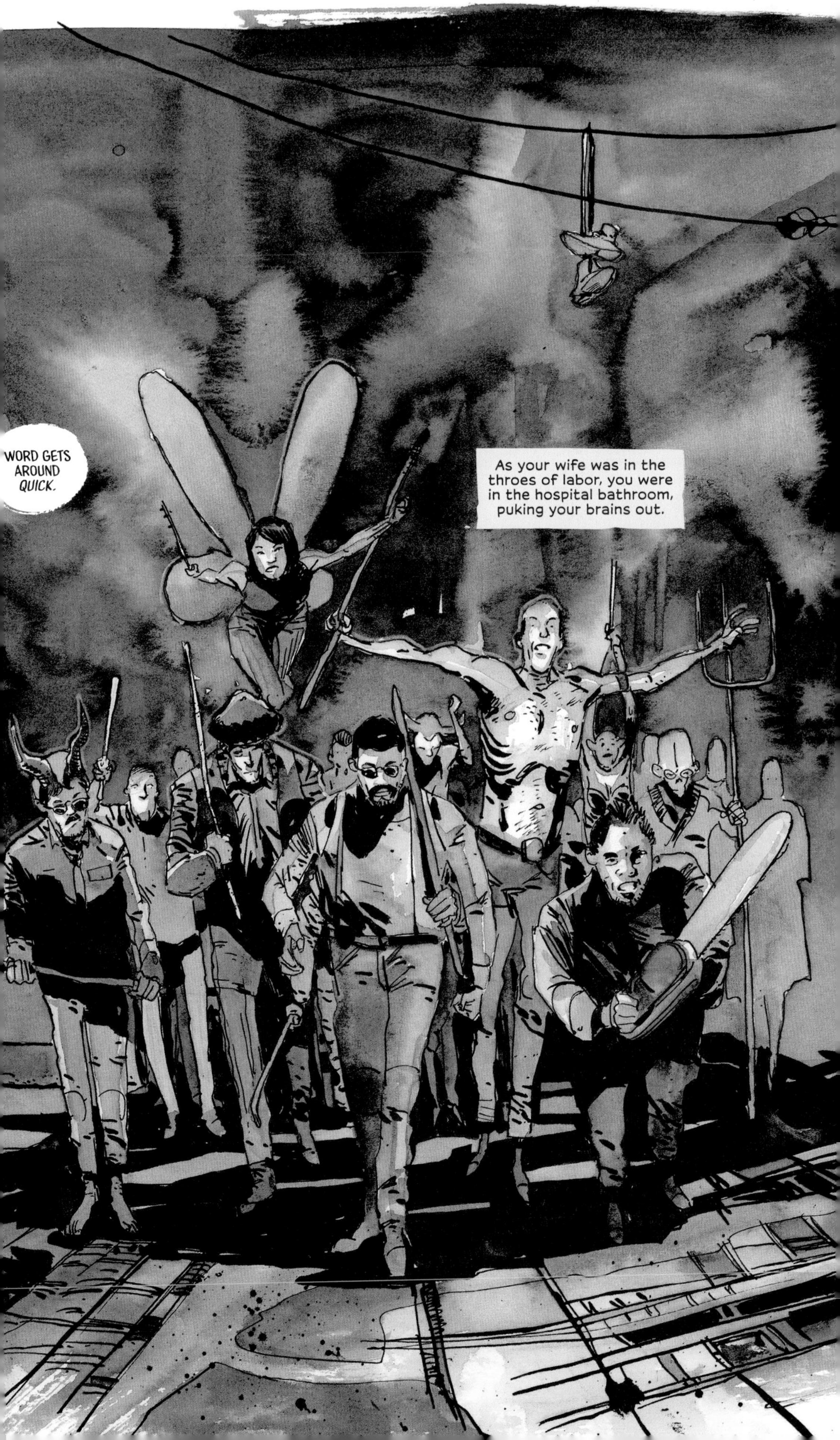
WORD GETS AROUND QUICK.
As your wife was in the throes of labor, you were in the hospital bathroom, puking your brains out.

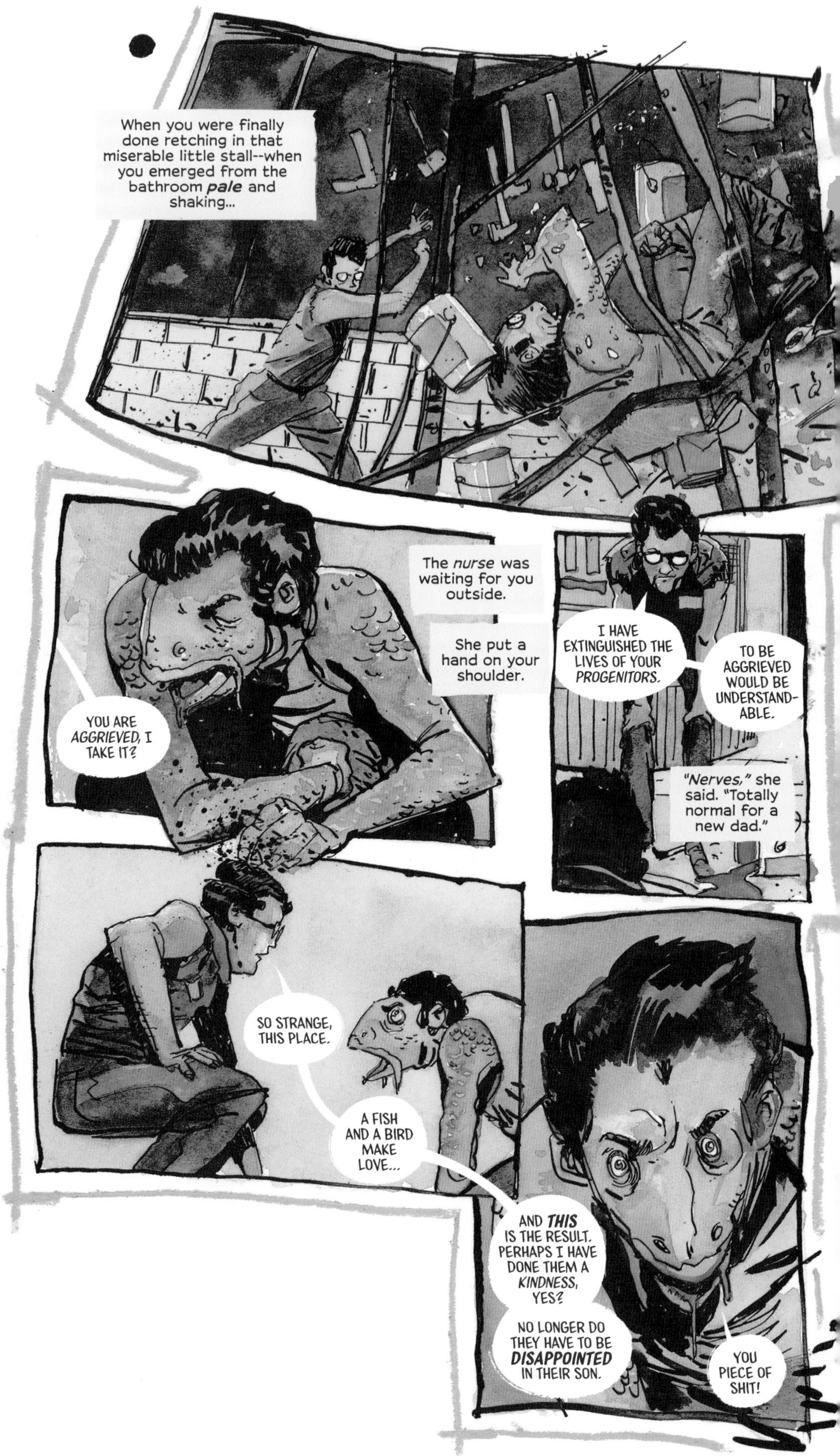
When you were finally done retching in that miserable little stall--when you emerged from the bathroom *pale* and shaking...
The *nurse* was waiting for you outside.
She put a hand on your shoulder.
YOU ARE *AGGRIEVED*, I TAKE IT?
I HAVE EXTINGUISHED THE LIVES OF YOUR *PROGENITORS*.
TO BE AGGRIEVED WOULD BE UNDERSTAND-ABLE.
"Nerves," she said. "Totally normal for a new dad."
SO STRANGE, THIS PLACE.
A FISH AND A BIRD MAKE LOVE...
AND ***THIS*** IS THE RESULT. PERHAPS I HAVE DONE THEM A *KINDNESS*, YES?
NO LONGER DO THEY HAVE TO BE ***DISAPPOINTED*** IN THEIR SON.
YOU PIECE OF SHIT!

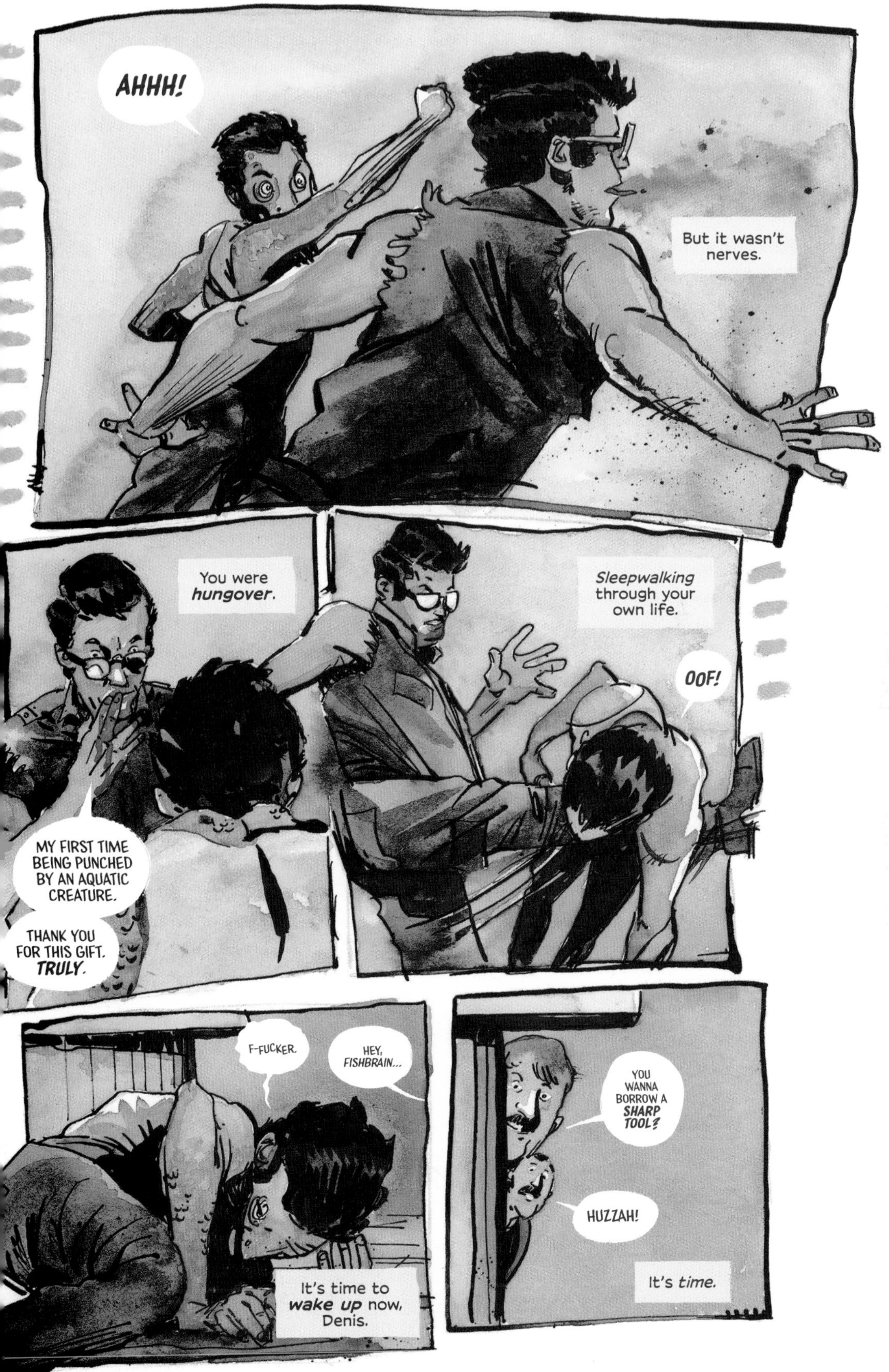
AHHH!
But it wasn't nerves.
You were hungover.
MY FIRST TIME BEING PUNCHED BY AN AQUATIC CREATURE.
THANK YOU FOR THIS GIFT. TRULY.
Sleepwalking through your own life.
OOF!
F-FUCKER.
HEY, FISHBRAIN...
It's time to wake up now, Denis.
YOU WANNA BORROW A SHARP TOOL?
HUZZAH!
It's time.

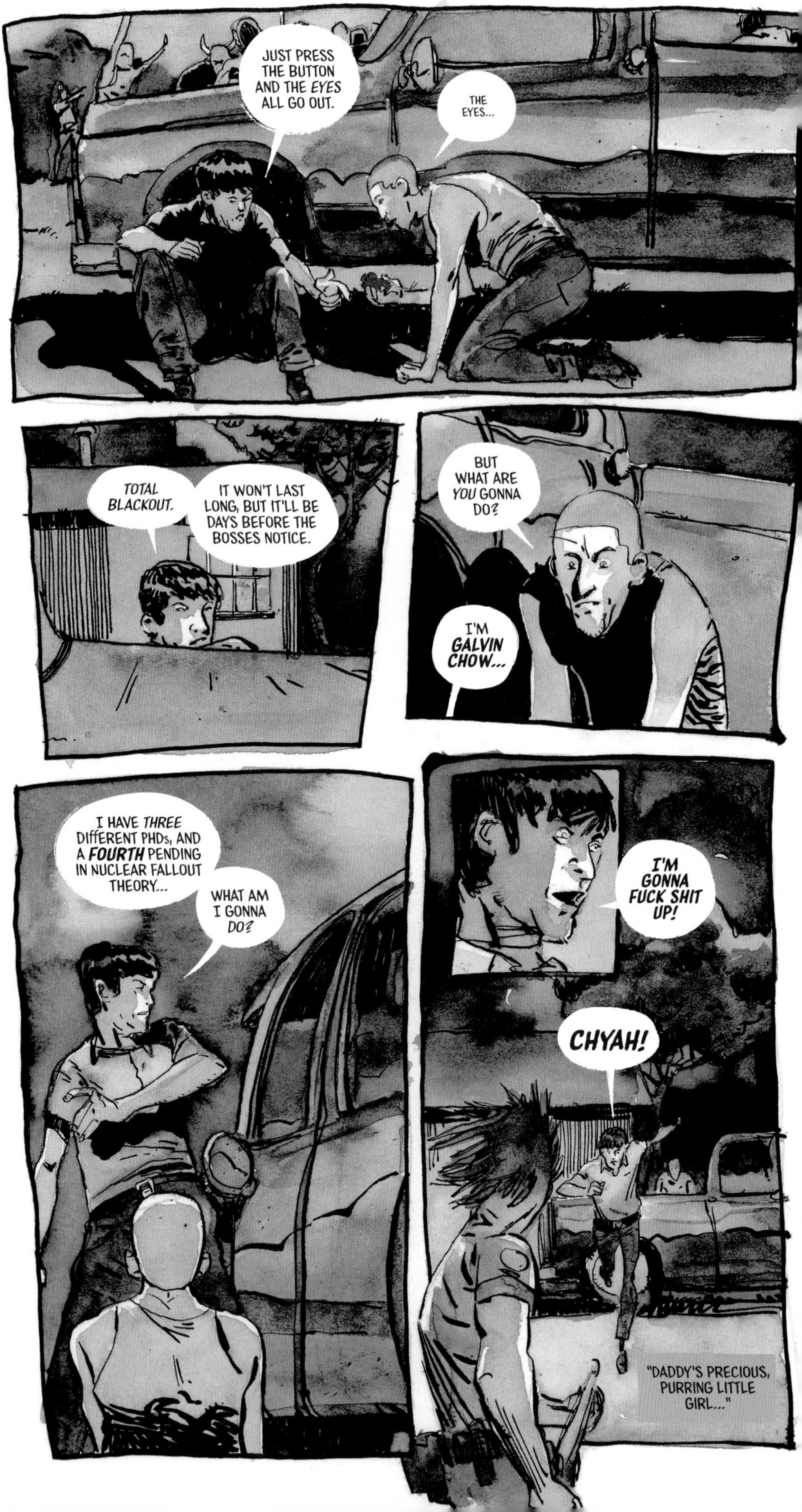
JUST PRESS THE BUTTON AND THE EYES ALL GO OUT.
THE EYES...
TOTAL BLACKOUT.
IT WON'T LAST LONG, BUT IT'LL BE DAYS BEFORE THE BOSSES NOTICE.
BUT WHAT ARE YOU GONNA DO?
I'M GALVIN CHOW...
I HAVE THREE DIFFERENT PHDs, AND A FOURTH PENDING IN NUCLEAR FALLOUT THEORY...
WHAT AM I GONNA DO?
I'M GONNA FUCK SHIT UP!
CHYAH!
"DADDY'S PRECIOUS, PURRING LITTLE GIRL..."

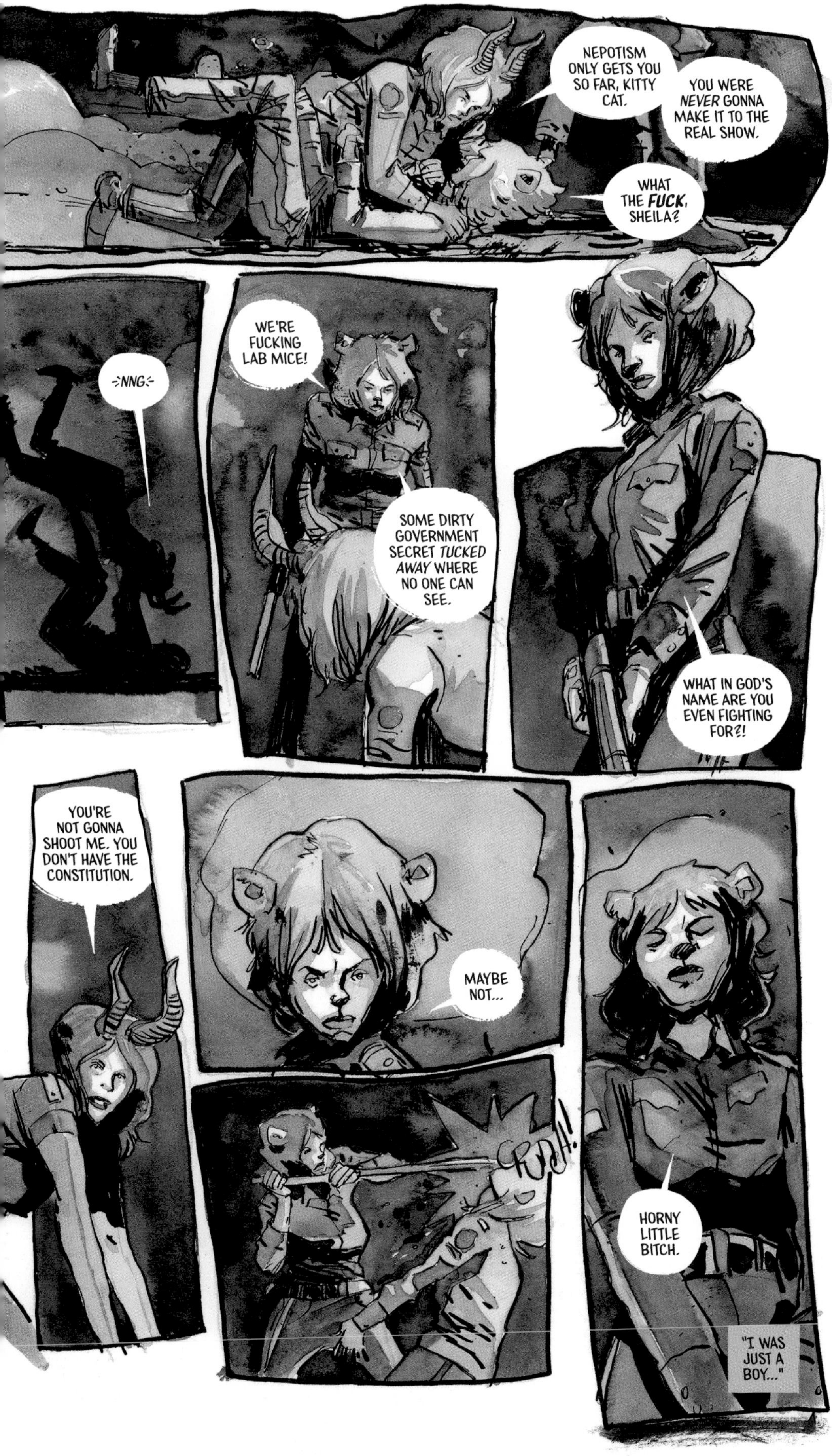
NEPOTISM ONLY GETS YOU SO FAR, KITTY CAT.
YOU WERE *NEVER* GONNA MAKE IT TO THE REAL SHOW.
WHAT THE **FUCK**, SHEILA?
NNG
WE'RE FUCKING LAB MICE!
SOME DIRTY GOVERNMENT SECRET *TUCKED AWAY* WHERE NO ONE CAN SEE.
WHAT IN GOD'S NAME ARE YOU EVEN FIGHTING FOR?!
YOU'RE NOT GONNA SHOOT ME. YOU DON'T HAVE THE CONSTITUTION.
MAYBE NOT...
HORNY LITTLE BITCH.
"I WAS JUST A BOY..."

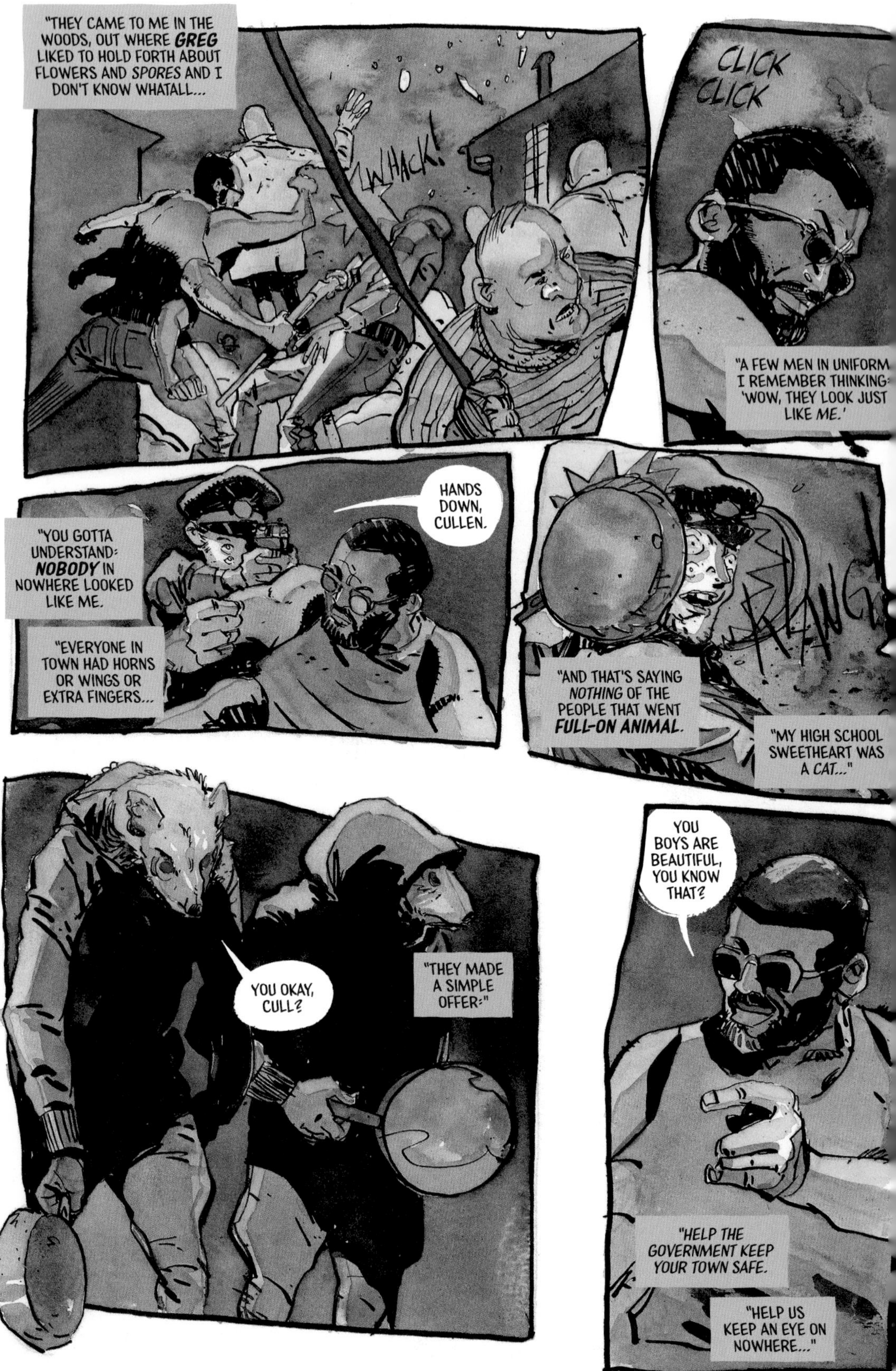
"THEY CAME TO ME IN THE WOODS, OUT WHERE GREG LIKED TO HOLD FORTH ABOUT FLOWERS AND SPORES AND I DON'T KNOW WHATALL...
WHACK!
CLICK CLICK
"A FEW MEN IN UNIFORM. I REMEMBER THINKING: 'WOW, THEY LOOK JUST LIKE ME.'
"YOU GOTTA UNDERSTAND: NOBODY IN NOWHERE LOOKED LIKE ME.
HANDS DOWN, CULLEN.
"EVERYONE IN TOWN HAD HORNS OR WINGS OR EXTRA FINGERS...
"AND THAT'S SAYING NOTHING OF THE PEOPLE THAT WENT FULL-ON ANIMAL.
"MY HIGH SCHOOL SWEETHEART WAS A CAT..."
YOU OKAY, CULL?
"THEY MADE A SIMPLE OFFER:"
YOU BOYS ARE BEAUTIFUL, YOU KNOW THAT?
"HELP THE GOVERNMENT KEEP YOUR TOWN SAFE.
"HELP US KEEP AN EYE ON NOWHERE..."

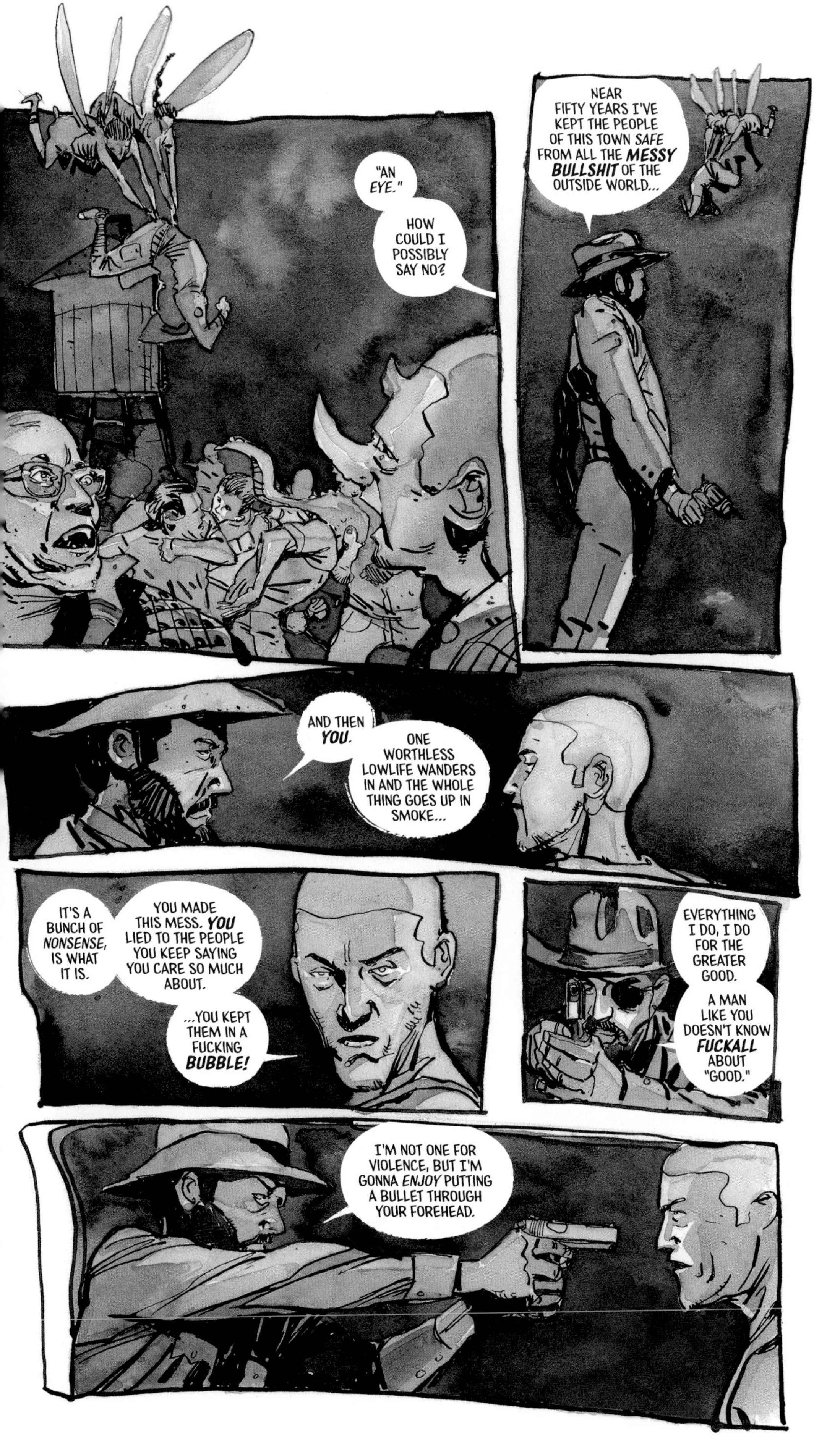
"AN EYE."
HOW COULD I POSSIBLY SAY NO?
NEAR FIFTY YEARS I'VE KEPT THE PEOPLE OF THIS TOWN SAFE FROM ALL THE MESSY BULLSHIT OF THE OUTSIDE WORLD...
AND THEN YOU.
ONE WORTHLESS LOWLIFE WANDERS IN AND THE WHOLE THING GOES UP IN SMOKE...
IT'S A BUNCH OF NONSENSE, IS WHAT IT IS.
YOU MADE THIS MESS. YOU LIED TO THE PEOPLE YOU KEEP SAYING YOU CARE SO MUCH ABOUT.
...YOU KEPT THEM IN A FUCKING BUBBLE!
EVERYTHING I DO, I DO FOR THE GREATER GOOD.
A MAN LIKE YOU DOESN'T KNOW FUCKALL ABOUT "GOOD."
I'M NOT ONE FOR VIOLENCE, BUT I'M GONNA ENJOY PUTTING A BULLET THROUGH YOUR FOREHEAD.

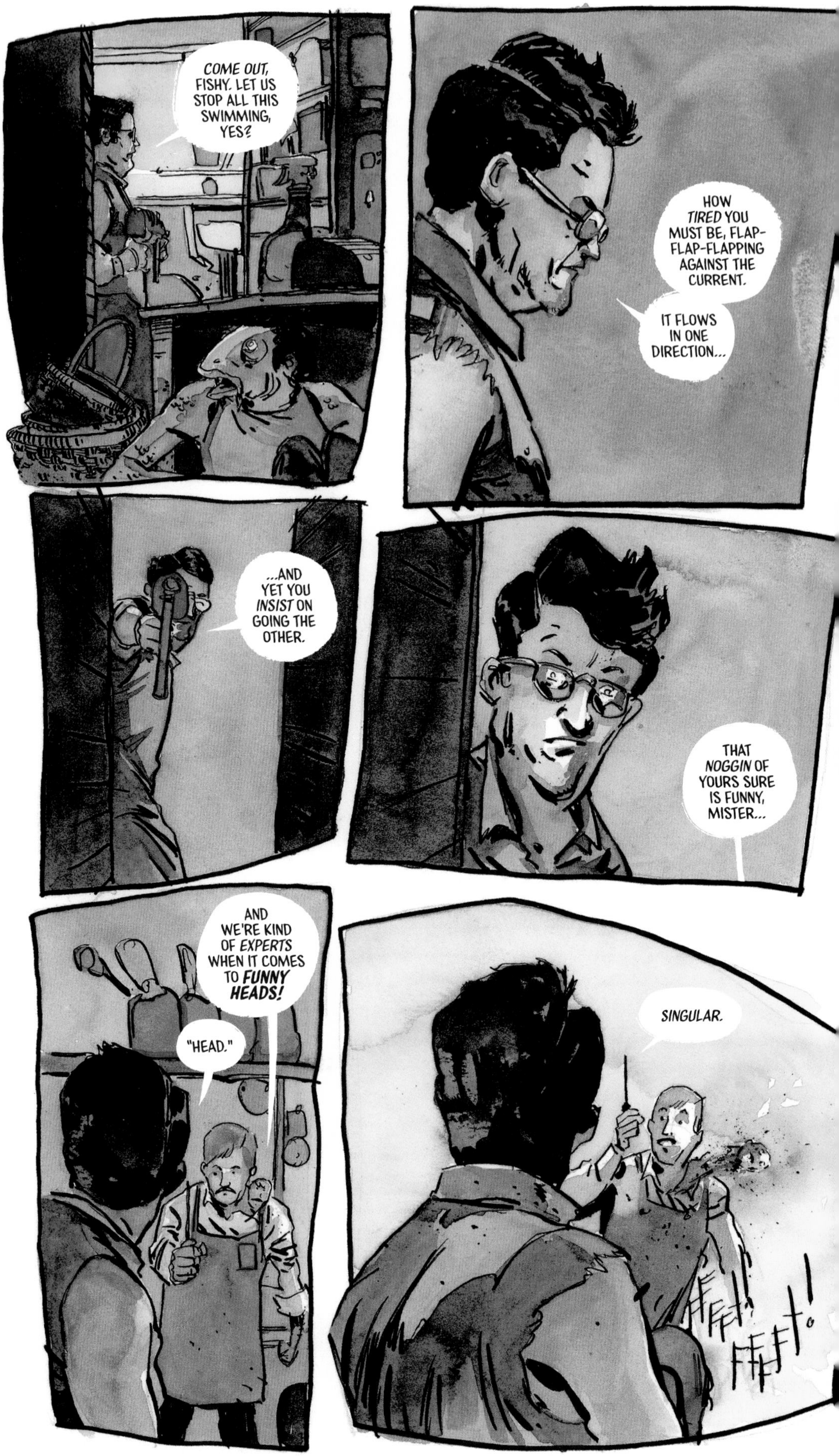
COME OUT, FISHY. LET US STOP ALL THIS SWIMMING, YES?
HOW TIRED YOU MUST BE, FLAP-FLAP-FLAPPING AGAINST THE CURRENT.
IT FLOWS IN ONE DIRECTION...
...AND YET YOU INSIST ON GOING THE OTHER.
THAT NOGGIN OF YOURS SURE IS FUNNY, MISTER...
AND WE'RE KIND OF EXPERTS WHEN IT COMES TO FUNNY HEADS!
"HEAD."
SINGULAR.
FFFT!
FFFT!

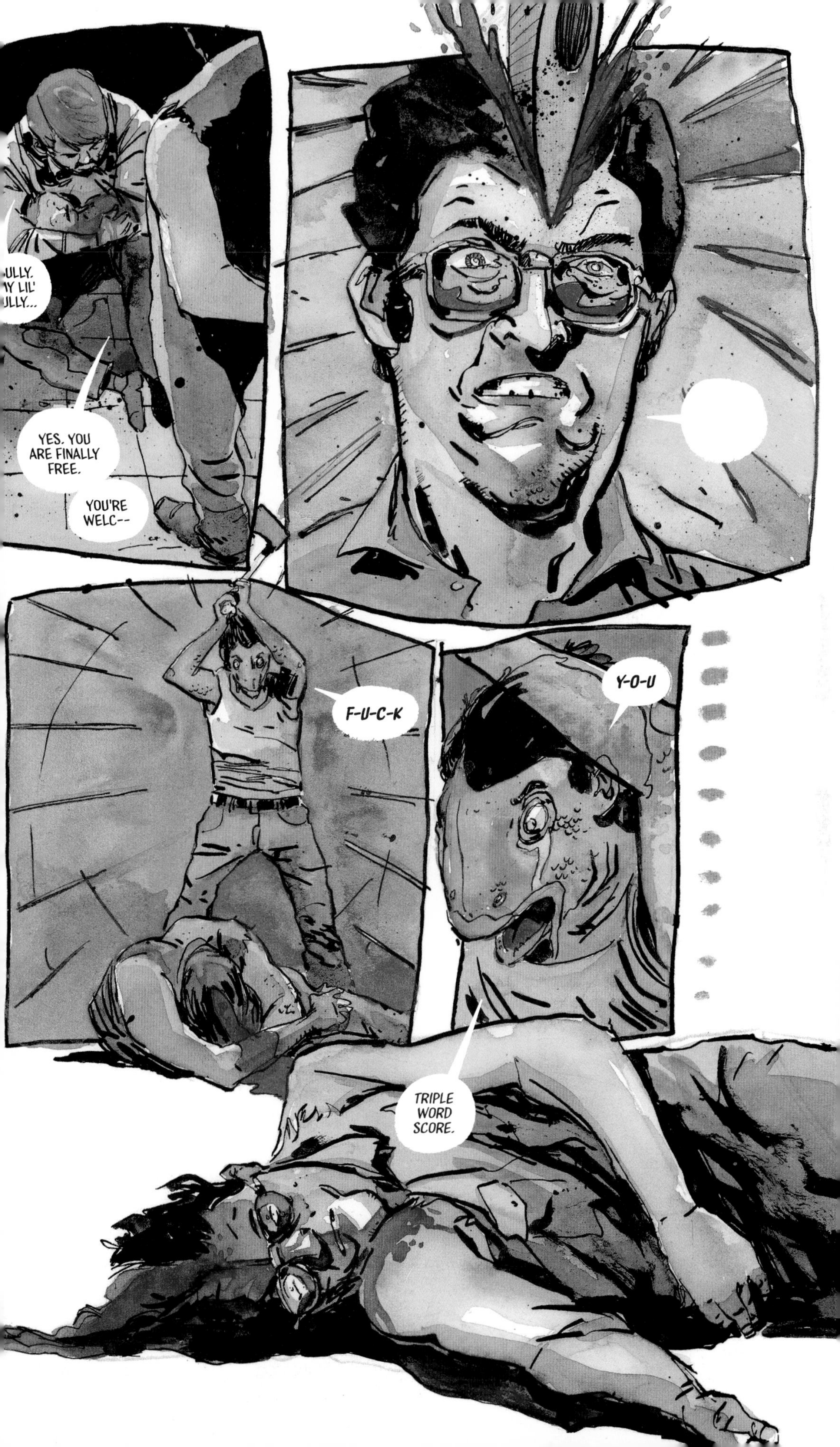
ULLY. MY LIL' ULLY...
YES. YOU ARE FINALLY FREE.
YOU'RE WELC--
F-U-C-K
Y-O-U
TRIPLE WORD SCORE.

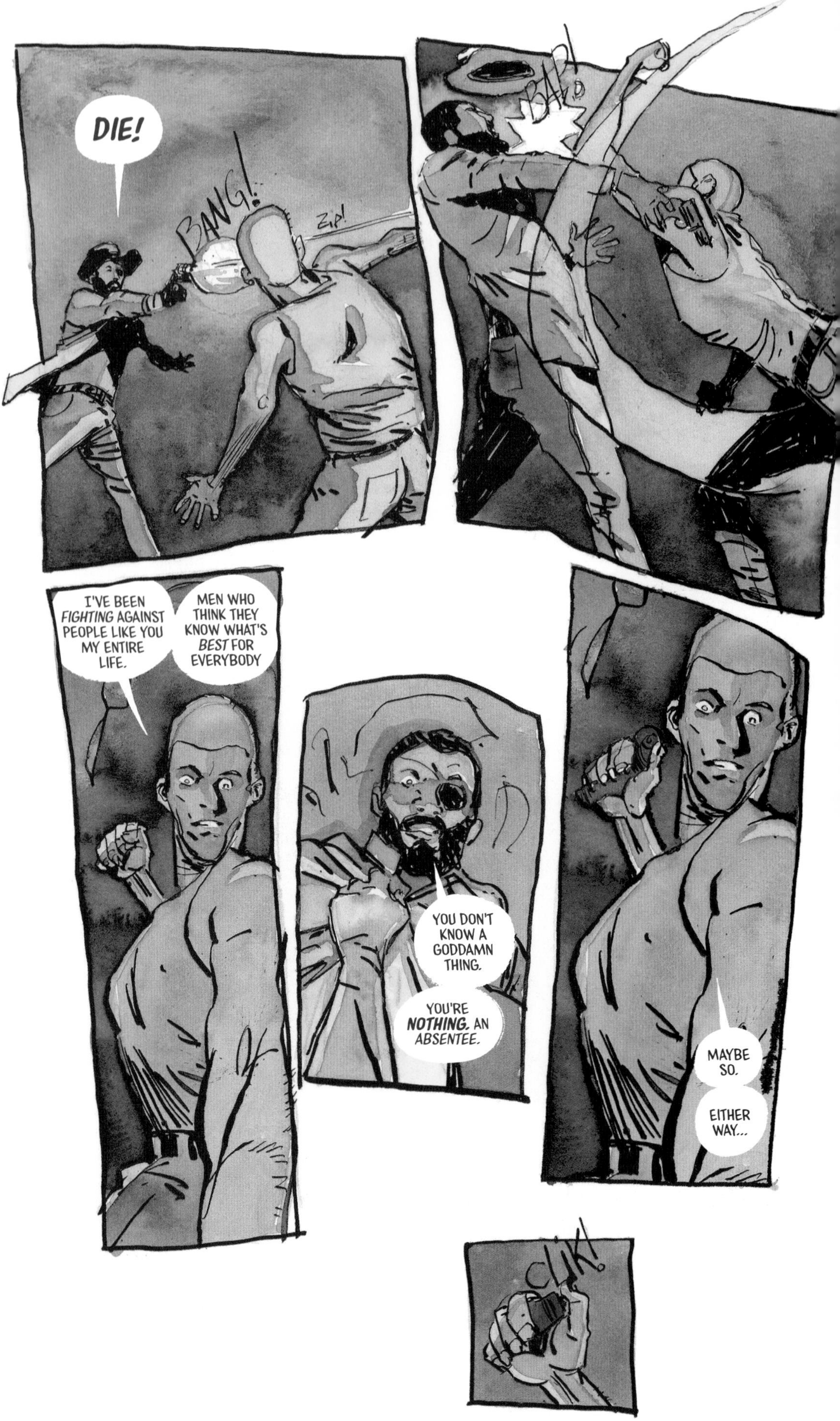
DIE!
BANG!
ZIP!
BAP!
I'VE BEEN FIGHTING AGAINST PEOPLE LIKE YOU MY ENTIRE LIFE.
MEN WHO THINK THEY KNOW WHAT'S BEST FOR EVERYBODY
YOU DON'T KNOW A GODDAMN THING.
YOU'RE NOTHING. AN ABSENTEE.
MAYBE SO.
EITHER WAY...
CLIK!

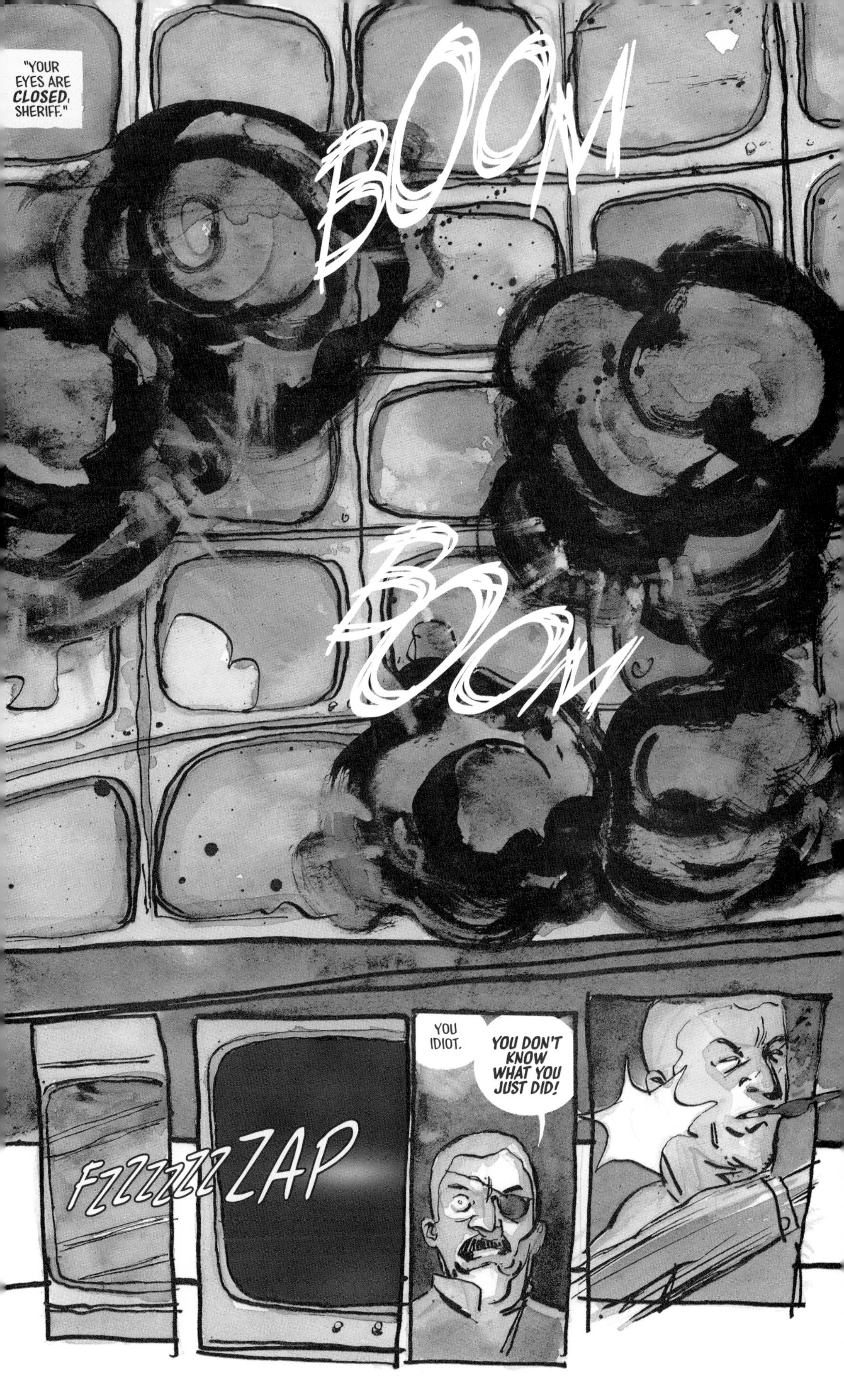
"YOUR EYES ARE CLOSED, SHERIFF."
BOOM
BOOM
FZZZZZZZZAP
YOU IDIOT.
YOU DON'T KNOW WHAT YOU JUST DID!

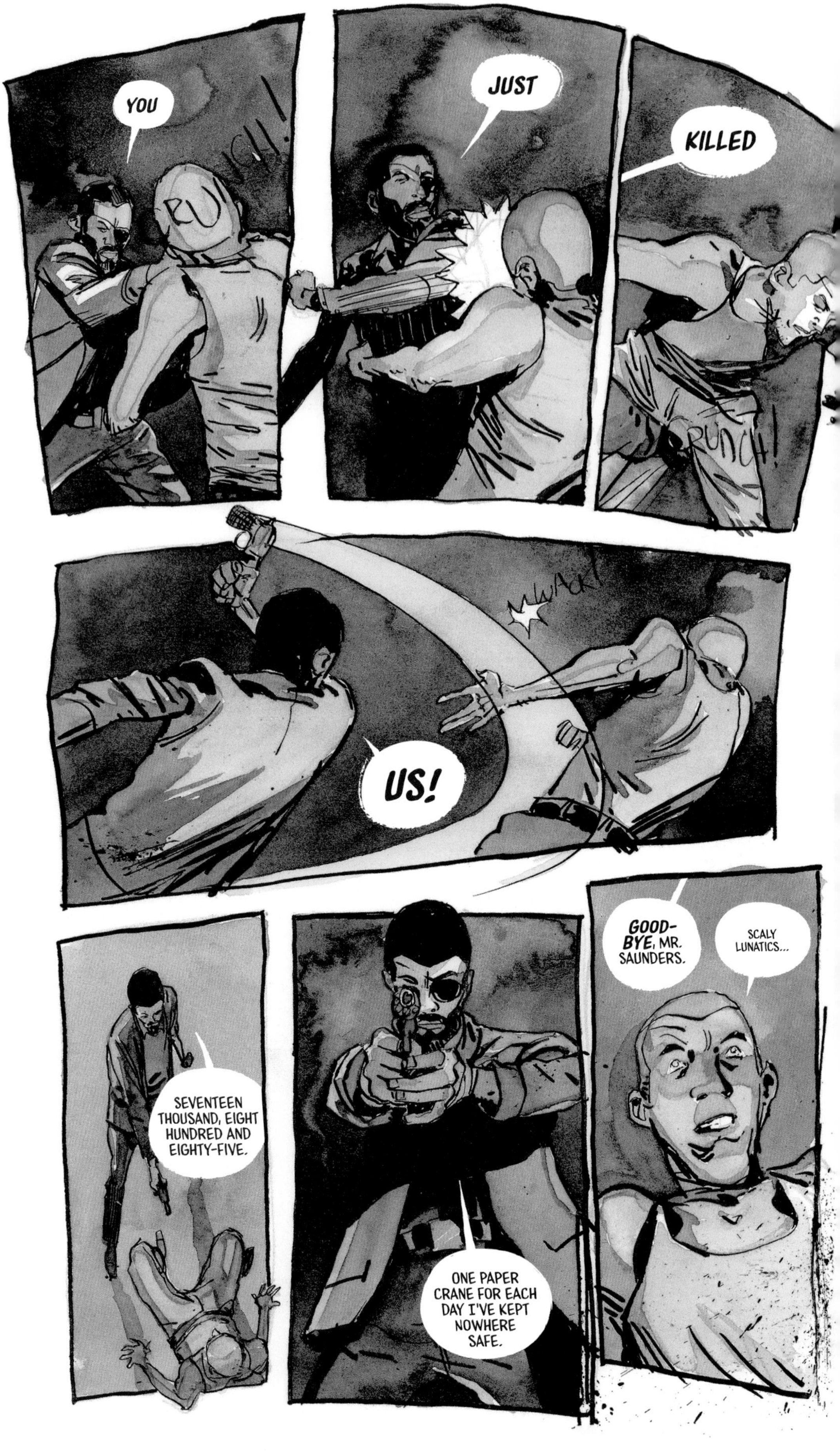
YOU
RUNCH!
JUST
KILLED
RUNCH!
WHACK!
US!
SEVENTEEN THOUSAND, EIGHT HUNDRED AND EIGHTY-FIVE.
ONE PAPER CRANE FOR EACH DAY I'VE KEPT NOWHERE SAFE.
GOOD-BYE, MR. SAUNDERS.
SCALY LUNATICS...

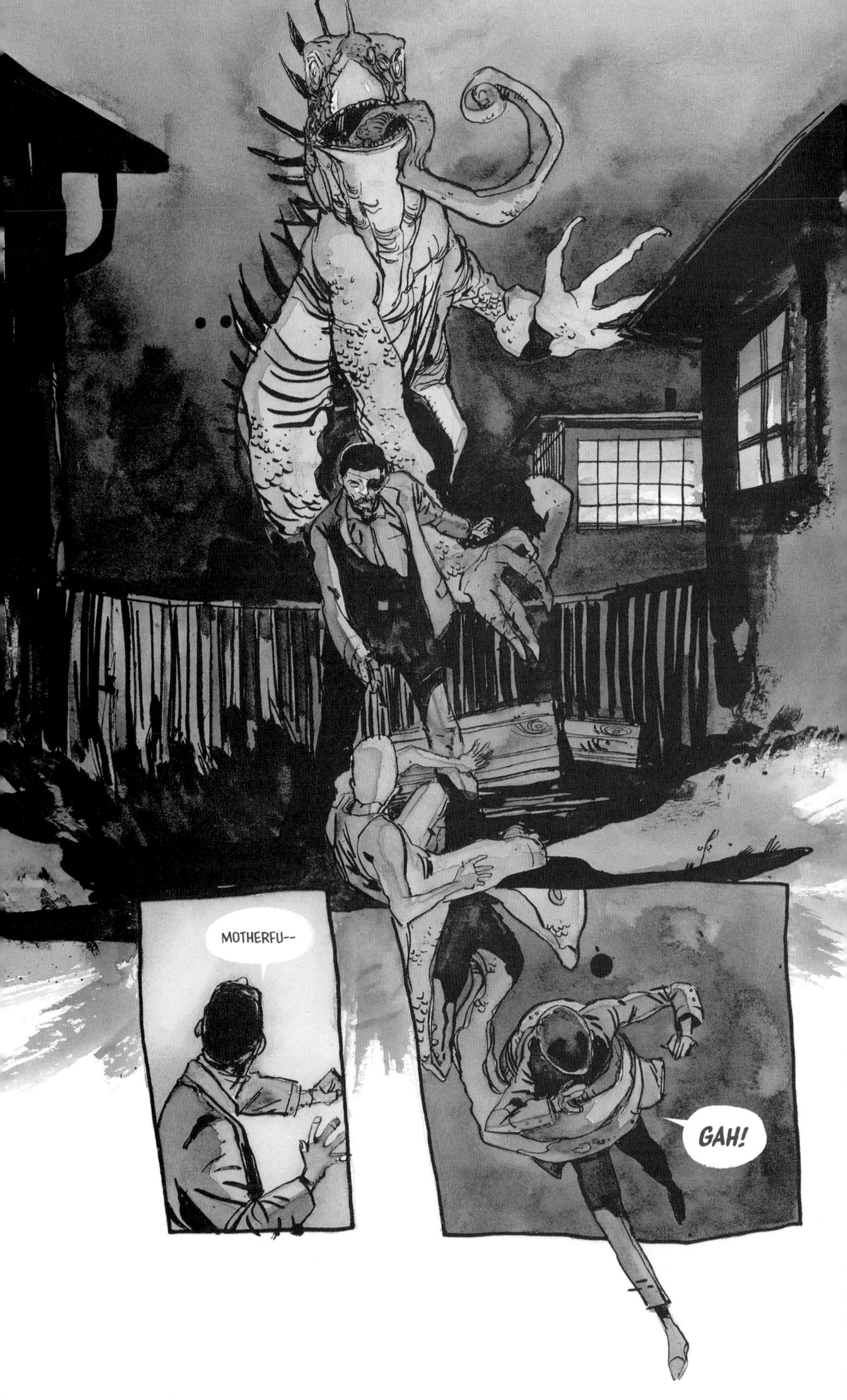
MOTHERFU--
GAH!

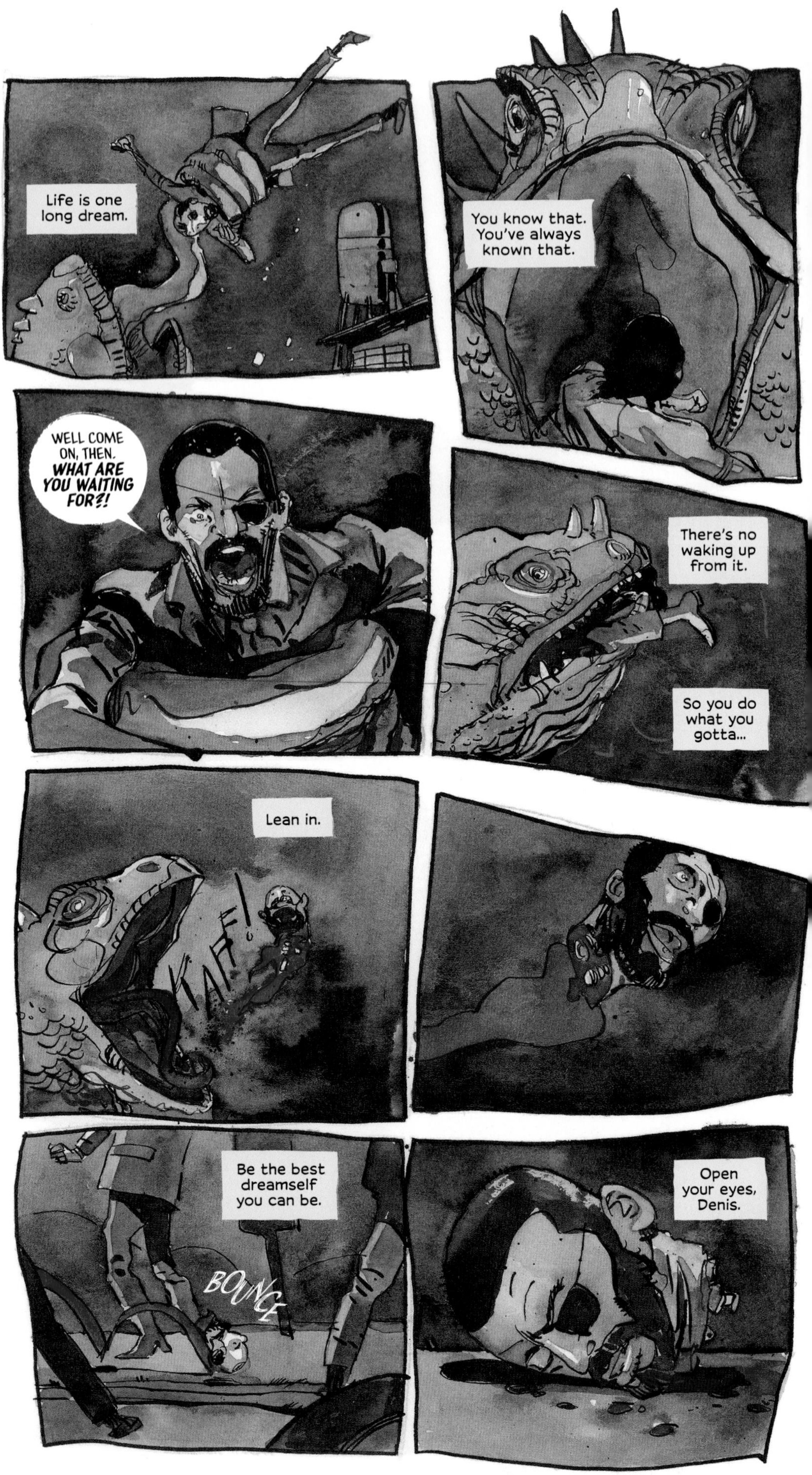
Life is one long dream.
You know that. You've always known that.
WELL COME ON, THEN. WHAT ARE YOU WAITING FOR?!
There's no waking up from it.
So you do what you gotta...
Lean in.
Be the best dreamself you can be.
BOUNCE
Open your eyes, Denis.

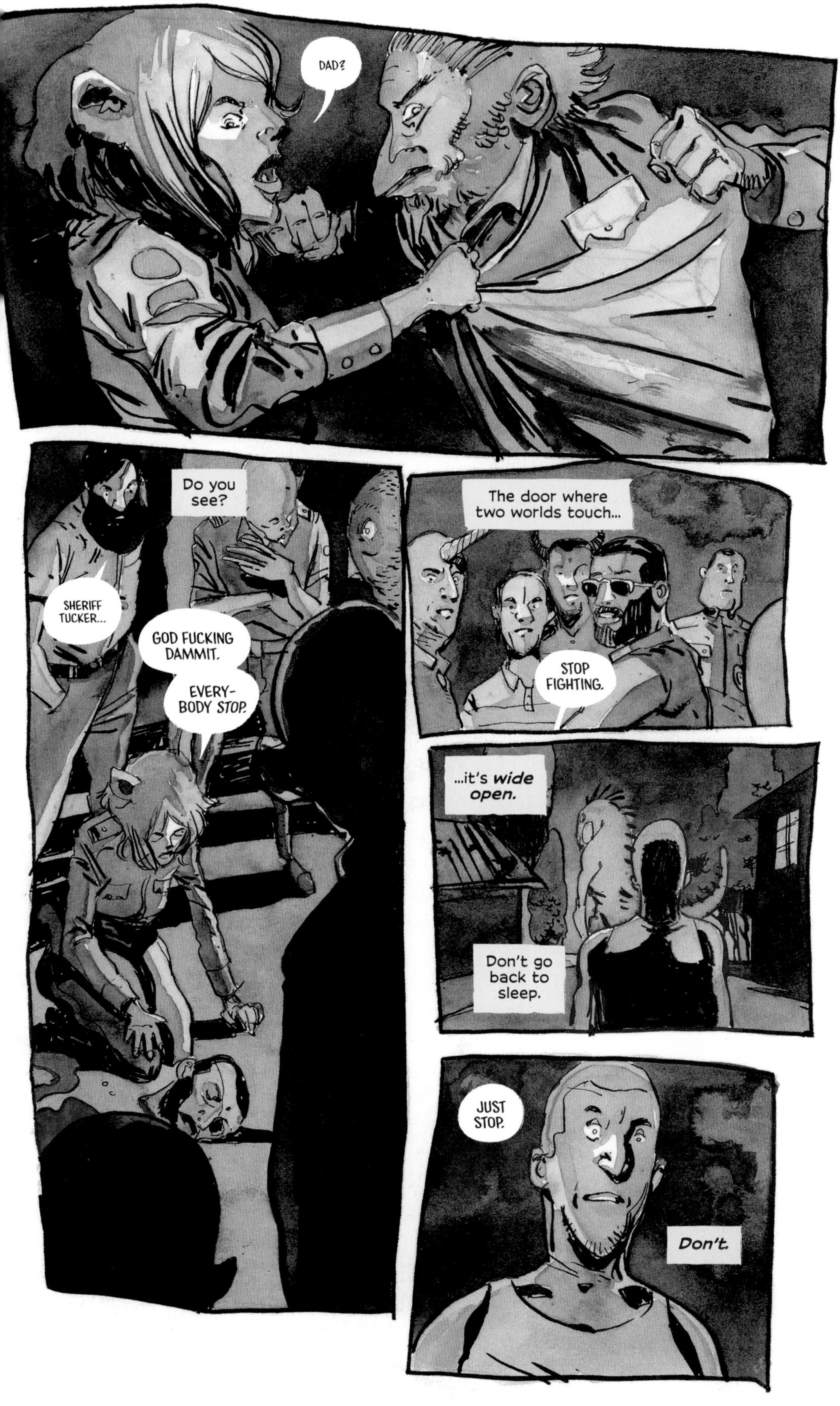
DAD?
Do you see?
SHERIFF TUCKER...
GOD FUCKING DAMMIT.
EVERY-BODY *STOP.*
The door where two worlds touch...
STOP FIGHTING.
...it's ***wide open.***
Don't go back to sleep.
JUST STOP.
Don't.

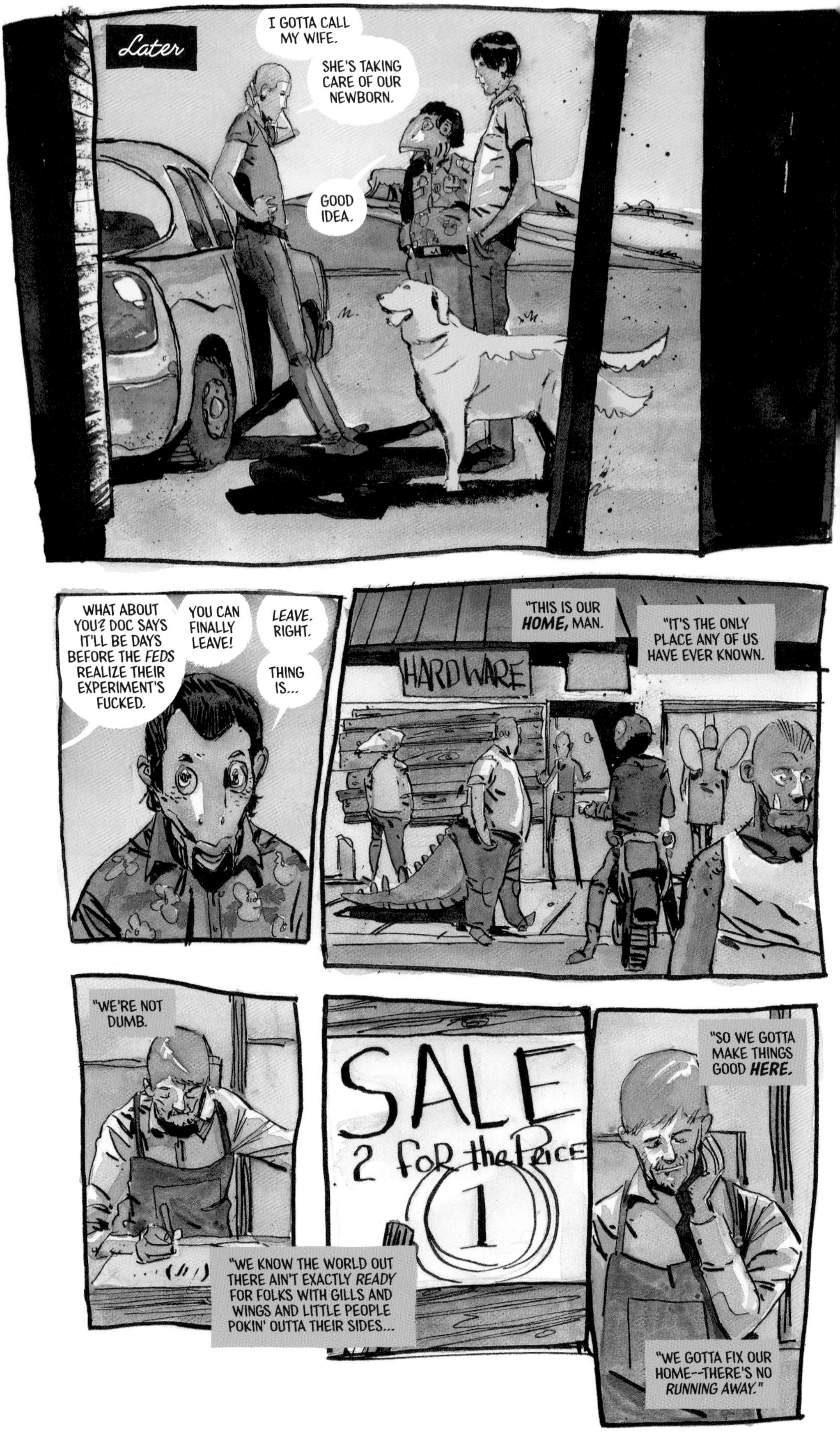

Later
I GOTTA CALL MY WIFE.
SHE'S TAKING CARE OF OUR NEWBORN.
GOOD IDEA.
WHAT ABOUT YOU? DOC SAYS IT'LL BE DAYS BEFORE THE *FEDS* REALIZE THEIR EXPERIMENT'S FUCKED.
YOU CAN FINALLY LEAVE!
LEAVE. RIGHT.
THING IS...
"THIS IS OUR ***HOME,*** MAN.
"IT'S THE ONLY PLACE ANY OF US HAVE EVER KNOWN.
HARDWARE
"WE'RE NOT DUMB.
"WE KNOW THE WORLD OUT THERE AIN'T EXACTLY *READY* FOR FOLKS WITH GILLS AND WINGS AND LITTLE PEOPLE POKIN' OUTTA THEIR SIDES...
SALE
2 FoR the Price
1
"SO WE GOTTA MAKE THINGS GOOD ***HERE.***
"WE GOTTA FIX OUR HOME--THERE'S NO *RUNNING AWAY.*"

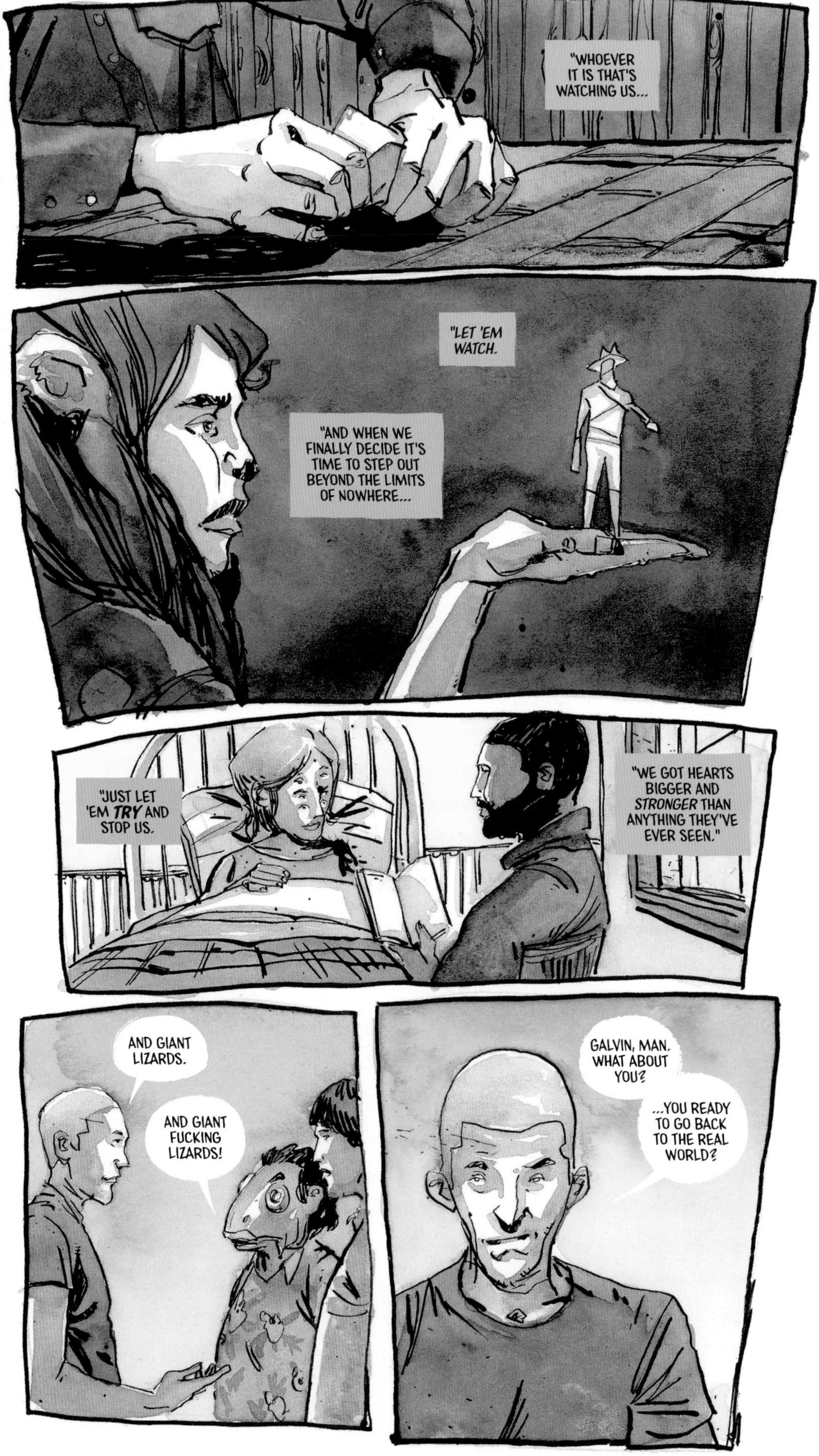
"WHOEVER IT IS THAT'S WATCHING US...
"LET 'EM WATCH.
"AND WHEN WE FINALLY DECIDE IT'S TIME TO STEP OUT BEYOND THE LIMITS OF NOWHERE...
"JUST LET 'EM TRY AND STOP US.
"WE GOT HEARTS BIGGER AND STRONGER THAN ANYTHING THEY'VE EVER SEEN."
AND GIANT LIZARDS.
AND GIANT FUCKING LIZARDS!
GALVIN, MAN. WHAT ABOUT YOU?
...YOU READY TO GO BACK TO THE REAL WORLD?

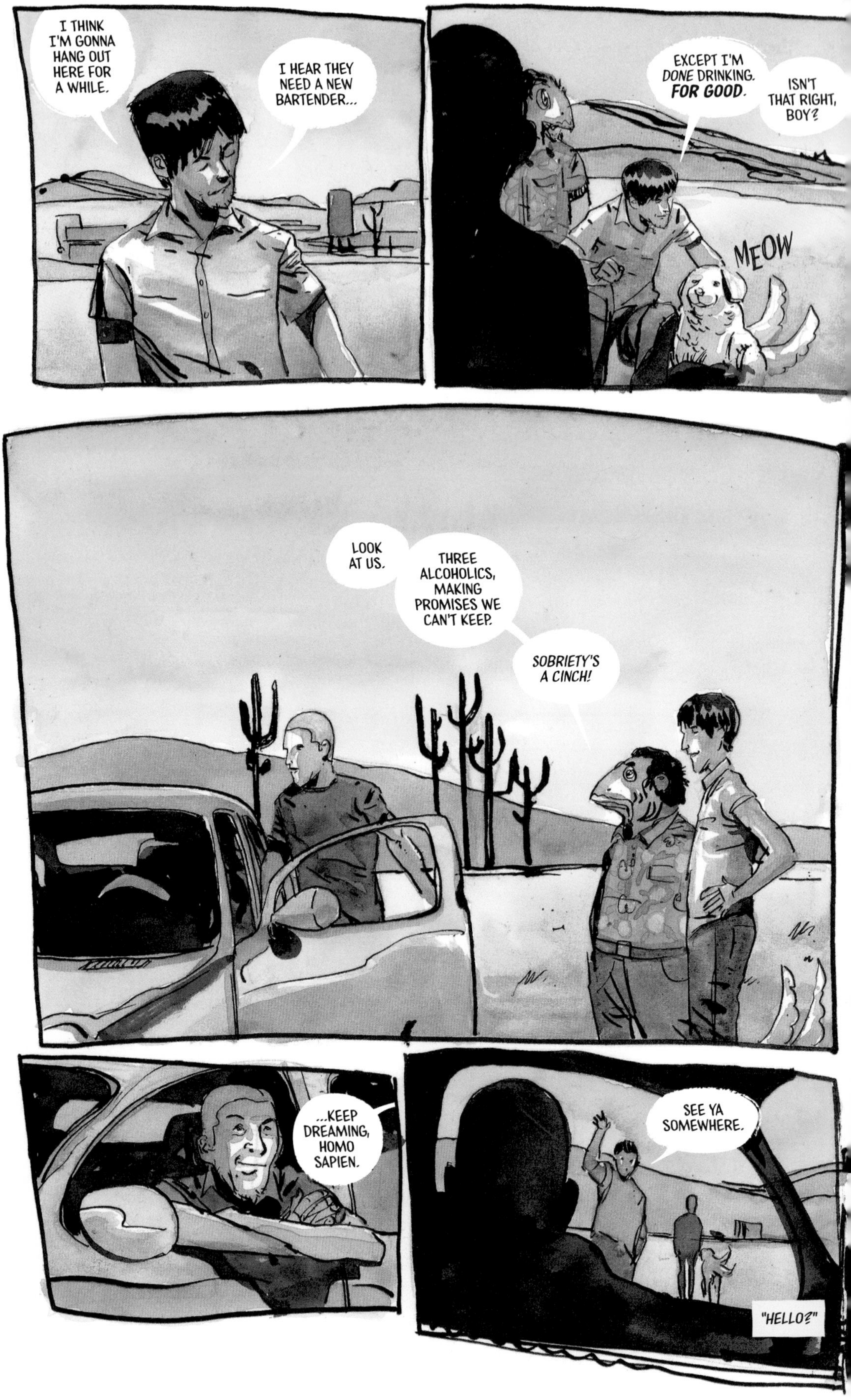
I THINK I'M GONNA HANG OUT HERE FOR A WHILE.
I HEAR THEY NEED A NEW BARTENDER...
EXCEPT I'M DONE DRINKING. FOR GOOD.
ISN'T THAT RIGHT, BOY?
MEOW
LOOK AT US.
THREE ALCOHOLICS, MAKING PROMISES WE CAN'T KEEP.
SOBRIETY'S A CINCH!
...KEEP DREAMING, HOMO SAPIEN.
SEE YA SOMEWHERE.
"HELLO?"

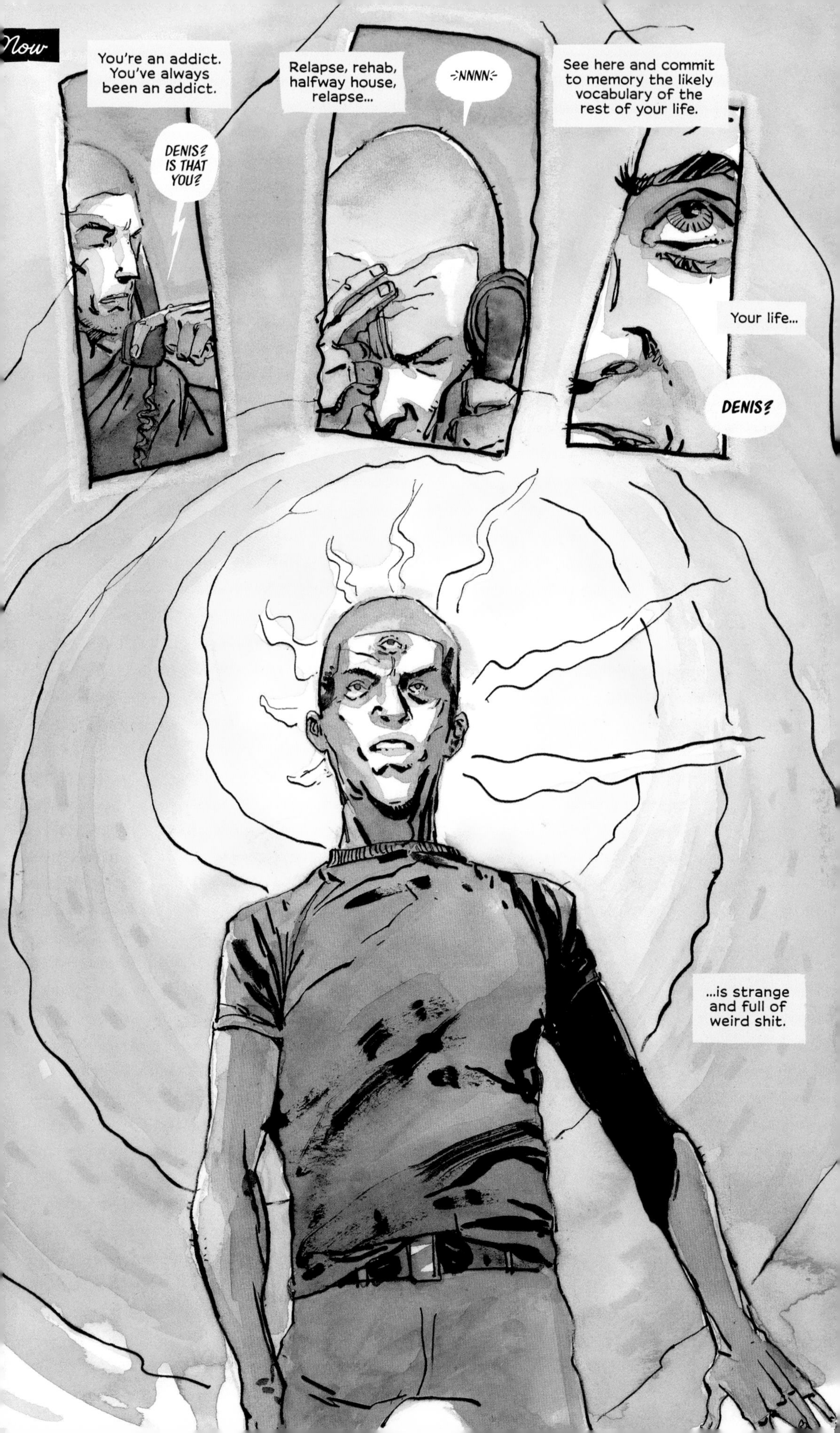
Now
You're an addict. You've always been an addict.
DENIS? IS THAT YOU?
Relapse, rehab, halfway house, relapse...
NNNN
See here and commit to memory the likely vocabulary of the rest of your life.
Your life...
DENIS?
...is strange and full of weird shit.

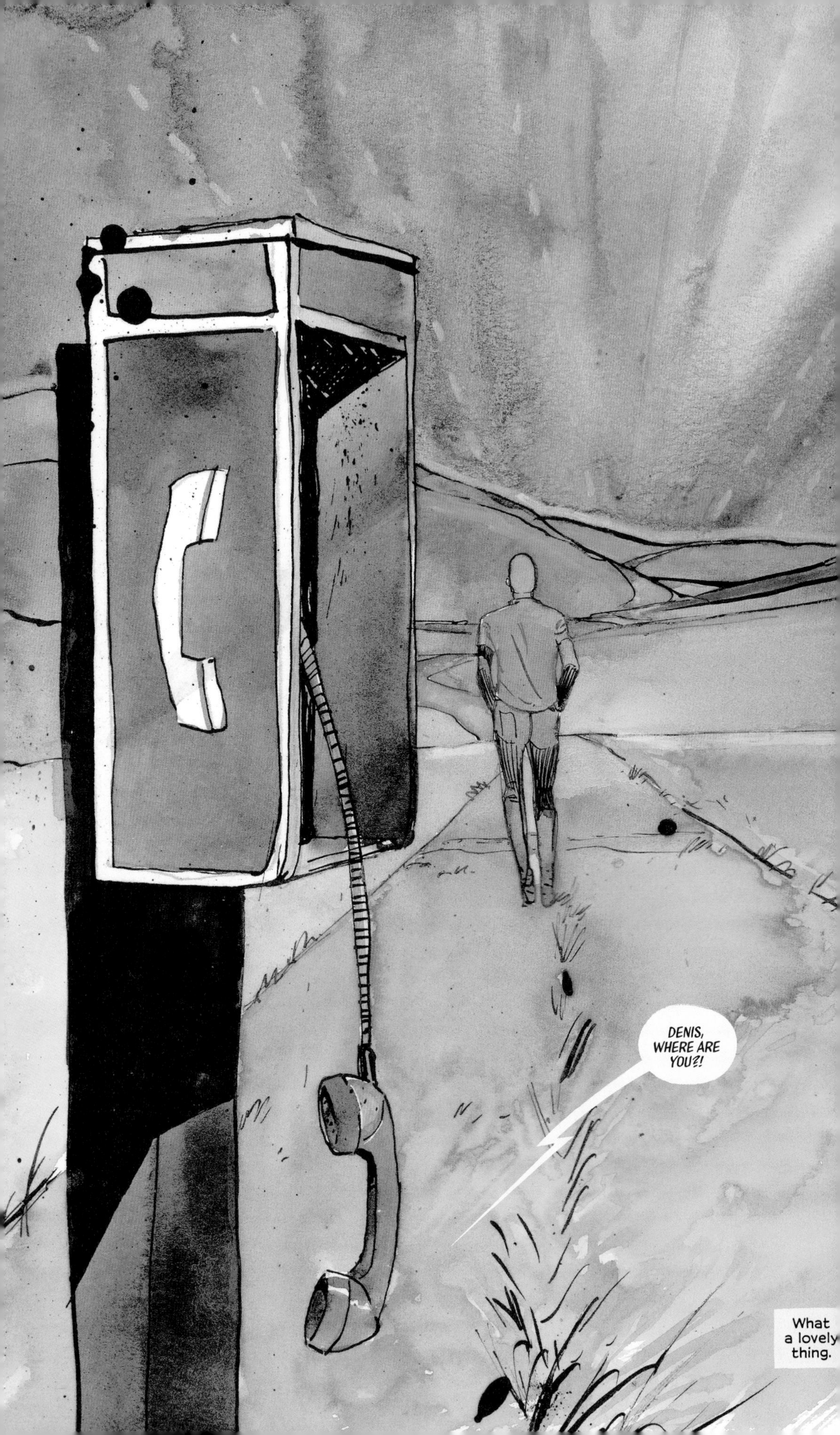
DENIS, WHERE ARE YOU?!
What a lovely thing.

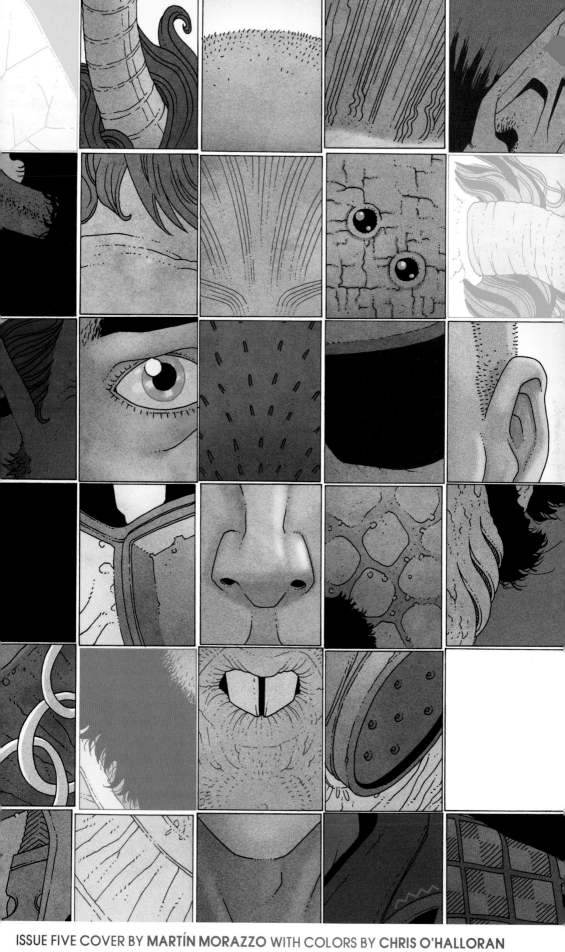

ISSUE FIVE COVER BY **MARTÍN MORAZZO** WITH COLORS BY **CHRIS O'HALLORAN**

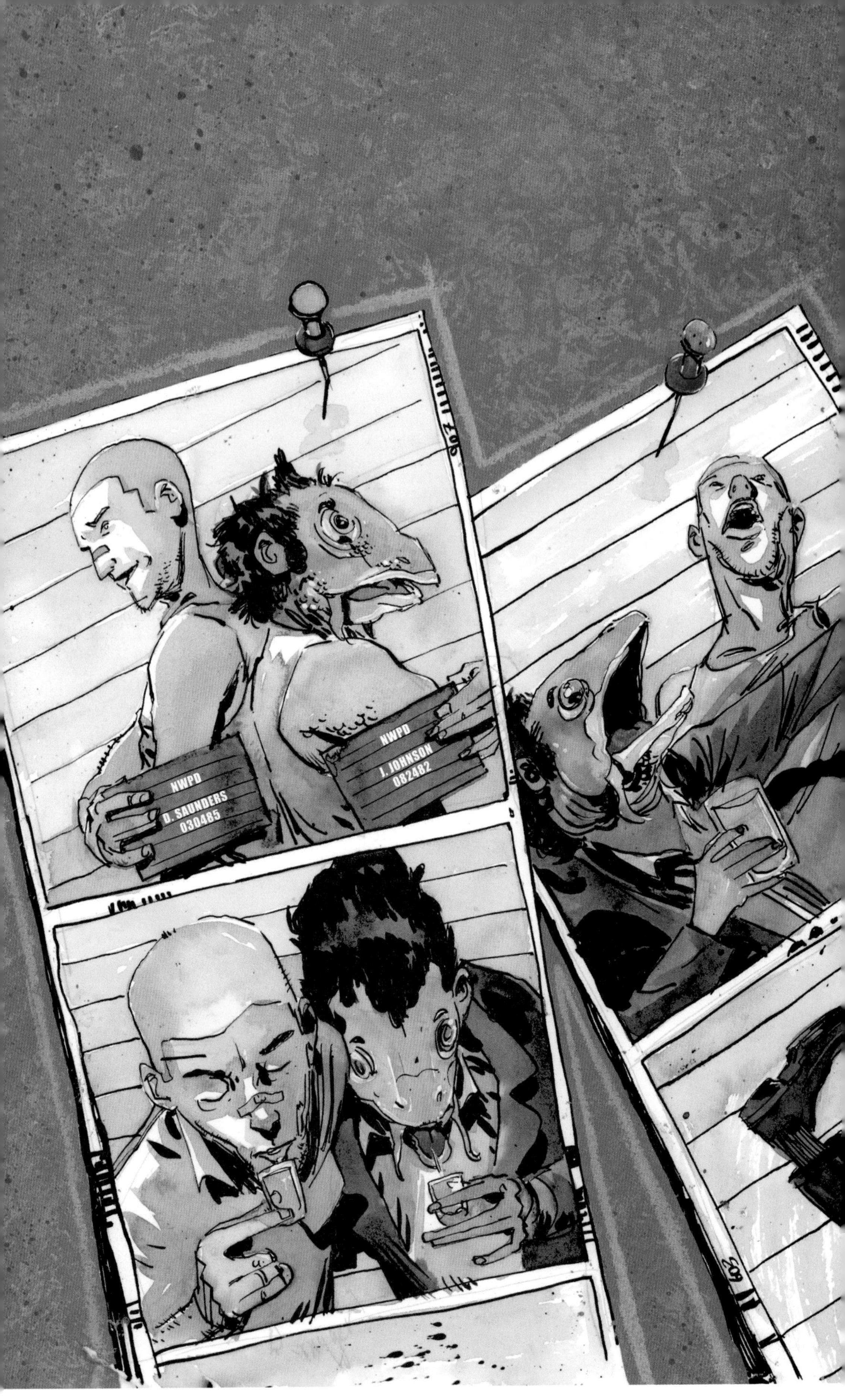
NWPD
D. SAUNDERS
030485
NWPD
J. JOHNSON
082482
ISSUE TWO COVER BY **TYLER JENKINS** WITH COLORS BY **HILARY JENKINS**

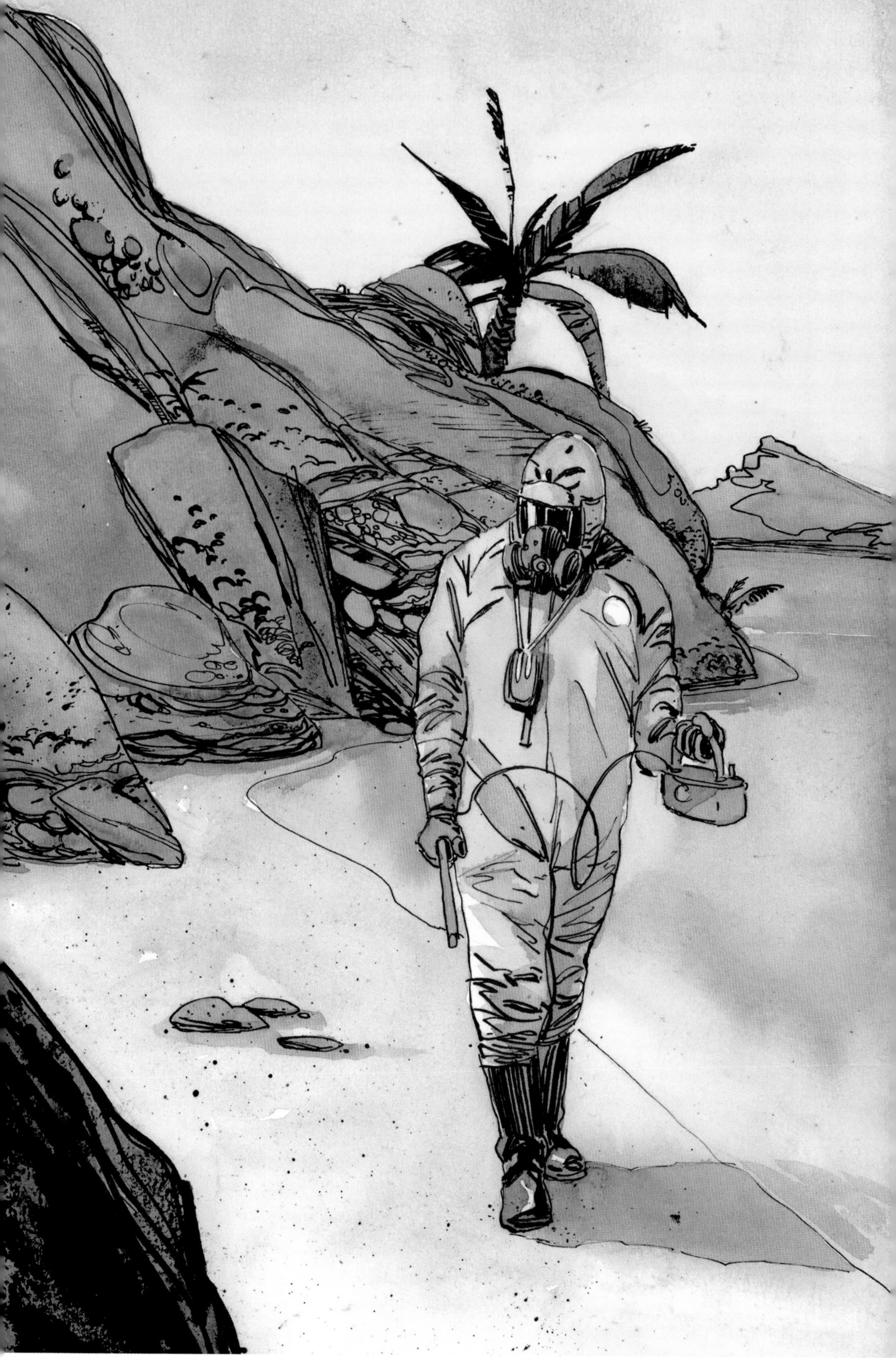

ISSUE THREE COVER BY **TYLER JENKINS** WITH COLORS BY **HILARY JENKINS**

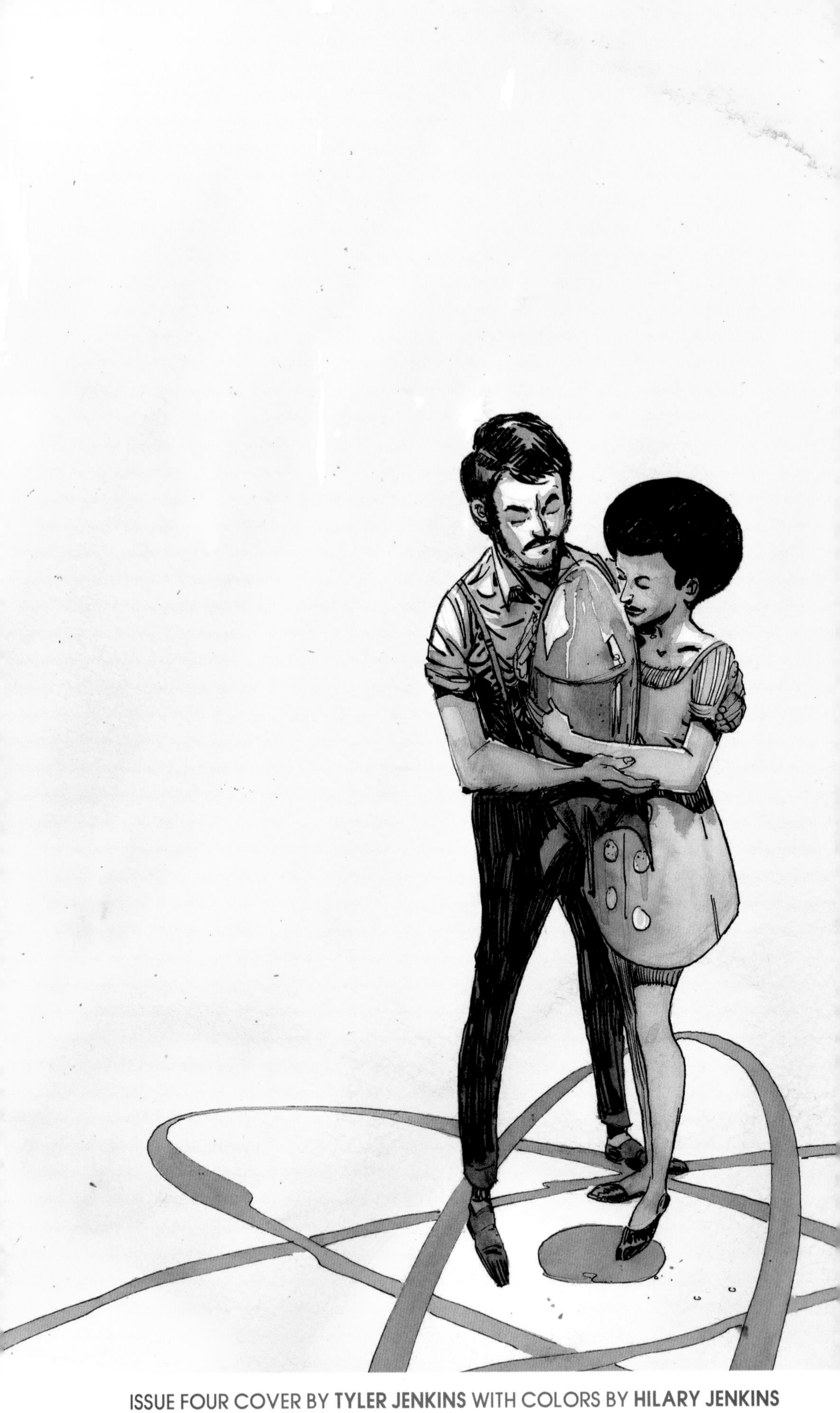

ISSUE FOUR COVER BY **TYLER JENKINS** WITH COLORS BY **HILARY JENKINS**

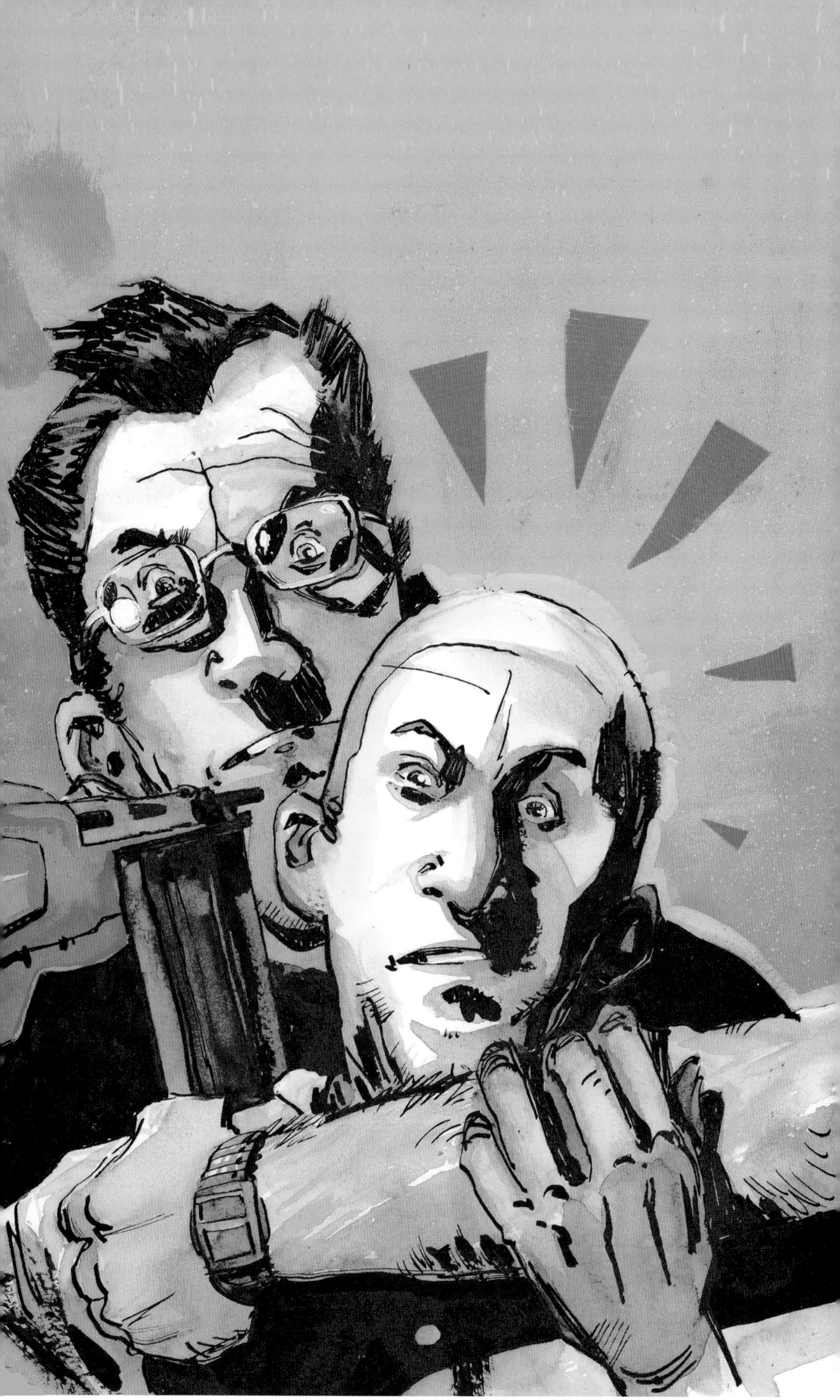

ISSUE FIVE COVER BY **TYLER JENKINS** WITH COLORS BY **HILARY JENKINS**

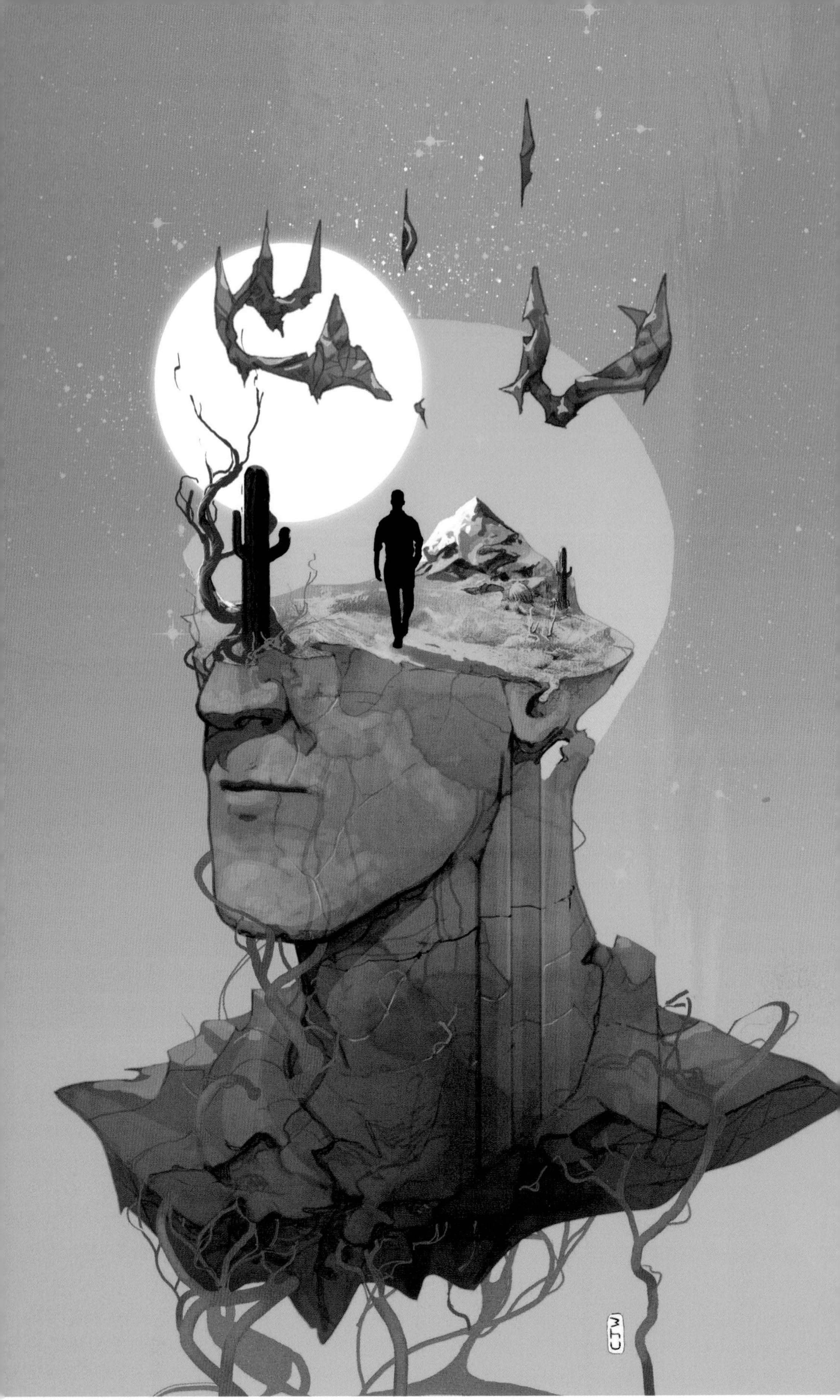
CTW

ISSUE ONE COVER BY **CHRISTIAN WARD**

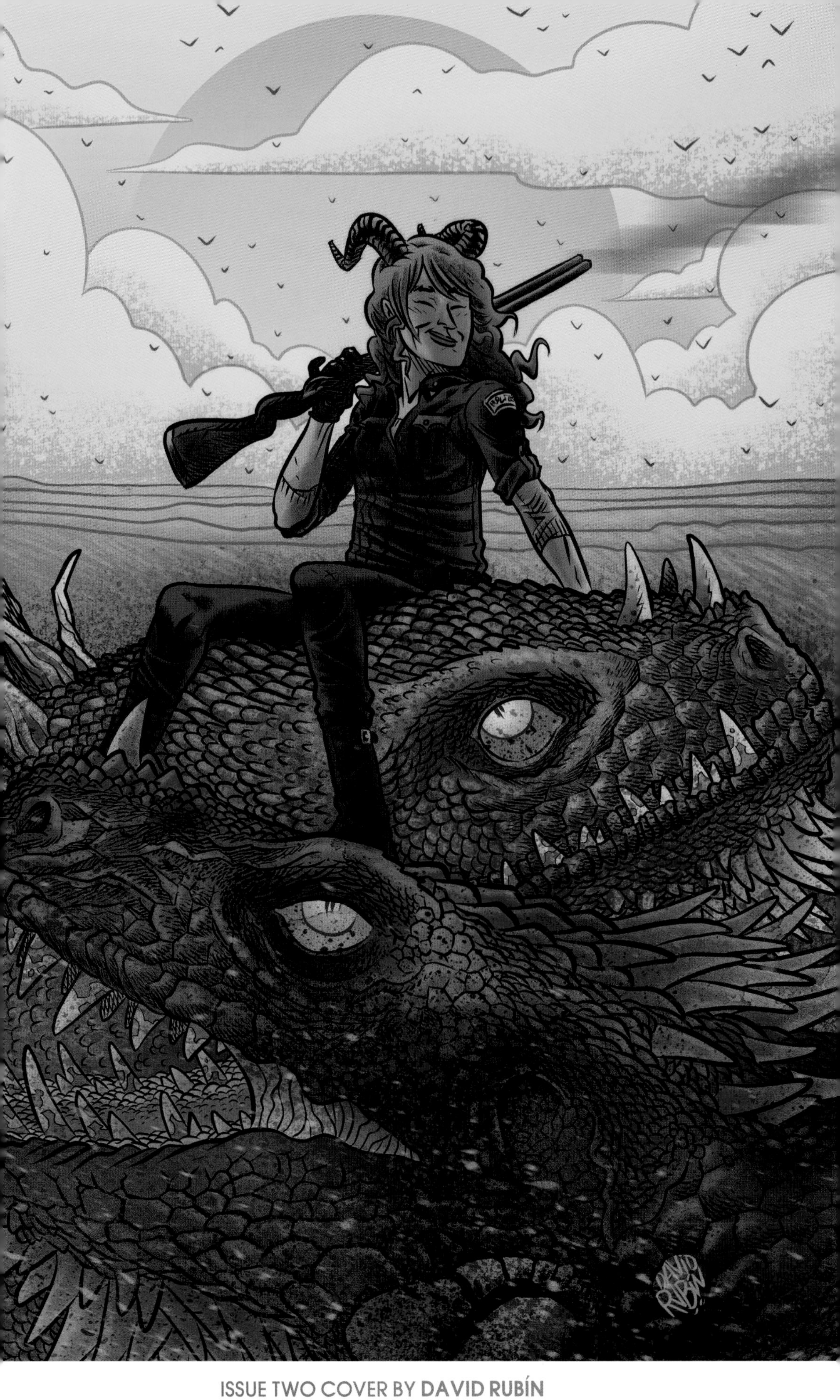
DAVID RUBÍN

ISSUE TWO COVER BY **DAVID RUBÍN**

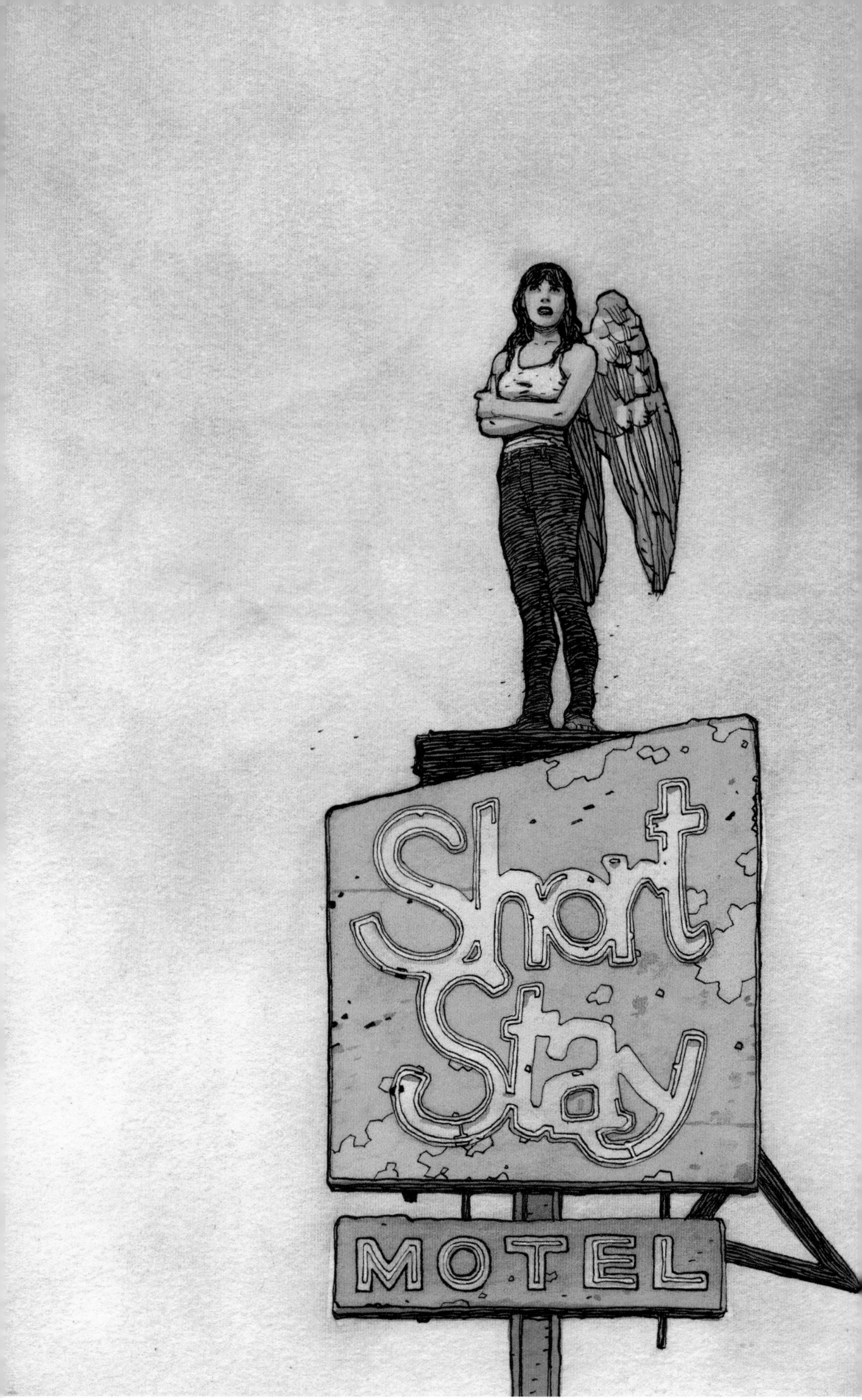

Short Stay
MOTEL

ISSUE THREE COVER BY **GABRIEL HERNÁNDEZ WALTA**

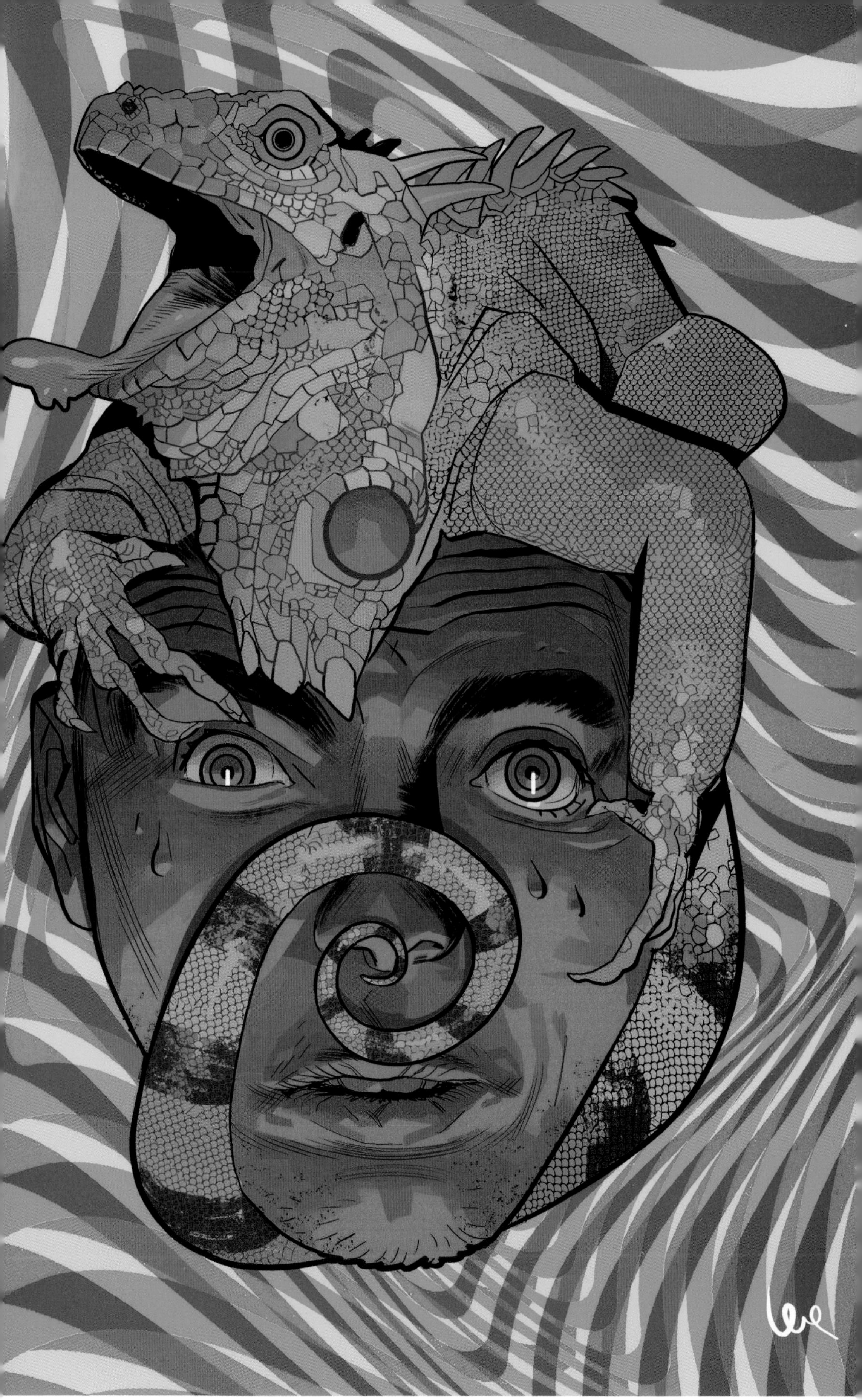

ISSUE FOUR COVER BY **LORENZO DE FELICI**